THE DISCIPLINE BOOK

*A Complete Guide to School
and
Classroom Management*

THE DISCIPLINE BOOK

*A Complete Guide to School
and
Classroom Management*

Richard L. Curwin

Allen N. Mendler

 Reston Publishing Company, Inc., Reston, Virginia
A Prentice-Hall Company

PHOTOGRAPHY BY RICK CURWIN

Library of Congress Cataloging in Publication Data

Curwin, Richard L.
   The discipline book.

   Bibliography: p. 241
   Includes index.
      1. School discipline. I. Mendler, Allen N.,
joint author. II. Title.
LB3011.5.C87   371.5   79-9349
ISBN 0-8359-1338-4

© **1980 by**
Reston Publishing Company, Inc.
A Prentice-Hall Company
Reston, Virginia 22090

10 9 8 7 6 5 4 3 2 1

PRINTED IN THE UNITED STATES OF AMERICA

To the love we still have for our fathers:

Louis J. Curwin (1903–1949)
Harold Mendler (1918–1971)

CONTENTS

PREFACE

Classroom and school discipline has consistently been rated as the number one problem issue in schools today. Our approach, which we call three-dimensional discipline (prevention, action, and resolution), provides the reader with a comprehensive survey of the issues related to discipline problems and offers numerous experiential activities that teachers can do alone, with a group of other teachers, with students in the classroom, and with parents.

The first section of the book provides the necessary theoretical formulations upon which three-dimensional discipline is built. The remainder of the book stresses practical activities and suggestions to help you set up your classroom in a way that minimizes or *prevents* discipline problems from occurring. Other discussions focus on what to do when misbehavior does occur and how to resolve problems with the student who chronically misbehaves; how to elicit parental support; how to enlist the aid of resource specialists; what can be done with the out-of-control student; how to choose techniques and methods according to your own unique style; and how our model can work on a school-wide basis.

The problem of discipline is a personal one for each teacher. How the teacher responds to any situation depends upon the teacher's values, beliefs, attitudes, and feelings, his/her knowledge of alternative approaches, an awareness of the needs of the misbehaving student, and the prevailing social attitude of the school community in which he/she works.

We offer you a framework within which you may develop your style of classroom management according to who you are, *not* according to who we tell you to be. Our emphasis is on discipline as a process that evolves in your classroom.

One obstacle we faced in writing this book was finding a suitable method of dealing with pronoun gender identity without being awkward or sexist. We eventually decided that no matter how we dealt with this issue, whether we used only plurals, "he/she," just "he," or just "she," we would be somewhat awkward or somewhat sexist. We finally resolved the issue by using all four of these constructs at various times throughout the book, depending on the context.

Many people helped us in writing this book. We wish to acknowledge their contributions and support. They are, alphabetically, Gladys Abraham, Karen Aragon, Robert Campbell, Barry Culhane, Patrick De-Marte, Pat Dichiaro, Hal Dobbins, Barbara Fuhrmann, Sam Graceffo, Lorraine Hahn, Stuart Horton, Liza McDaniel, Barbara Mendler, Linda Moscowitz, Millie Ness, Holly Sandiford, Jo Vance, and all the teachers who tried our approach and were kind enough to tell us about their experience. We also wish to thank the Rush-Henrietta School System of Henrietta, New York for allowing us to photograph its teachers and students.

RICK CURWIN
ALLEN MENDLER

THE DISCIPLINE BOOK

*A Complete Guide to School
and
Classroom Management*

1

INTRODUCTION

Everyone involved with education in America is deeply concerned about discipline, including teachers, administrators, parents, and even students. Educators rated it the number one concern in a *Phi Delta Kappan* poll (September 1977), and when parents were asked in a Gallup poll (1972, 1975), "What do you think are the biggest problems with which the public schools in this community must deal?"[1] discipline was again rated number one. The setting of the school has little bearing on whether or not there are discipline problems. The types of problems differ in rural, urban, and suburban settings as they do in different economically stratified communities, but nevertheless, it appears that discipline problems cause all schools to experience frustration.

Because of the widespread need for improved methods of dealing with discipline, a plethora of approaches and theories have been developed and tried in colleges of education and school classrooms throughout

[1] George H. Gallup. *Gallup Poll Public Opinion 1972–1977.* (Wilmington, Del.: S.R. Scholarly Resources, Inc., 1978) p. 500.

Despite the many books on the subject, teachers and schools are still searching for solutions to the problems of discipline.

the country. These different approaches include such models as drug therapy, behavior modification, reality therapy, client-centered therapy, teacher effectiveness training, moral reasoning, values clarification and others. Yet, despite these books, workshops, courses, and in-service training programs, teachers and schools are still searching for solutions to the problems of discipline and the frightening, tiring effects of disruptive youth.

We believe that most approaches do not take into account the needs and feelings of teachers and often ignore the needs and feelings of students. Our approach, which we call *three-dimensional discipline*, does not advocate any particular theory, nor is it tied to a particular model. We help you, the teacher, discover your own unique needs and then provide a structure to help you deal with discipline effectively. All of the above mentioned approaches can be utilized within the framework of *three-dimensional discipline*.

Three-dimensional discipline is a flexible, systematic process. You will learn what you can do to prevent discipline problems, what to do when a problem occurs, and what to do to decrease the possibility of problems recurring. Our model is equally effective in minimizing school-wide problems should an entire school decide to adopt it (see Chapter 13).

Because the three-dimensional approach is eclectic, encompassing a variety of theories and approaches, it may not be an easy process for you to implement immediately. We have found in extensive work with teachers that improving discipline requires hard work which involves recognizing and accepting feelings, developing an awareness of self and of students, and establishing a classroom structure for dealing with classroom events that may cause discipline problems to occur. We know teachers who classify themselves as "humanistic" and who enjoy the awareness part, but see the structure as rigid and overly traditional. We also know more "traditional" teachers who relate well to the structure, but have reservations about "getting in touch with feelings" and getting to know their students in a more personal way. We find that labels such as "humanistic," "behavioral," or "traditional" interfere with improved discipline. It takes an integration of many ideas and methodologies to make a meaningful difference in the area of classroom or school-wide discipline. We also believe that each one of us has a "traditional/structured" side and a "humanistic" side, and the three-dimensional approach is designed to give energy and aliveness to each of these sides as well as to any other that might also exist. We see value in mobilizing all that we are rather than in picking and choosing limited parts of ourselves.

Our book provides numerous activities which invite you to risk the excitement of new awareness, to struggle with the pain of confronting discipline problems, and to experience the joy of discovery which may lead you to more effective interactions with students and fewer disruptive events.

Before we begin explaining our approach, we want to share our thoughts and feelings about how this book can best help you. When we were young, we played with activity books and relished them. They were filled with games and activities ranging from follow the dots, to coloring, to finding out what's wrong with a picture. But as adults, when we are intrigued by a book that includes any related activities, we are more apt to enjoy reading the book without taking the time to complete the suggested exercises. While we have no objection to this approach, we strongly encourage you to let yourself become involved in a positive and active way in the activities that we offer (the root word for activity is *action*). You can begin the process of effective classroom management by paying attention to each activity, "trying on" some of our suggestions, and assessing for yourself how well they "fit" for you.

We equate improving discipline conditions with losing weight. As much as we wished it were otherwise, we never lost a pound by reading a diet. Only the rigorous and often painful execution of the diet made any difference in our weight regardless of how well we intellectually understood the diet and the philosophy behind it. On the other hand, diets that loomed as more work and more frustration than we could tolerate actually increased our propensity to put on weight for we resigned ourselves to the inevitability of overeating. The impossibility of the task encouraged our failures. Discipline can have the same effect. We have seen many teachers accept an attitude of resignation which says, "I can do nothing. I am powerless." Teachers who have had success in preventing *major* classroom problems are sometimes willing to accept gradual classroom erosion caused by many minor events as being part of the job. We do not think that resignation is necessary or even tolerable. A weight gain may have desultory consequences for the obese, but an eroded classroom has desultory consequences for the entire school and ultimately, the community.

It is our hope that readers will become doers. We suggest that you read each activity and begin experiencing by choosing those that you believe have current possibilities for yourself and/or your classroom. We are advocates of gradual change(s) which is best accomplished by fitting and adapting the activities to you rather than adapting yourself to them. So, we encourage you to pass over those activities that you imagine would create dissonance for you until you feel ready. Some are easy to do and can be experienced individually, while others require intensive work that may be done best with a partner or in a small group.

Group support has a strong positive effect in working toward solving discipline problems.

One of the reasons for the success of diet workshops and organizations like Weight-Watchers is the strong positive effect of group support. Maybe the formation of a "discipline workshop" in which you and your peers work through the process of three-dimensional discipline may be helpful in providing the support needed for some difficult yet exciting days ahead.

2

WHAT

IS

DISCIPLINE?

Discipline is a word frequently used by teachers, parents, and administrators, yet there is little common agreement on its meaning. For many it refers to punishment: "If you don't stop misbehaving, I will discipline you, but good." For others, it means classroom management, or what the teacher does to control student behavior. This meaning implies that students are discipline problems when they do not act the way the teacher wants. The key to the management definition is student *behavior*. One other common perception of discipline relates to students' attitudes. Students with "bad" attitudes and/or feelings are discipline problems.

We find the same dynamics operative at all levels in schools. The nonconformist teacher who chooses to behave differently from the administrative or peer norm and the pushy parent who insists that the school is not doing enough for his/her child are frequently viewed as discipline problems.

One common concept is inherent in all these definitions. The blame or responsibility for improvement is put upon the one who is different. The one who refuses to conform to the classroom or school code is either presented options for improvement which are determined by others, and/or is confronted with some type of punishment.

In the classroom, it is generally the teacher who decides what is right, be it behavior or attitudes, and the student is expected to go along, or is labelled "a discipline problem." These "right" attitudes and behaviors can change and vary within a school depending upon the unique expectations of each individual teacher. We define discipline differently. First of all, we do not define discipline as a person. The sentence, "Bobby is a discipline problem because . . ." makes no sense to us because it ignores both the teacher and the classroom environment. Discipline problems do not occur in a vacuum; they are part of a total social system. Secondly, the common definitions mentioned above do not provide a framework for change. They tend to blame or accuse, but do not provide the teacher with any real way of making things better. We believe that the first step toward improvement is to define discipline in a way that provides a concrete framework for that improvement.

To help you understand our definition of discipline, we have designed the following experiment which will provide you with a framework for understanding our concept.

AN IMPOSSIBLE CHOICE

For this simple experiment, all you have to do is choose between two extreme alternatives for eliminating discipline problems in your class (or school). The experiment is difficult since neither alternative seems to be what school is about. However, each alternative, if it could be implemented exactly as it is described, would theoretically eliminate all discipline problems.

PROBLEM: Suppose you, the teacher, had only two choices for describing your classroom environment. Which would you choose?

Choice A: There are no rules—everything goes. The teacher and student can do whatever they want in the room, and each person has the authority to do whatever he/she believes is right. Naturally in this situation, discipline is never a problem because there are no rules to break.

Choice B: There are rules for everything in your classroom, and you alone, have the authority to determine what the rules are. Every single behavior is governed by a rule, and moreover, no student ever breaks any rule in your class; they are all followed to the letter. Naturally in

There are no rules in this classroom.   **This classroom has a rule for everything.**

this situation, discipline is never a problem because no rule is ever broken.

Make your selection and write a brief paragraph and/or discuss in a small group the reasons for your choice. Begin most of your sentences with the word "I."

_____

_____

_____

_____

_____

_____

Let's examine each of these choices. In Choice A, it is apparent that the needs of each individual within the group are more important than the needs of the group. Each person may do whatever he or she wants, and in that way, can take care of himself/herself. The group may still have needs, but they are secondary to the needs of each individual.

In Choice B, the needs of the group, or the needs of the authority who represents the group (in this case, the teacher), are more important than the needs of the individual. Again, the individual still has needs, but they are not as important as the needs of the group or authority who represents the group.

We define a discipline problem as a *situation or event in which the needs of the group or authority conflict with the needs of an individual who is part of the group.* When an individual behaves in a way that meets his needs or at least that he perceives meets his needs, and these behaviors prevent the group from meeting group needs, a discipline event occurs.

The process of preventing discipline problems is simple to state, yet difficult to accomplish. It is a matter of establishing an environment where both individual and group/authority needs can be met with minimum conflict. The three-dimensional approach is based upon this simple premise. The group in this instance is comprised of the students and the teacher in the class.

The case of Ron, a fourth grade student, serves to illustrate how a discipline problem can be prevented. Ron, who was a new student to his suburban school, would make noises and wander around the classroom disturbing other students during quiet seatwork time. A very brief assessment of his achievement skills placed him two years below grade level—the lowest functioning student in his class. Although he was receiving both reading and math help with a resource teacher, he was expected to do the same English and workbook assignments as his peers. Ron saved face and hid his academic deficiencies by avoiding the workbook in favor of noisemaking and classroom wandering. This behavior created a discipline problem. Ron's avoidance behavior was interfering with the needs of the

Mrs. B. suggests an alternative method of instruction to Ron.

authority (teacher) and of the group. His teacher, Mrs. B., was a person who genuinely wanted both to solve the discipline problem and to help Ron. She sought help from the school psychologist and was advised to set up a conference with Ron to share her impressions and concerns with him. She told Ron that she knew that he was a smart boy who, for one reason or another, was working far below his potential. She suggested that while the other students worked assignments from the English workbook, she would provide instruction for him in a different way. She accomplished this by simply obtaining a second grade level workbook for Ron to work in during workbook time. She also informed him, in a firm, supportive manner, that she would no longer accept his noisemaking and wandering. If he felt compelled to continue such behavior, he would be required to leave the classroom and sit in the vice-principal's office until such time as he felt he could behave more appropriately. Within two days of this conference, Ron's irritating behaviors had all but ceased.

In this situation, Mrs. B. went through the following process:

1. Became aware of her angry feelings toward Ron.
2. Shared these with the school psychologist.
3. Did a brief diagnostic assessment of his academic standing.
4. Defined her problem with Ron.
5. Suggested to him an alternative method of instruction.
6. Set clear and enforceable limits.
7. Confronted Ron when only he was present.

In effect, Mrs. B. set up an environment in which future problems with Ron would be minimized.

NEEDS IDENTIFICATION

The following activity is designed to help you understand our definition of discipline from your own experiences.

1. Describe a recent classroom or school discipline problem in which you were the authority. List the sequence of events.

    _____

    _____

    _____

    _____

2. List your needs as best you can recall them. Begin with the phrase, "I needed" or "I wanted."

   _____

   _____

   _____

   _____

3. List the needs of the student(s) involved as best you can imagine them:

   _____

   _____

   _____

   _____

4. Recall a time when you were a student, preferably the same age and/or grade of the student listed in the previous section. Remember in detail a time when you were a discipline problem for a teacher. Take some time remembering, envisioning as many details of the situation as possible. (If you are working in a group, you might role play this situation with you being the student and a group member the teacher.) Describe the situation and list the sequence of events:

   _____

   _____

   _____

   _____

5. List as best you can your needs as a student.

   _____

   _____

   _____

   _____

6. List the needs of the teacher involved as best you can imagine them.

   _____

   _____

   _____

   _____

7. Answer the following questions about the previous steps:

   a. In what ways were your needs as a student similar to the needs of the student described in Step 3? How were they dissimilar?

   _____

   _____

   _____

b. In what ways were your needs as a teacher similar to the needs of the teacher described in Step 6? How were they different?

_____

_____

c. In what ways were your needs as a teacher in Step 2 similar to your needs as a student in Step 5?

_____

_____

d. List as many ways as you can to meet the sets of needs of the teacher and student in Steps 2 and 3.

_____

_____

e. List as many ways as you can think of to meet the needs of the teacher and student in Steps 5 and 7.

_____

_____

f. Write your impressions of the following definition of discipline as a result of this activity.

"A discipline problem occurs when the needs of the individual conflict with the needs of the group or authority (teacher) who represents that group."

_____

_____

_____

_____

There are two important concerns raised by our definition of discipline:

1. What happens when the authority (the teacher) is not representing the group, but is meeting his/her own needs, and because of the position of power, can do so regardless of what the group or individuals within the group want? Certainly any teacher who wants to meet his own needs regardless of what the group (class) needs has the power to do so, but there are predictable consequences, such as rebellion, either open or subversive, a decrease in learning, constant

tension, resentment, and in a very real way, mourning. Few teachers ever actively choose this alternative, but many often confuse their own needs with the needs of the group. On the other hand, it is impossible to conceive of teachers with the ability to meet only group needs without meeting any of their own needs. We believe that the most effective teachers can and do take care of themselves, and at the same time can and do take care of the group. When there is conflict between the two sets of needs, a resolution is worked out.

2. An even more difficult problem occurs when the real needs of the students and of the teacher are different from their perceived needs. In this case, either the student or the teacher is out of touch with himself and is trying to meet a need which has been mistaken for a different need. One typical example is a student who tries to meet what he perceives as a need to talk with his friend in class, but really needs to be noticed and wants interaction with the teacher. If the teacher tries to meet the student's need by providing a time to talk to the friend, the student's underlying need would still not be met, and the solution would eventually fail. We offer the three-dimensional model to help teachers prevent, act, and resolve these situations.

3

TEACHERS' AND STUDENTS' NEEDS

In the previous chapter we defined discipline as a conflict between the needs of the individual (the student) and the needs of the group (the class) or the authority who represents the group (the teacher). We now wish to explore the relationship between these sets of needs in greater depth.

Our first task in exploring this relationship was to discover what were the basic school needs of both teachers and students. When we talked with various groups of students and teachers at all grade levels we found the following general sets of needs (the list is not in any order of priority).

NEEDS OF STUDENTS IN SCHOOL SETTINGS

- Peer approval.
- Teacher approval.
- Academic success.
- Social success.
- Popularity.
- A voice in "school life."
- A fair and just environment.
- A feeling of worth and importance.

- A feeling of belonging (they belong to the school and the school belongs to them).
- A positive relationship between school and home.
- A feeling that the school will take care of them (support).
- Skills and knowledge (or credentials) for career success.

These are general basic needs that most students identified as important for positive school experiences. Notice the similarity between this list and the following one we developed out of our contact with teachers.

NEEDS OF TEACHERS IN SCHOOL SETTINGS

- Peer respect.
- Administrative respect and support.
- A feeling that students are learning.
- Authority to run classroom without interference.
- Working in a safe school environment.
- A voice in the running of the school.
- A feeling of worth and importance.
- Fair relationship with administration.
- A good living and job security.
- To be liked and respected by students.

There are common themes that run through each of these lists. In *Making Urban Schools Work*, Mario Fantini and Gerald Weinstein developed a model for looking at student needs. Their model identifies three basic issues that we can use to clarify how the needs in our lists fit together. Their three issues (needs) are as follows:

By *identity* issues, we mean those aspects of a person's behavior which aim at providing him with a sense of worth. This area includes all the questions pertaining to the process of self-evaluation and the consequences of these evaluations. It is referred to by such terms as self-image, self-concept, identity, self-awareness, self-esteem, ego, ego-strength, and the like. All of these surround the basic questions: Who am I? What am I worth?

By *connectedness* issues we mean those aspects of a person's behavior which aim at providing him with a sense of positive affiliation with others. This is the relations-with-others domain, ranging from the primary face-to-face relations to secondary relations with less direct groups. Connectedness issues involve the questions: To whom does the individual feel an allegiance? To whom does he feel he belongs? What are people to him? Who are the significant others? How does he relate? With whom does he *integrate?*

By *power* issues we mean those aspects of a person's behavior which aim at providing him with a sense of control or influence over what is happening and will happen to him. Does the individual feel that he has a significant part to play in the construction of situations that will affect him? If he does, does he act in accordance with these feelings?[1]

We have added one more category which we call *achievement*. We define the fourth category as follows:

By *achievement* issues we mean those aspects of a person's behavior which aim at being successful in a given professional or educational endeavor. Achievement issues involve the questions: What do I need to be able to do a good job? How can I measure my success in my work (schoolwork)? Is what I am doing now going to provide me with the kind of job fulfillment and security I desire?

These four sets of needs—identity, connectedness, power, and achievement, become the central focus for the three-dimensional discipline approach. We can modify our basic definition of discipline to: A conflict between the needs of individuals (students) for identity, connectedness, power, or achievement, with the needs of the group (class) for its needs for identity, connectedness, power, or achievement; or with the authority which represents the group (teacher) for meeting needs of identity, connectedness, power, or achievement. The conflict can arise out of competing needs within a category; for example a teacher and a student both desiring power. Or conflict can arise out of different sets of needs; for example, a student's need for power conflicting with the class need for achievement. Note the following examples of typical discipline problems.

1. Teacher asks student to be quiet, and the student refuses to do so. Now they are locked in a power struggle to see who can win. Neither cares any more about the student's talking, only coming out ahead in the argument is important. This is a classic power to power conflict.

Individual	Authority
Student	*Teacher*
Identity	Identity
Connectedness	Connectedness
Power ——————————————————— Power	
Achievement	Achievement

Group
Class
Identity
Connectedness
Power
Achievement

[1] Mario Fantini and Gerald Weinstein, *Making Urban Schools Work* (New York: Holt, Rinehart and Winston, 1968), p. 5.

2. A student has been separated from her friends by the teacher because of excessive talking. The student later becomes sullen and refuses to do any work. This is a conflict between the student's need for connectedness and the teacher's need for achievement ("I can't do my job if you keep disturbing me").

Individual	Authority
Student	*Teacher*
Identity	Identity
Connectedness	Connectedness
Power	Power
Achievement	Achievement

Group
Class
Identity
Connectedness
Power
Achievement

3. A group of students is making fun of one student who later throws wads of paper at them and refuses to work in a group with them. The student's need for identity (protecting one's self-concept) is in conflict with the group's need for connectedness. The group has one common factor, picking on the student, which is their connectedness, but by banding together they are attacking the self-concept of the other student.

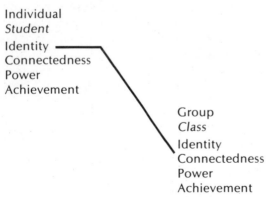

Individual
Student
Identity
Connectedness
Power
Achievement

Authority
Teacher
Identity
Connectedness
Power
Achievement

Group
Class
Identity
Connectedness
Power
Achievement

4. Some students are making fun of a teacher who accidentally overhears them. Later the teacher calls on one of these students when he sees that the student is not paying attention. The teacher then embarrasses the student in front of the class. This example shows the self-concept or identity needs of both the teacher and student in conflict.

Individual
Student
Identity ────────────────────────────
Connectedness
Power
Achievement

Authority
Teacher
Identity
Connectedness
Power
Achievement

Group
Class
Identity
Connectedness
Power
Achievement

Try the following experiment. In Chapter 2 you recalled an incident in which you had a discipline problem as a teacher and you listed your needs and your student's needs as they related to the discipline problem. You then did the same, recalling a problem you had when you were a student. Go back to Chapter 2, page 12, and list the student needs and teacher needs below.

Student Needs: *Category:*

Teacher Needs: *Category:*

Now categorize each need or set of needs as best you can into one or more of the categories: identity, connectedness, power, and achievement. Do the same for the teacher's needs. In the diagram below, draw a line from the major category of the student to the major category of the teacher.

Student	*Teacher*
Identity	Identity
Connectedness	Connectedness
Power	Power
Achievement	Achievement

This method of categorizing and diagramming can be used for diagnostic purposes when you have discipline problems. One of the first steps in solving discipline problems, based upon our definition, is to attempt to meet the conflicting needs of the individual and the group or authority. Identification of the type of conflict will give you clues as to what steps you must begin to take to improve the situation. For example, if you notice a conflict between identity issues, you can spend some time building self-concepts, or if the problem is a power struggle, you can begin to establish situations which enable students to have and use power in constructive ways.

4

THE
PREVENTION
DIMENSION

The first goal of the three-dimensional approach is to set up an environment in which discipline problems are prevented. The *prevention* dimension is designed to minimize or prevent classroom problems from occurring. We think of the prevention dimension as similar in many ways to a subject curriculum. The purpose of a curriculum is to provide the teachers and students with a well thought out plan to guide the learnings of a particular lesson or course. The best curricula are flexible enough to allow day to day changes as new needs arise and to incorporate evaluations as to how well the plan is working. The prevention dimension is a plan which is designed to provide you a structure and a direction, yet is flexible enough to accommodate both day to day changes and long-term developmental changes as you and your students develop new needs and new awarenesses. Like content curriculum, our prevention dimension includes cognitive, behavioral, and affective components, blended together so that awareness leads to understanding which leads to action which leads to awareness.

This chapter and the chapters that follow include a variety of experiences, activities for you to try, examples, and information. Through active participation, you will create your plan for the prevention or minimization of discipline problems in your class.

The six stages of the prevention dimension are as follows:

1. Increasing self-awareness (teacher).
2. Increasing awareness of students.
3. Expressing genuine feelings.
4. Discovering and recognizing available alternatives.
5. Establishing social contracts.
6. Implementing social contracts.

Increasing Self-Awareness

The first stage of the prevention dimension is increasing awareness of self (teacher). We have discovered that those teachers who are the most effective at classroom management also have a high degree of congruence between their real and ideal teaching selves.

> The ideal self is comprised of values, feelings, attitudes, past experiences, influence from significant others, and self-perceptions. This ideal is not a fantasy, like childhood dreams of superhuman feats, but rather has its basis in real people as they really are. Given who people are, with all their assets and limitations, it's what they can be at their best. It is potentially within them, and is obtainable. Before they can attain it, though, each individual must personally discover and identify his/her own unique ideal self. Each individual also has a real self, which is comprised of his/her feelings, attitudes, and behaviors *right now*. The real self is not static; it changes from moment to moment, and is always available for inspection by both the individual and others.[1]

There is little difference in effective classroom management between those teachers who are permissive, authoritarian, or moderate. What does make a difference is knowing what you are, allowing yourself to be what you are, and permitting your students to see you as you are. Many classroom discipline problems occur because of double messages (a symptom of lack of congruence) that the teacher gives the students. For example, Mrs. Satkir, a second grade teacher, wants to see herself as an open

---

[1] Richard Curwin and Barbara Fuhrmann, "Mirror, Mirror on the Wall: Developing Teacher Congruency," *Humanist Educator*, September 1978, p. 34.

teacher who allows her students to solve problems and make their own decisions. There is a wide discrepancey between what she wants to be (open and permissive) and what she actually is. Scolding and lecturing are her two main discipline weapons and outside observers clearly see this. However, she lacks self-awareness as to what she is actually doing and what her beliefs, attitudes, and values tell her she should be doing. While her students hear one verbal message ("You have responsibilities in this classroom," and "It's up to you to solve a problem when Jenny takes Billy's pencil"), she really has a very strict internal code, and when this code is violated, she becomes angry. She implicitly wants the problem to be solved her way, and when it is not, she scolds and lectures. So the double message is: (1) "Solve your own problems;" but (2) "Solve them the way I believe they should be solved." Double messages and mixed signals often lead to agitation and anxiety in students, particularly those who for other reasons are already sensitive to such feelings. They often culminate in conflict, confusion, and classroom management problems. Mrs. Satkir would benefit herself by closing the gap between what she wants to be as a classroom manager and what she actually is. We will provide activities and experiments to help you develop this increased self-awareness.

Increasing Awareness of Students

The second stage of the prevention dimension is increasing awareness of your students. The three-dimensional approach is an interactive one that takes into account your students as real people who are living with you in a classroom micro society. Their needs and desires play a major role in developing a preventive environment. The more aware you are of your students, the more effective you will be in working with them.

Margaret Franklin was a first year ninth grade English teacher who spent the greater part of her summer before her first teaching assignment preparing for her class. She wrote out detailed lesson plans that had her every minute structured with what she believed to be helpful and enjoyable learning activities. She was forced to drastically change her plans when she discovered the first day that three of her twenty-five students did not get along and spent the entire first class arguing and acting out with each other. A fight destroyed her chances to get through her lesson before the class was half over. She soon discovered that her definition of helpful and enjoyable was very different from that of her students.

Steve Jones had a similar experience under entirely different circumstances. He had taught in the same school for many years and had learned effective methods for dealing with his students. For the last five years he had begun his class with the same lecture and activities. This time, though, the class was not receptive to his presentation because many of the students were bored.

Their friends had Mr. Jones as a teacher the year before and had told them what to expect. The attitude of the students was a collective, "You don't care very much about us if you are going through a standard routine."

Expressing Feelings

The third stage of the prevention dimension is the expression of genuine feelings. Although this process is one of the most important steps in preventing discipline problems, it is traditionally ignored in most, if not all, teacher preparation programs, both in-service and preservice. It is also ignored by many of the philosophical-psychological approaches offered by theoreticians who focus on classroom behavior. In this stage you will learn how to genuinely express your feelings and how to use these expressions to help yourself manage your classroom more effectively.

Unless you're in touch with your feelings toward your students and learn ways to safely express these feelings, you will be blocked from using your powers of reason to help yourself solve discipline problems. Most teachers do little to take care of themselves prior to engaging difficult students. We are reminded of Mrs. Meyer, a fourth grade teacher who, after months of migraine headaches which yielded dozens of sleepless nights and disputes with her husband and children, finally asked for help. Being a well-trained teacher with fifteen years of experience, she had learned all of the "right" humanistic concepts such as loving, understanding, and caring for those in her class. But her image of herself as a caring teacher prevented any acknowledgment of the raging feelings that she secretly harbored toward some students in her problematic class. We tried to help her first by recognizing and then accepting her negative feelings. We suggested that she imagine the presence of her troublemakers and tell them exactly how they make her feel. We used the fantasy dialogue technique (see pages 41 and 69).

After a period of initial reluctance, which is common for those who are unaccustomed to talking to empty chairs, she contacted her hurt feelings and began to cry; then she began to shout and yell at the bothersome students. We asked her to tell her troublemakers (represented by empty chairs) what she resented, what she demanded, and finally what she appreciated. After approximately forty-five minutes of this experience, she was surprised to discover that her headache was gone.

Expression of feelings, especially negative feelings, is very difficult for most of us because of all the injunctions we have learned against such expressions early in our lives. And while most teacher education programs pay considerable attention to curriculum, methods, and other cognitive "how to's," it is rare that any attention is given the feelings of the teacher. Many in our school society have becomed narcoticized to their own feelings and mechanistically go about their business day to day as if feelings were not a part of teaching. It indeed can become frightening when disruptive students challenge our sense of equilibrium and refuse to follow our rules and guidelines. It is these difficult students who often get us in touch with feelings that we have learned through the years to value as "bad." As part of an effective program of classroom or individual student management, it is important that the teacher take care of himself or herself by both recognizing and learning to express feelings.

Discovering and Recognizing Alternatives

The fourth stage of the prevention dimension is discovering and recognizing many different alternatives or models of behavior, theories of discipline, and some of the research into psychology and education as they apply to discipline. This knowledge alone will not make you a better classroom manager, but along with the other stages, knowledge can generate viable alternatives that you can borrow from, adapt, or use as they are. Once you have personal awareness, you can use the work of others in your own way. Chapter 8 provides an overview of much of the current thinking about discipline and classroom management.

Establishing Social Contracts

The fifth stage of the prevention dimension involves establishing social contracts with your class. A *social contract* is a list of rules and consequences governing behavior, either in class or on a school-wide basis, that you and your class agree to. You will make a list of rules and consequences for your class, and then ask your students to develop a list of rules and consequences for you, and finally, rules and consequences for each other. Some teachers resist the use of the word *rule* because they see it as conceptualizing a rigid classroom structure which constricts the development of humanistic teacher-student relationships. To us the word, *rule*, means an agreed upon standard of behavior intended to facilitate an understanding of the limits that are necessary to meet individual and group/authority needs.

The lists are then discussed and evaluated by the total class, and when agreement has been reached, this list of rules and consequences becomes the *classroom social contract*. Thus, your class will be involved in a process of setting rules and consequences and will feel ownership of the contract. It is not only you, the teacher, who will decide the rules; but rather the class as a whole will assess needs and come to decisions about rules that will govern behavior.

Implementing Social Contracts

The sixth and final stage of the prevention dimension involves a transition into the *action* dimension. By implementing the social contract you will set up a classroom environment that is governed by the rules, and when misbehavior occurs, a consequence is implemented or acted upon.

In the following chapters we examine each of the prevention dimension stages in depth.

5

AWARENESS OF SELF AS TEACHER

The first step of the prevention dimension is to develop awareness of yourself as a teacher and classroom manager. In this way we believe you will be able to find areas of congruence in your attitudes, values, and ideals with your behaviors in teaching. We offer the following activities to help you begin the process of self-examination to determine what you want of yourself as a classroom manager. Many of these activities can be done alone or with a group of peers. Please feel free to modify any of the directions to best fit your unique teaching situation.

CLASSROOM MANAGEMENT: WHAT'S YOUR STYLE?

There are many factors that affect the atmosphere of a classroom and can be responsible for creating or maintaining disruptive student behavior. This activity is designed to help you become better aware of how you manage your

classroom and what you need in order to make your personal style of classroom management consistent with your beliefs and values.[1]

Directions: Read each statement on pages 29–32. Some statements are "most
like" you (column one) while others are not like you (column two). If you do
what that statement says as often as you want to, then check column five. If
you want to do more of it, check column three. If you want to do less, check
column four. For example, if you never arrange your desks in rows and that's
the way you want to run your classroom, check columns two and five because you are doing the right amount for you (which is nothing). (Complete
this activity before proceeding to activity below.)

PRIORITIZING SHEET

A. Look at your responses to "Classroom Management: What's Your Style"
   and choose the six responses from the column, "I do the right amount
   of," that are most reflective of you as a classroom manager.
   1. _____
   2. _____
   3. _____
   4. _____
   5. _____
   6. _____

B. Look at your responses to the columns, "I wish I did more of" and "I wish
   I did less of," and choose the six that you'd most like to attain for yourself
   as a classroom manager.
   1. _____
   2. _____
   3. _____
   4. _____
   5. _____
   6. _____

C. Now that you've identified six behaviors that you'd like more of or less of,
   answer the following questions:
   1. How do you stop yourself from becoming more of what you want to
      be? (For example, if you checked "I wish I did more of #33," try to dis-
      cover how you stop yourself from laughing more in class.)
   2. What do you imagine would happen if you permitted yourself to do
      more of or less of what you want? (What would happen if you did
      laugh more?)
   3. List all the negative consequences that might happen if you made real

[1] Adapted from Richard Curwin and Barbara Fuhrmann, *Discovering Your Teaching Self: Humanistic Approaches to Effective Teaching* (Englewood Cliffs, N.J.: Prentice-
Hall, 1975), pp. 47–50.

Check the column that fits best for you

	This is most like me (I do this most of the time)	This is not like me (I rarely or never do this)	I wish I did or was more of	I wish I did or was less of	I do the right amount of
1. Desks in my classroom are usually arranged in rows.					
2. I encourage students to speak spontaneously, without necessarily raising their hands.					
3. I allow my students to call me by my first name.					
4. Papers being turned in follow a standard format in my classroom.					
5. The bulletin boards in my classroom are usually decorated by me, rather than by the students.					
6. I usually follow and complete my lesson plans.					
7. I expect my students to ask permission to leave the room.					
8. I allow students to go to the bathroom at just about any time.					
9. My students may chew gum and eat most of the time.					
10. I have assigned seats or places for my students.					
11. I often threaten punishment of one kind or another for misbehavior.					

Statement	This is most like me (I do this most of the time)	This is not like me (I rarely or never do this)	I wish I did or was more of	I wish I did or was less of	I do the right amount of
12. I frequently contact parents.					
13. I do not tolerate swearing or other unacceptable language in my classroom.					
14. When I monitor a study period, I insist that the students be quiet.					
15. I often stand or sit behind a lectern or desk when teaching.					
16. My students and I sit on the floor.					
17. Students are permitted to remove their shoes in my class.					
18. I believe in dress codes for students and teachers.					
19. I act in ways that students consider traditional.					
20. I act in ways my principal considers traditional.					
21. I encourage students to work independently in self-directed activities.					
22. I allow my students to make decisions about classroom management.					
23. I often depart from or discard my lesson plans.					

This is most like me (I do this most of the time)	This is not like me (I rarely or never do this)	I wish I did or was more of	I wish I did or was less of	I do the right amount of	
					24. I keep students after school when they misbehave.
					25. I tell my students a great deal about myself.
					26. I allow students to openly disagree with me.
					27. I find it difficult to say, "I don't know."
					28. I often ask students for feedback concerning my teaching.
					29. I am likely to be asked to keep my students quieter.
					30. I ignore student misbehavior.
					31. I attend or chaperone student parties and events.
					32. I am likely to be advising student groups, formally or informally.
					33. I laugh a lot in class.
					34. I enjoy team-teaching.
					35. I am careful about checking attendance.
					36. I usually reprimand students who are tardy.
					37. I get tense when my principal comes into my room.

Item	This is most like me (I do this most of the time)	This is not like me (I rarely or never do this)	I wish I did or was more of	I wish I did or was less of	I do the right amount of
38. I probably let students take advantage of me.					
39. I enjoy being friends with my students.					
40. I frequently touch students.					
41. I expect respect from students.					
42. I have carefully read my students' cumulative records.					
43. I feel and act differently with students outside of class.					
44. I send students to see the principal, vice-principal, or counselor when they misbehave.					
45. I sometimes use sarcasm to win a point with a student.					
46. I use my curriculum to reflect the wants and needs of the students in my class.					
47. I take time to share appreciations with my students, and to have them share appreciations and resentments with me and each other.					

your second group of six statements. (If I laughed more—the principal would think I'm a hyena; I'd never get through the curriculum; etc.)

_____

_____

4. List all of the advantages to yourself and your students if your actual behavior matched your preferences. (What are the advantages of my laughing more either to myself and/or to my students?)

_____

_____

D. Look at your responses to the "this is most like me" column. If you were a student, what statements would you make about this teacher's style of teaching and ability to communicate with students? Would you choose to have this person as your teacher?

_____

_____

E. Look at the "this is not like me" column. Are there any items that you would like to move into column one? Are there any items in column one that you would like to transfer to column two? For example, if most of the time you use sarcasm to win a point with a student, and you would like to use less sarcasm, what do you imagine would happen if you expressed less sarcasm? One problem that many teachers face is not knowing other substitute responses for sarcasm that might yield a more effective result. Think of alternative responses for those behaviors you would like to change.

_____

_____

F. Write down one or more specific things that you are willing to do tomorrow that you believe can make you a more effective classroom manager (i.e., I'm going to allow myself to laugh at least once when I think that something is funny).

_____

_____

G. From your responses to the forty-nine statements, write a paragraph describing the characteristics and behaviors of your personal style of classroom management. (What about your style are you proud of, and what are you going to change?)

_____

_____

COMPARATIVE RULE INVENTORY

All teachers have rules for themselves and for their students, although sometimes these rules are never stated. When everybody knows what the rules are and when teachers have rules for themselves that are congruent with those that they have for their students, discipline problems are minimized. Clear rules stated and consistently enforced by a congruent teacher have the effect of removing double messages (saying one thing while meaning something else) that can lead to confusion and disharmony.

Directions: List one or two rules that you have for yourself and one or two rules that you have for your students in each of the following categories. These rules can be explicit (everybody knows what they are) or implicit (rules that exist but are never stated). Try to state your rules positively; for example, instead of "No fighting," for anger, state how anger *can* be expressed, such as "Angry feelings may be shared verbally without put-downs by expressing how *you* feel."

Categories	Rules for Me	Rules for My Students
1. Having homework and lesson plans done on time		
2. Doing what a superior (teacher or principal) wants you to do when you don't really want to do it		
3. Being flexible, changing plans on the spur of the moment		
4. How to dress in school		
5. Making a decision for which no rule exists		
6. The use of killer statements (put-downs, sarcasm)		
7. Expressing anger		
8. Expressing fear		
9. Expressing sadness		
10. Expressing love		
11. Caring for school property		
12. Movement in the classroom		

FOLLOW-UP QUESTIONS

1. How specific are each of your rules? How many are implicit (those rules you never tell your students until they are broken)? How many are explicit (those rules you tell your students before they are broken)?

_____

_____

_____

_____

_____

2. What categories show the greatest harmony between "rules for me" and "rules for my students"?

_____

_____

_____

_____

3. What categories show dissonance between the two?

_____

_____

_____

_____

4. What steps can you take to narrow the gap between "rules for me" and "rules for my students"?

_____

_____

_____

_____

5. If you were a student in your class, how would you feel about the rules that the teacher has for you?

_____

_____

_____

_____

6. As this student, write a short paragraph listing the characteristics and attributes of this teacher's rules.

_____

_____

_____

_____

7. As this student, what statements can you make of this teacher's fairness, consistency, believability, and firmness?

_____

_____

_____

_____

8. Identify the two categories in which you would like to narrow the gap, and with each of these categories, brainstorm all of the possible rules with which you imagine both you and your students could live. When

you have finished, select the one rule that fits most comfortably for you.

_____

_____

_____

_____

9. We suggest that you use this activity with your students in class, and you can modify the categories if you wish. Instead of "rules for my students," substitute "rules for my teacher." We also advise you to add a third column, "rules for each other." This can provide you with invaluable feedback from your students and can serve to tell you what it is that the students want regarding rules in the classroom.

_____

_____

_____

_____

SENTENCE STEMS

Sometimes just looking at your feelings in writing can provide an awareness that is helpful in dealing with discipline. Complete the following open-ended sentences with the most appropriate and honest responses.

1. The most effective method of discipline I have is _____
   _____

2. Discipline _____

3. When people yell at me, I feel _____
   _____

4. When I was a student in school I was disciplined once when _____
   _____

5. My teacher (re:#4) _____
   _____

6. One teacher that I most respected was _____
   _____

7. His/her style of classroom management was _____

8. One thing that I presently want from my students is _____
   _____

9. The kid who gives me the most trouble in my class(es) is _____
   _____

10. The thing I most dislike about this student is_____
   _____

11. With this student, I've tried _____
_____to modify his/her behavior.

12. What I believe to be the cause of most discipline problems is _____
_____

13. The two major classroom causes of discipline problems are _____
_____ and _____ _____

DISCIPLINE SCAVENGER HUNT [2]

The scavenger hunt is an activity designed for small groups (or large groups divided into small groups), but if you do not have access to a group you can do it by yourself as well. The purpose of this activity is to help you look at your behaviors and enhance your awareness in relation to discipline.

Directions: If you are working in small groups, you may do the activity by keeping score or just for fun without a score. The goal of the activity is to find through verbal interaction as many of the items on the following list as possible. If you keep score, give your group one point for each like and one point for each dislike on the first list and five points for each common experience on the second list. You can score a total of thirty-five points.

 If you are doing the activity alone, give yourself one point for one thing you like about yourself and one thing you dislike about yourself on the first list and five points for each experience you can vividly recall on the second list.

 Once you have written down your answers and tabulated your score (if you are doing so), you may compare the experience of each group and then answer the following questions. If you are doing the activity by yourself, go on immediately to the questions.

Find one like and dislike that your group (or you, if doing this alone) can unanimously agree fits each of the following categories:

	Like About Myself	Dislike About Myself
1. A time when you talked with a parent (parents) about discipline.		
2. A time when you talked with an administrator/teacher about discipline.		

[2] Adapted from R. Curwin and G. Curwin, *Developing Individual Values in the Classroom* (Palo Alto, California: Learning Handbooks, 1974), p. 17.

	Like About Myself	Dislike About Myself
3. A time when you talked with teachers in the lounge about students who are disruptive.		
4. A time when you punished a student (students).		
5. A time when you praised a student (students).		

Find one common experience that each member of your group (or you, if done individually) has shared (experienced) that fits each of the following categories:

1. An experience that would not go away (you thought about for over two days) that involved you as a disciplinarian.
2. A time you were caught breaking a rule as a student or as a teacher.
3. A time you got away with something and how you felt.
4. One thing you did to subvert the disciplinary "system."
5. One instance when you were proud of yourself (related to discipline).

FOLLOW-UP QUESTIONS

1. What do your responses have in common?
2. List the ways that your negative behavior helps you as a classroom manager.
3. How did you feel before you were caught breaking a rule? What did you want that the rule didn't allow you to have?
4. How did you feel when you were caught breaking a rule?
5. What statements can you make about yourself when you get away with something or when you subvert the system and get away with it?
6. How do you give yourself power as a classroom manager?
7. What is one way that you would like to be in your classroom that you believe would improve the atmosphere, but you have stopped yourself from being or doing for fear of nonvalidation or punishment from higher up?

TAKING OWNERSHIP

Many times we feel powerless with the methods we use to manage our classrooms. Although the methods available are often dependent upon the prevailing values and attitudes that exist in the community and school, it's important to give ourselves as many choices and options as we can when working with disruptive students. One way of immediately losing the respect of a student and encouraging more disruptive behavior is by imposing rules with which we feel no ownership. Yet, often it can be dangerous and risky to follow our beliefs, particularly when these are in conflict with those of the prevailing system. But if we do not, we can expect classroom disruption to increase. Consider the dilemma of a physical education teacher, Sally Borden, who has an eight-year-old boy who is so terrified of closeness to people that the only way he feels safe in making contact with other children is by whizzing a basketball at their heads. The school rule for such behavior is to send the student to the principal's office for punishment, which at the discretion of the principal may include paddling. Sally does not personally believe in the physical punishment of acting-out children but she has chosen to work in a school which has such a rule. If she follows the rule, she is in conflict with her personal beliefs and if she doesn't, she is in conflict with the social system. The consequences of not following the rule might include the loss of her colleagues' esteem, cries of inconsistency, and charges of insubordination. This is a classic "no win" situation for Sally which is common in disciplinary situations. On one level, Sally has a bigger problem than her disturbed student.

What can Sally do? We suggest that she accept herself as being in conflict. She needs to accept her problem and discover a solution which makes sense for her. If she decides to send Jimmy to the office, then she has actively chosen a solution that will create conflict for her, but *she* has decided and chosen a solution. At the very least, this leaves her with a sense of being a teacher with choices and options, and although limited, the end result is that Sally contacts the power in her to decide and to accept the consequences of her choice. And Jimmy gets to see his teacher as a feeling person who experiences conflict and can make decisions while she learns to live with this conflict.

Consider the following messages to Jimmy:

1. *Sally:* I have to send you to the office because you broke the rule and hit Mary in the face with the basketball.
2. *Sally:* (firmly) Jimmy, the rule here is that basketballs are not for throwing at people. While I don't like sending you to Mr. Hamilton's office, I am choosing to do this because of the school rule.

In the first example, the message is that *you* (the student) broke a rule and I *have to* carry out school policy. The second example states clearly that a rule was broken and although Sally is in conflict, she has *chosen* a course of action despite her lack of total comfort with it.

The following activity is designed to help you contact some of the conflict you may have in relation to your choices for discipline.

DIRECTIONS

A. List all your classroom behaviors and methods of disciplining that you believe you *have* to do in order to maintain classroom contol.

1. I have to _____

2. I have to _____

3. I have to _____

4. I have to _____

5. I have to _____

6. I have to _____

B. Now change all of the above I have to's to I choose to's. If you stated "I have to scold a student when he steals," change this to "I choose to scold a student when he steals."

1. I choose to _____

2. I choose to _____

3. I choose to _____

4. I choose to _____

5. I choose to _____

6. I choose to _____

FOLLOW-UP QUESTIONS

1. Which "choose to" statements elicit in you the strongest negative feelings?

2. Which "choose to" statements do you feel are not true for you?

3. For those statements that don't fit for you in the "choose to" category, what can you do to give yourself choices that are different from those listed?

4. Usually the "have to" statements that are not comfortably changed to "choose to" suggest conflict. What are you afraid would happen to you if you decided to discard those statements that you believe give you no choice? Have you checked out your fears, or are you silently living with them?

5. Look at your lists. Those statements that you feel are not true for you are good indicators that you have other preferences that you would like to act on.

6. For the statements that apply in "A," complete the following:

I have to _____ ,
and I would rather _____ ,

7. What do you need from yourself or others to begin to act on your preferences?

8. How can you get what you want? Who or what is blocking you, and what steps can you take in an effort to remove these obstacles?

DISCIPLINE FANTASY

This fantasy is designed to help you become aware of some of your feelings related to discipline. It can be done alone or in a group. If you participate in a group, have someone lead the fantasy by slowly reading the following directions. If you do it alone, read the directions in parts, fantasize that part and continue in this manner until you finish.

We suggest that you experience this activity during a quiet time when few distractions are present. Find a comfortable position and let yourself relax.

Now think of one of your students who makes life difficult for you in your classroom. Visualize him/her clearly; notice how he/she looks, what he/she is wearing, what his/her gestures are. Pay attention to how you feel as you experience this student. Now try to become this student and speak silently as if you were talking to your teacher. Talk to your teacher about yourself. Tell what you are like and what your life is like. (Pause.) Tell your teacher what you do and what your interests are. (Pause.) Now express how you feel toward this teacher or about the classroom. (Pause.) Start making some demands of your teacher (You should or shouldn't _____ ; I demand that you _____). Tell the teacher what you resent (I resent or I'm angry when _____). (Pause.) Now tell the teacher what you appreciate. Now see if you have anything else you'd wish to express to your teacher and express it. (Pause.) Now become the teacher again and respond to this student. Tell him/her what you're feeling and what you want. Make some demands (You should/shouldn't or I demand _____). Share your resentments (I resent you when you _____). Now tell this student what you appreciate in him/her.

FOLLOW-UP

1. Imagine yourself as a third person (somebody who has been observing this interaction) and see if you can discover some middle ground for both sides.
2. Write down all of the middle ground suggestions that this third person has just given you (do not censor your thoughts).
3. Choose one suggestion that you believe may be of use.
4. Remember this when you next encounter the student and try it. For example, you might say to the student, "I've been thinking of some

ways that we could get along that would make me feel more comfortable with you. I'd like to suggest_____. Is this suggestion something that makes sense to you?"

5. Don't be discouraged if the student chooses not to respond to your suggestion. At least you've made contact with him/her and have opened the way to problem identification and mutual problem solving.

RESOURCE DIRECTORY

This activity is designed for use in small groups or on a school-wide basis.[3] It reflects our belief that teachers have a great deal to offer each other based upon their personal experiences with classroom management methods.

In your group (or groups) of teachers answer the following questions (preferably on paper).

1. Do you believe that if a colleague visited your classroom, he or she would learn anything about effective classroom management? What?
2. Are you willing to allow a colleague to visit your classroom?
3. Which of your colleagues would you like to visit that you believe would help to make you a more effective classroom manager?

On a ditto master, briefly describe what you do that would be helpful for a colleague to see and sign your name, class times and room.

We suggest that a central person in the school, such as a principal or guidance counselor collect the dittos and put together a staff resource manual for school-wide distribution.

Finally, encouragement of classroom visits and discussions can be made by the school administration.

STUDENT PERCEPTIONS OF TEACHER

This activity is designed for you to see how well your students know you. Seeing yourself through the eyes of your students can provide valuable insights into how you are presenting yourself. It is possible that some of your

[3] We wish to thank the staff of the Hawthorne Middle School in Yonkers, N.Y. for their help in developing and testing this activity.

behaviors, of which you are unaware, can influence events in the classroom and may lead to discipline problems.

Directions: Tell your students that you would like to know how they perceive you, and that you would like them to answer the following questions. To avoid or minimize the student fear (or relish) of criticizing the teacher, have them do this activity anonymously.

Please answer the following questions:

1. What is one thing that your teacher enjoys doing?
2. What is his/her favorite saying or expression?
3. What is something that students do in class that makes the teacher unhappy?
4. What does the teacher do when he/she's unhappy or angry?
5. What is something that students do in class that makes the teacher happy?
6. What does the teacher do when he/she's happy or pleased?
7. What does your teacher do that you wish he/she did differently?
8. Where does your teacher live?
9. What does he/she say or do when he/she's made a mistake?
10. What is your teacher's favorite way to discipline?
11. How are you like your teacher?
12. How are you different from your teacher?

TEACHER AWARENESS CONTINUUM

One way of continuing to develop your self-awareness is through obtaining periodic feedback from your students regarding your management behavior. The Teacher Awareness Continuum should be administered anonymously at first, although as trust develops, it might be of interest to you to see how specific individuals perceive you. The students are encouraged to respond honestly and should be told that the purpose of the information is to help you to be more responsive to their views.

Administer the Awareness Continuum on approximately a monthly basis so that you may have an ongoing record of comparison of how your management style is being received by your students.

Directions: Tell the students to place an x on the continuum according to how they perceive each of these behaviors in you.

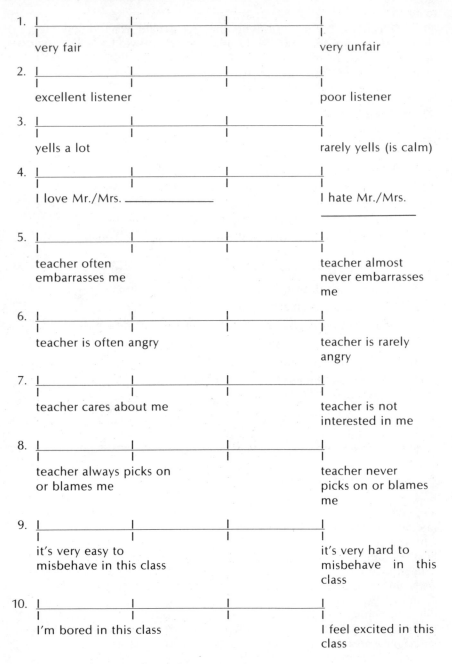

1. |_____|_____|_____|
   very fair   very unfair

2. |_____|_____|_____|
   excellent listener   poor listener

3. |_____|_____|_____|
   yells a lot   rarely yells (is calm)

4. |_____|_____|_____|
   I love Mr./Mrs. _____   I hate Mr./Mrs.
                                                _____

5. |_____|_____|_____|
   teacher often   teacher almost
   embarrasses me   never embarrasses
                                                me

6. |_____|_____|_____|
   teacher is often angry   teacher is rarely
                                                angry

7. |_____|_____|_____|
   teacher cares about me   teacher is not
                                                interested in me

8. |_____|_____|_____|
   teacher always picks on   teacher never
   or blames me   picks on or blames
                                                me

9. |_____|_____|_____|
   it's very easy to   it's very hard to
   misbehave in this class   misbehave in this
                                                class

10. |_____|_____|_____|
    I'm bored in this class   I feel excited in this
                                                class

FOLLOW-UP

After you have had time to examine the classes' responses, you might want to elicit more specific details to gain further understanding of their responses and perhaps change some of your behavior(s). You may, for example, say in class, "I looked through your responses to the form that I asked you to fill out the other day and I noticed that several of you think that I'm not interested in you. I also discovered that a number of you see me as picking on some students unfairly. I was really happy to see that most of you find the class to be exciting. I'd like to spend a few minutes today to see if anybody is willing to let me know how I show my disinterest. I know that it's a little strange to tell the teacher such things, but I sure would appreciate any help I can get."

We've found that honest sharing by the teacher often results in the building of trust and gives the students an opportunity to participate in risk taking (telling the teacher something unpleasant) and problem solving (seeing that teachers aren't perfect and are willing to grow and change). Be sure to tell the students that there will be no negative consequences for their input. Such modeling can have a powerful impact particularly on those students whose self-concepts are too rigid to allow for change and growth.

NONVERBAL MESSAGES/BODY INVENTORY

The messages that you express with your body, and gestures are at least as important as those that are spoken. The music of your message is contained in *how* you deliver your words. When your verbal message is incongruent with your gestures, tone of voice, and/or body language, then you may be perceived as inconsistent and unclear. Because of the complexity of human behavior, it is impossible for anybody to be consistent all of the time. However, the more your nonverbal behavior approximates your verbal message, the easier it will be for your students to be clear about what is acceptable or unacceptable to you. An incongruent teacher unknowingly encourages misbehavior, as students will predictably test his/her limits of tolerance until they are fairly sure that a certain student behavior will be met with a certain teacher response that is consistently given both verbally and nonverbally.

One clue to the presence or absence of verbal/nonverbal congruence is the degree of daily tension that you experience. If you're leaving school with frequent headaches, stomachaches, tightness in the neck, shoulders, face, legs, or chest, it's a good bet that you're holding your body back from expressing what it wants. Becoming aware of the messages that your body wants to express but isn't, and following through with action can lead you to a clearer understanding of how you allow yourself to respond to your students based upon your needs, how you stop yourself from responding, and how you can free more of your energy through an integration of your mind with your body.

We suggest that you do a *body inventory* during your break time, during your five-minute interval between classes, or after school on a regular basis, be it daily or weekly.

1. Sit down in a relatively quiet location and verbally finish the following sentences (either silently or out loud):

    a. Right now, my face feels _____

    b. Right now, my neck feels _____

    c. Right now, my shoulders feel _____

    d. Right now, my chest feels _____

    e. Right now, my back feels _____

    f. Right now, my legs feel _____

    g. Right now, my feet feel _____

    h. Right now, my behind feels _____

    i. Right now, my thighs feel _____

    j. Right now, my ankles feel _____

2. Now, for each body part in which there is tension, change the "My _____ feels" to "I feel." For example, if you discovered tension in your shoulders and neck, change "My neck and shoulders are tense" to "I'm tense."

3. Now, take responsibility for your tension. Although events outside of you can contribute to your tension, you ultimately either make yourself tense or not tense. So instead of saying, "I'm tense," say, "I'm tensing my shoulders and neck right now."

4. Now exaggerate this tension. Make your neck and shoulders even tighter than they were before. Squeeze each body part that is tense, and then relax that body part until you feel some loosening. It sometimes helps to put words to your actions; for example, say "I'm tightly tensing my shoulders and neck" or "I'm loosening my shoulders and neck," as you're doing it.

LETTING YOUR BODY SPEAK

1. Do the first step described in "body inventory" which calls for becoming aware of any tension in your body.

2. Now give this body part a *voice*. Let it speak as if it had a voice of its own. We often find that beneath tension lies a host of unspoken or unexpressed feelings which find expression in the body musculature. By giving this part a voice and a personality, you can help yourself to lower your level of tension.

3. Now what does this part want to say or do? (For example, say "I'm my tense shoulders. I want to squeeze Johnny right now. I want to give him my tension. Debbie, I can't stand you when you lie about your homework assignment. Sam, I make myself tense, but what I really want to do is force you to pay attention in class.") We advise you to say what you want to say and do *not* censor. As noted in the "Fantasy Dialogue') in Chapter 7 the student isn't really there, so you are your only censor. You need not hold back.

SILENT MEDITATION

With the vicissitude of demands that are daily made upon teachers, it's incumbent that time be allowed for a siphoning off of the tension associated with others' demands. Meditation has been associated by some with mysticism, voodoo, magic, and religion. While most forms of meditation have their origins in Far Eastern beliefs and practice, the modern day adaptation of these approaches makes it possible for most teachers to benefit from relaxation through meditation. The meditator is usually encouraged to spend a minimum of twenty minutes twice daily. We believe that while this may be optimal, it is possible to benefit from meditating for even shorter periods of time. Meditation can be effective in lowering blood pressure and leading one to a more relaxed state.

Since a variety of techniques is available, we encourage the interested teacher to read or scan Patricia Harrington's book *Freedom in Meditation*, which offers an excellent, easily readable, comprehensive overview of meditation and its various practices. In our workshops, we have used an adaptation of a Zazen technique which we will briefly describe here.

1. Find a comfortable, quiet environment in which the likelihood of your being disturbed is minimal.
2. Find a comfortable position either seated on the floor or in a chair. Some prefer a lotus or half-lotus position, while others are more comfortable in a chair. You decide for yourself.
3. For one minute, just let yourself experience any thoughts or feelings that you have. Let thoughts come and go and make no effort to continue with them.
4. Now pay attention to your breathing. Fill your lungs with air and then let the air out. Continue this for another minute. Do not try to breathe differently, just pay attention to how you breathe.
5. Close your eyes, or if you prefer, leave them open and fix them upon an immobile object.

6. Now, on each "out" breath, silently count. The process is
   1. In-breath   2. ONE (on out-breath)
   1. In-breath   2. TWO (on out-breath)
   1. In-breath   2. THREE (on out-breath)
   1. In-breath   2. FOUR (on out-breath)
   1. In-breath   2. ONE (on out-breath)
7. Some people report that they lose count. Should this happen to you, then simply start with "one," when you're aware that you've lost count. If thoughts come as you meditate, then stay with them until you're aware that you're thinking. When you become aware that you're thinking, simply return to counting. A few people experience some initial nausea and dizziness when they begin to meditate and this is a normal reaction for them. Within a short time, these side effects usually disappear.

The purpose is to provide you with another way to gain awareness of yourself as well as to give to yourself. You simply cannot meditate and give to another person at the same time. Since so much of the teacher's time involves giving to others, we believe that your ability to give will be enhanced when you first give to yourself. By giving yourself a time to relax, you'll have more energy to respond to the demands of others.

VOICE AWARENESS

Directions: Bring a portable cassette player to class with a one-hour tape. Leave the cassette player on and record the events of your class during different times. Pay particular attention to your voice and its qualities. As you listen to your voice, what does it sound like? Is it high pitched or low? Loud or soft? Demanding or reassuring? Parental or childlike? What is its emotion? Is it joyful, sad, angry, worried, or lacking in expressiveness?

Now listen for the content. Do you do most of the talking or is there shared involvement? Are your words blaming, reasoning, threatening, instructing, helping, or hindering? What do they convey?

Now imagine that this voice belongs to someone other than yourself. What are your immediate impressions? Is this a person from whom you'd seek help? Do you like him or her? If you misbehaved, is this a person whom you would listen to, respect, want to accept caring from, be afraid of? If you had to be in school, is this a teacher you'd like to have?

Write a brief paragraph regarding the characteristics of the person on the tape. Include those qualities of classroom management that you can attribute to this individual. You might wish to ask a few trusted (and honest) colleagues to listen and give you feedback.

6

AWARENESS OF STUDENTS

Simply stated, the better you know your students, the more opportunities you will have to prevent discipline problems from occurring. The alienated, frustrated student will most likely become a discipline problem. To the degree that each individual student feels a sense of power and control in himself, he will have less need to hurt others in order to feel his power. The powerless bully, and the alienated agitate.

Youngsters who chronically misbehave tend to feel that both the school and their parents are disinterested in them. These students are unable to realize their potential in a world in which they feel uncared for and alone. They usually lack respect for authority and are hard to like. Feeling defeated, the teacher understandably resorts to such methods as blaming, scolding, punishing, calling parents, taking away privileges, referring for psychological relief, and using other power-based methods that are often doomed to failure. The powerless student has only his defiance to protect him from an environment that he experiences as unresponsive to his needs. When he shows his defiance, at least he elicits a response.

It is certainly no easy task to change things meaningfully. But we agree with the notion that an ounce of prevention is worth a pound of cure. By paying attention to *who* your students are, how they think, and what they feel, you are doing quite a lot toward the prevention of discipline problems.

Finding out who your students are and how they feel requires a willingness to be open with them and an acceptance of *any* feelings that they may have. It is our belief that there are no *bad* feelings and that any feeling is acceptable. Limits around expression of feelings (behavior) are essential, but limits around feelings make no sense. The impulsive student has not learned to separate feelings from action because both are regarded as unacceptable. When one learns to put limits on behavior and none on feelings, a great deal of creative potential is released which can lead the student on a wonderful journey to rich and heretofore undiscovered self-knowledge and self-esteem.

The following activities will be useful only when the students feel that they can trust you and when they know that they will not be punished for expressing their genuine thoughts and feelings.

INTEREST INVENTORY

The interest inventory is a brief way of quickly finding out some information about your students.[1] We suggest that you modify this sample inventory to meet the needs of children at different grade levels. There might be some particular information that you may wish to include that does not exist on this form.

name _____   *date* _____

1. What do you like to read?

    a. _____

    b. _____

2. What are three things that coming to school means for you?

    a. _____

    b. _____

    c. _____

[1] Adapted from John Stellern, Stanley F. Vasa, and Jack Little, *Introduction to Diagnostic-Prescriptive Teaching and Programming* (Glen Ridge, N.J.: Exceptional Press, 1976), p. 166.

3. What are your hobbies or favorite interests?

    a. _____

    b. _____

    c. _____

4. If you could spend your time doing anything you want, what would you do?

    a. _____

    b. _____

    c. _____

5. The thing that I want most from this class is _____

    _____

6. The best reward anybody can give me is _____

7. Name your favorite grown-up. _____

    What I like best about this person is _____

8. Name your three favorite television shows. _____

9. When I do well at school I wish my teacher would _____

    _____

10. When I do poorly at school I wish my teacher would _____

    _____

11. The other kids in this class _____

12. Something I really want is _____

13. My sisters and/or brothers _____

14. The class in which I learned the most was _____

15. My favorite teacher _____

16. Name three things that people do to punish you.

    a. _____

    b. _____

    c. _____

17. How well do each of these punishments work?

    a. _____

    b. _____

    c. _____

18. Which is most effective? _____

19. I will do almost anything to avoid _____

    because _____

20. Name as many things as you can that you would like to change in this class.

PEER SOCIOGRAM

Knowing how the students perceive each other can tell you a lot about your class makeup and which students might be most likely to be viewed as different. Students who are perceived as different by their peers are likely to be more sensitive to rejection and may choose to attack others as they feel attacked. We strongly suggest that you allow your students to remain anonymous for this activity.[2]

1. The three students that I like most in the class are

    a. _____

    b. _____

    c. _____

2. The three students I dislike most in the class are

    a. _____

    b. _____

    c. _____

3. One student in this class I'm afraid of is _____

    I'm afraid of him/her because _____

4. If I could choose three other students to do a class project with, they would be

    a. _____

    b. _____

    c. _____

5. The student who I think the teacher likes the most is _____

6. The student who I think the teacher dislikes the most is _____

Instead of using "three students I like" and "three students I do not like," you may substitute "three students I would like to work with in a group" and "three students I would prefer not to work with in a group" to make the sociogram less threatening for your students.

SUGGESTED FOLLOW-UP

There are many possible ways that you can use this information to benefit yourself and your students. Some of these are as follows:

1. Pair off students who are generally well perceived with those who are not and have them do group assignments together.

---

[2] This activity has been controversial because of the potentially negative information generated. It will be wise to check with your school to make sure there is no policy against it and to explain it carefully to the students to make sure they know that no one will be singled out or ridiculed. A high degree of trust is important for this activity to work. The sociogram is, however, a device of long standing and of good repute.

2. Choose poorly perceived students for high status jobs such as safety patrol; this can serve as a self-concept and peer status booster.

3. Put the poorly perceived youngster in the role of helper, either in the classroom with academics, or if not academically proficient, with children who are younger.

FEEDBACK LETTER

In most classrooms, there is little daily feedback to the teacher from his/her students. Teachers are usually left to their own impressions as to how the day went. We believe that one way for you to have a direct way of knowing where your students are is to ask for feedback.

For students even as young as third graders, we suggest that you ask them to write a brief letter to you toward the end of the school day. Ask them to describe how they felt about school, to name one or two important things they learned that day, and to list any problems they had which they'd like help with. You might wish to give more structure to the letter by limiting its focus. (For example, say to them, "I'd like to know what you learned today from the math assignment" or "Tell me what you liked most in school today and what you liked least.") When most students experience the teacher as caring and willing to accept both positive and negative feedback, their need to act out in inappropriate ways can diminish significantly.

With older students who see you for only forty to fifty minutes a day, we suggest you ask for feedback letters once a week.

You can also use the letters to open up issues to the class. After a day or class in which you sensed something was wrong, but had no direct incident, you can ask for letters and read them to the class anonymously (include a letter of your own). In this way you and the class can see how the other students are feeling. If an issue comes up, you have a framework for discussion and resolution.

SHOW & TELL

There probably is not a kindergarten or first grade classroom in the country that doesn't have *show and tell*. Traditionally, this is a time for children to gain confidence in self-expression by showing objects to their classmates of which they are proud and talking about them, or by telling something to the class which has meaning for the child. Why then, does show and tell cease to exist in most schools after the first grade? Perhaps show and tell is dismissed because of the competing curriculum needs and the always present classroom time shortage. After grade one, if a youngster brings his new model car to class unannounced, it's likely that it will wind up in the teacher's desk before the day is over. Students who are poor academic achievers are more likely to be disruptive in school because of the daily lack of affirmation they receive. When they attend school and know that some time will be set aside for discussion of their life experiences and out-of-school interests and talents, their sense of connectedness with school strengthens and their need to disrupt weakens.

Show and tell has the advantage of giving you daily input as to the interests, concerns, difficulties, and excitements that your students experience. We believe that by staying in touch with these you will enhance your sensitivity to the changing needs of your students. With children ages seven to eighteen, we suggest that you have a "checking in" time at the very beginning of the day. This time is used to allow students to share anything they would like to with the class. With the younger children, it would be wise to structure the activity by suggesting they discuss their breakfast, bus ride to school, what they did last night, and any feelings they would like to share. The children should be told in advance that they will have fifteen minutes for this. With high school or junior high school students, discussion can be limited to five minutes.

DISRUPTIVE BEHAVIOR CHECKLIST

We define disruptive behavior as events which prevent the teacher from teaching what he/she wants to because the events require teacher intervention. Disruptive behavior may also affect other students, as they are distracted from their expected tasks by the event causing the disruption. We suggest that you use the checklist as a way of giving yourself information regarding disruptive events, as well as providing specific feedback to the student regarding his/her disruptive behavior.[3] Using this activity can set the stage for developing *resolution dimension contracts* with chronic rule breakers which will be discussed in detail in Chapter 11. In addition, you can use this data to formulate rules and consequences for students as discussed in Chapter 9.

DIRECTIONS

We suggest that you make a chart which includes the names of all students, potentially disruptive classroom events, and the date. Then use an outside observer (who might be another teacher, aide, or somebody else you

---

[3] We advise you to check with your school administration regarding its policy on record keeping and confidentiality before you use the checklist.

are comfortable with) to record disruptive events on the chart by placing a check mark in the square next to the student's name. You may also act as observer during specific classroom periods when the students are working independently. You may also choose to make frequent use of the checklist by keeping a copy on your desk and simply recording events as they occur each day. We include a sample checklist for your use. Each time a disruptive event occurs, simply place a check mark in the appropriate column next to the student's name. See our sample checklist on page 56.

Note: Our sample checklist is not meant to be a complete list of disruptive behaviors, but simply a guide for your use. We urge you to tap your creativity in developing a checklist that is relevant and meaningful for you and your students.

FOLLOW-UP

The information can be used in many different ways and can serve as a basis for individual, small group, or total classroom problem solving. For example, if the data is collected during reading group time, and Student X has incurred several check marks indicating a pattern for him, then it is fair to assume that he wants something other than what he's getting during this time. His teacher can say, "Today you were out of your seat five different times instead of doing your workbook assignment, and yesterday it was six times. Johnny, this tells me that getting out of your seat is better for you than doing your workbook. Now, do you need extra help from me to do your workbook or is there something else that would make it easier for you to stay seated?" A similar approach could be used with groups.

You could also use this data to consider ways of changing the classroom structure, particularly if you see that several students are frequently disruptive. The data could also be used to help plan a specific change. With Johnny, for example, the teacher who's comfortable with behavior modification could choose to use out of seat time (which is obviously rewarding) for improved in seat behavior. In this way, Johnny is rewarded for in seat behavior by being given x minutes of time to be out of his seat.

FREE TIME ACTIVITY COOKBOOK

When students feel that some of their wishes and preferences can be realized in the classroom, they experience a higher degree of connectedness to the class and are less likely to subvert the system to get what they want. While it is impossible and undesirable to meet the needs of all students all of the time, a number of discipline problems can be prevented by providing students with choices of activities that are initiated by them. We've found that many problems requiring teacher intervention occur during those times

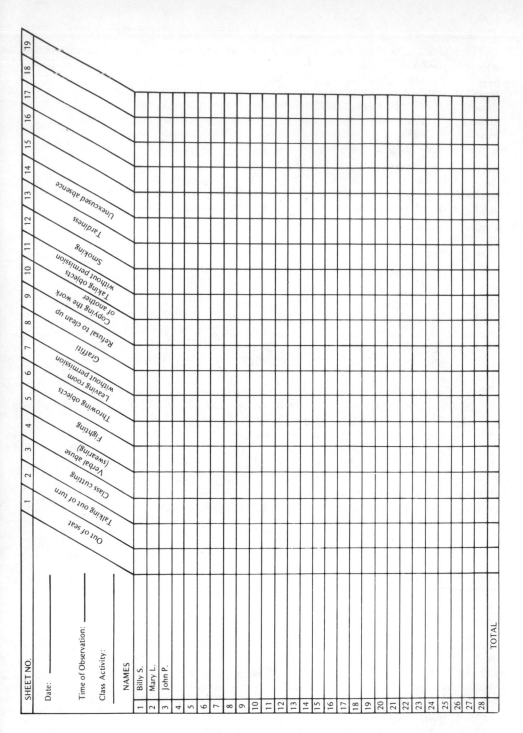

SHEET NO. _____

Date: _____

Time of Observation: _____

Class Activity: _____

NAMES	Out of seat	Talking out of turn	Class cutting	Verbal abuse (swearing)	Fighting	Throwing objects	Leaving room without permission	Graffiti	Refusal to clean up	Copying the work of another	Taking objects without permission	Smoking	Tardiness	Unexcused absence						
	1	2	3	4	5	6	7	8	9	10	11	12	13	14	15	16	17	18	19	
1 Billy S.																				
2 Mary L.																				
3 John P.																				
4																				
5																				
6																				
7																				
8																				
9																				
10																				
11																				
12																				
13																				
14																				
15																				
16																				
17																				
18																				
19																				
20																				
21																				
22																				
23																				
24																				
25																				
26																				
27																				
28																				
TOTAL																				

which are relatively unstructured and nonteacher directed. Allowing students to choose high interest activities during these times can help to significantly reduce the incidence of discipline events in your classroom.

DIRECTIONS

Tell the class that it's important to you that each student has a chance to choose things to do in the classroom from time to time. Direct each student to write down two activities that he/she likes to do; these can be activities he/she has done either at school or elsewhere. (The students need not identify themselves.) Once they finish, they will give their papers to you, and you will read each suggestion aloud, and offer your thoughts as to the classroom appropriateness of each. We also encourage you to invite discussion from the students.

If you should object to any suggested activity, then let the group know of your objection and be as specific as possible, explaining how this activity would *not* be acceptable in the classroom. Be careful during class discussion to point out that not all activities will be desirable to all or even many students and that this is okay. Student objections should be limited to *how* any given activity would interfere with them and prevent them from doing what they want to do in the classroom. For example, "If kids were allowed to walk around the class during free time, then I would be bothered because I like to read silently during free time." Class discussion is for the purpose of finding ways to allow the activity (if possible) while at the same time not interfering with the needs of others. Sometimes students or the teacher may have a suggestion as to how the activity can occur without disturbing others.

After all discussion has been completed, ask for a group of volunteers to make a "free time activity cookbook" which lists all acceptable student suggested activities.[4] The students then may choose activities from the cookbook during free time.

FOLLOW-UP

Sometimes problems occur which were not anticipated. For this reason, it is important to periodically monitor and review the activity selections from the cookbook and modify some, add others, and omit some. Any additions, subtractions, or modifications can be discussed with the class prior to making any changes.

---

[4] Adapted from Gay Hendricks and Thomas Roberts, *The Second Centering Book* (Englewood Cliffs, N.J.: Prentice-Hall, 1977), p. 100.

7

EXPRESSION OF FEELINGS

Dealing with your feelings is tough enough for most people, and when a teacher lives in a classroom with twenty-five to thirty students, difficulties can quickly intensify. It is difficult to find acceptable outlets for expressing feelings. This difficulty causes students and teachers to engage in a battle of wills that often leads to classroom discipline problems.

As mentioned in Chapter 6, we believe that all feelings that anyone has about *anything* are acceptable. It is one's inability to accept himself as a feeling person that leads to destructive behavior. It is incumbent upon educators to encourage students to become aware of and alive to their feelings, and to teach the difference between "bad feelings" and "bad behavior." The young child often equates feelings with action, so that if he even wishes his parents or teachers harm, he's a "bad boy." Very quickly we learn that feelings such as anger and sadness are not to be experienced, for if we allow ourselves to feel these feelings, then we will release much harmful energy to other people. This belief is the antithesis of how we actually function. We simply have no way of completely denying ourselves recognition of our feelings without hurting ourselves or each other. Paradoxically, the most healthy way of not feeling angry is to let ourselves experience the anger by fully recognizing its existence. The same is true of all other feelings such as excitement, sadness, sexuality, and joy. When we stifle an emotion, we pay a heavy price.

We are reminded of Lorraine Hanley, a teacher who wanted help in dealing with what she felt was racial tension. She reported that her six black students had alienated themselves from others and were creating management problems for her. When Mrs. Hanley was asked, "What would happen if you told the class that you felt that the blacks and whites were not getting along and that this was creating problems for you," her voice started quivering. She imagined that the classroom racial tension would be intensified, that kids would go home and tell their parents, and that the parents would mobilize and accuse her of being a racist. Obviously, with all these anticipated catastrophic fantasies, she paralyzed herself and rendered herself helpless to deal with the problem.

Let's examine one more example. Don Riley teaches tenth grade general science in a middle class suburban school. In his fourth period class he has a problem with Clara, an attractive student who rarely works and who spends most of her class time talking with her girlfriend. Don is regarded as a tough disciplinarian with few rules, but they are consistently enforced. When he asked for help, it was the first time he had done so in three years. It was agreed that a few classroom observations might be useful in helping Don to gain insight into Clara and what could be done to minimize the frequency of her disruptive behavior.

The classroom observer noticed (1) a lack of firmness in Don's voice and gestures when telling Clara to stop talking; (2) a lack of consistent eye contact when disciplining her; and (3) a tendency for Don to be in close physical proximity to Clara. For Clara, the observer recorded (1) provocative clothing and gestures and (2) consistent eye contact with Don coupled with such behaviors as licking lips and softly touching her legs when he was in view.

In short, there were nonverbal sexual messages being frequently communicated between the two. The hunch was that Clara was sexually provoking Don. His response was to approach her by being in close physical proximity, while at the same time to avoid her by showing no firmness in his discipline and avoiding eye contact. Don was attracted to Clara but full of injunctions that made him deny these feelings. Family, religious, and professional ethics continually reminded him that he should not have sexual feelings for a student.

A series of activities to be done while Don drove home by himself after school was suggested to help him accept his attraction to Clara. By allowing himself to feel his desires and establish his limits, he was able to put to test the uneasiness he felt when he was in Clara's company. After the first week, Don reported that he was still having trouble with Clara. We worked together using this technique for one month, after which time Don reported that things had considerably improved in the classroom. He was still aware of Clara's provocative behavior (which eventually diminished), but was in control of himself.

Don Riley needed to become aware of and accept his sexual feelings for Clara, which was no easy task. This didn't mean that he should act on them or even make them public. In fact, never once did he deal with Clara directly, which would have been at the least, a very risky venture. Once he allowed himself to experience his sexual feelings (in the safety of his car ride home with no one else present) and to acknowledge them as part of himself, the better able he was to deal with Clara's classroom misbehavior.

These examples illustrate the importance of acknowledging one's feelings. If Lorraine Hanley really wants to deal with the racial tension in her class, she must first start with the tension in herself. She needs to pay close attention to her catastrophic fantasies which are frightening to her and prevent her from resolving the problem in her classroom. As long as Lorraine is intimidated by her fantasies, she won't have the power to think clearly and begin to find solutions to her very difficult problem. By contrast, Don was willing to acknowledge his sexual feelings for Clara and to find a safe method of expressing these feelings. By paying attention to what was going on in him, he cleared himself emotionally and stopped his game with Clara.

The following activities are suggested methods for both you and your students to learn how to accept and safely express feelings.

CATASTROPHIC FANTASIES

Teachers often stop themselves from acting because of fears that if they did a certain thing, then psychological harm would befall either themselves or their students.[1] By examining the thoughts that underlie a fear, we can discover whether the fear is reality based or is mostly irrational. We can then decide if we want to continue to listen to what we fear and behave accordingly or if we want to risk behaving differently. Most fears are based upon the anticipation of negative consequences. Some common fears expressed by teachers include losing control of one's class; losing the respect of colleagues; being criticized by administrators; being disliked by students; devel-

[1] We wish to thank Sam Graceffo of the Gestalt Institute of Syracuse for making us aware of this concept.

oping a poor image with parents, and seeing oneself as an unworthy teacher. When we allow ourselves to become aware of how we make ourselves afraid to act, it becomes possible for us to arrive at other options if we choose to.

A. List five things that you had an impulse to do in your classroom during the last week but decided not to do (be specific). These can include such behaviors as yelling at a student, giving a test, or calling a parent. (Your list can include behaviors and /or feelings.)

   1. I wanted to _____ and I didn't.

   2. I wanted to _____ and I didn't.

   3. I wanted to _____ and I didn't.

   4. I wanted to _____ and I didn't.

   5. I wanted to _____ and I didn't.

B. Now for each behavior on your list, write down all the negative consequences that you imagine would have happened to you if you'd allowed yourself to act on these behaviors. (It's very important that your list include all anticipated negative consequences.)

   1. Behavior (I wanted to yell at Johnny and I didn't).
      List your anticipated negative consequences (If I did yell at Johnny, this is what I fear would happen).

      a. _____

      b. _____

      c. _____

      d. _____

   2. Behavior

      a. _____

      b. _____

      c. _____

      d. _____

   3. Behavior

      a. _____

      b. _____

      c. _____

      d. _____

   4. Behavior

      a. _____

      b. _____

      c. _____

      d. _____

5. Behavior

    a. _____

    b. _____

    c. _____

    d. _____

C. Now go back to your list of "I wanted to . . . and I didn't," and in a safe environment (e.g., your car, study, kitchen) express all of those behaviors and feelings that you didn't allow yourself to express in the classroom. (It's important that you don't hold back. Remember, the source of your conflict is not really here, so you can hurt no one. That is, unless you choose to whip yourself for having such terrible feelings and fantasies. If you want to hit a student, substitute a soft pillow for the student and let him have it!)

D. After each expression, check out your feelings and thoughts. Again, ask yourself, "What would happen if I behaved this way in my classroom?" (Be sure to consider the positives as well as the negatives.)

E. For each of these statements write down what it is that you *do* that's different for each of these behaviors. (For example, if you stated, "I wanted to punch Johnny in the nose when he called me an S.O.B.," state now what it is that you did that was different (e.g., ". . . but I ignored him").

F. Now compare your lists from step "A" and from step "E", keeping in mind the consequences of each action. Are you thinking that you'd like to continue your classroom behavior as is, or would you like to change?

G. For each behavior in step "A" that you choose to maintain, repeat the following: "I want to punch Johnny in the nose when he calls me an S.O.B. and I choose to continue to ignore him."

H. What will I do?
    We suggest that you allow yourself to make very gradual changes. For example: "I want to punch Johnny in the nose and I won't (for personal and moral reasons) and I won't ignore him. I will tell him firmly, 'Johnny, I'm very angry when I hear that and I will not tolerate that any longer.' "
    Usually some compromise solution between the two polarities and closer to what you're currently doing is advisable. Big changes, quickly done usually lead to even more anxiety.

GRIPE BOX

The purpose of this activity is to provide an on-going, daily account of difficulties and annoyances that students are experiencing during each day. It's important that little daily annoyances and resentments are not allowed to accumulate but are rather dealt with each day. It's the accumulation of resentments, often minor, that ultimately lead to blowups, chaos, confusion and discipline problems.

We suggest that you use a shoe box or cardboard box and decorate it with the words "gripe box." Explain to your students that each day various things happen to us which leave us feeling upset, sad, annoyed, or angry. These events can occur on the school bus, playground, in the cafeteria, or in the classroom. Explain that they may feel resentful toward you, other students, hall monitors, security guards, or other people in the school. But from now on, when they think that they've been mistreated and they are feeling resentful, angry, sad, or upset, you would like them to write down on a piece of paper what happened and how they feel. After they've written this down, suggest that they put their gripe in the classroom "gripe box." Then explain that during a prearranged time you will read each gripe and together with them see if there are some things all of you can think of that would help the student with his or her problem. It's important that you, the teacher participate in this process as well and contribute your annoyances to the "gripe box" along with your students.

FOLLOW-UP

After you or a student has read each gripe, we suggest that you encourage your students to brainstorm as many solutions to the described problem as possible. You might direct the discussion by saying, "Billy felt angry when Mr. Paulsen scolded him in the hall today. If you (class) were Billy, what are all the things that you could do to make yourself feel less angry?" We suggest that you list all proposed solutions on the blackboard (even the silly ones) and leave it to Billy to either publicly or privately choose those which best fit for him. It's been our experience that publicly stating a problem is often sufficient help for students. The empathy and concern they experience from their classmates serves to help them feel that they are not entirely alone with a problem and that the classroom can be a place to receive emotional support.

TENSION RELAXATION

Many students who become involved as discipline problems are observed to be "anxious," "tense," "sitting on a powder keg," "aggressive," "hostile," and "hyperactive." By learning *not* to express feelings verbally, these students keep their resentments and other feelings inside and convert these feelings to muscular tension. This muscular tension may lead to physical aggression. As a way of helping them to "drain off" this tension, we offer the

Tension relaxation can help students "get off the powder keg."

following activity.[2] (Each "pause" should be of approximately a ten second duration.)

> I'd like you each to find a comfortable seated position either on the floor (rug or mat if possible) or in your chair. Try to face away from each other. Let yourself relax and pay attention to your breathing. Listen to yourself breathing in and out. Now picture yourself in a very quiet, peaceful, happy place where you can do whatever you want. (Pause.) Nobody is going to tell you what to do unless you want somebody to do this. Close your eyes if you wish. What are you doing? Where are you? Just let yourself be wherever you are. (Pause.) Now again pay attention to your breathing. (Pause.)
>
> Now I would like you to think of one word that makes you feel very peaceful and relaxed. Words such as *friend, love, peace, quiet, calm* are but a few that might be relaxing words for you. (Pause.) Now choose your relaxing word. (Pause.) Take in a deep breath and as you let it out, say this word quietly to yourself. Now let yourself breathe naturally and each time you exhale say this word. (Pause.) Keep your eyes closed or if you insist upon opening them, find a spot right in front of you and keep your eyes fixed on this spot. Continue breathing and quietly saying this word as you exhale. Keep doing this until I tell you to stop. (About 5 minutes.)

FOLLOW-UP

Some students will find both their eyes and minds wandering. Tell them that when this happens, to just let themselves wander. Then when

[2] There are two other helpful relaxation activities in *The Second Centering Book* by Hendricks and Roberts (Prentice-Hall, 1976). See "Deep Relaxation" (p. 41) and "Instant Relaxation" (p. 46).

they're ready to return their attention to their fixed spot on the floor, tell them to continue their breathing while quietly saying their word.

We suggest this as a daily activity, not to exceed ten minutes with older children or five minutes with younger children.

PREVENTIVE PUT-DOWNS

We define put-downs as critical words, statements, or actions whose purpose is to hurt the self-concept of the victim. The victimizer ordinarily lacks any feelings of power and control. He gains a sense of power only at the expense of someone whom he perceives as more helpless and vulnerable than himself. You can use the following activities to reduce or eliminate put-downs in your class.

ACTIVITIES

1. *Bulletin board.* Any time a student or the teacher experiences a put-down from somebody, we suggest that either a picture (e.g., of a gun, sword, or knife) or a statement such as "I hurt" be placed on a bulletin board. If no put-downs are heard for a class period or a day, a picture is removed from the board. Special class privileges can be earned by keeping the board free of pictures for a specified time, such as three days or a week.

2. *Agreeing with the put-down.* In addition to the power felt by the victimizer, one need that he/she's often expressing through put-downs is the need for attention. By removing attention from the victimizer, the power of the put-down often diminishes. Fitzhugh Dodson, in his *How to Discipline with Love*, describes a process which has classroom adaptability. The intent of this method is to frustrate the victimizer's attempt to control with power, by teaching the victim to passively agree with everything the victimizer says. The use of this method in the classroom may go as follows:

   Judy (*victimizer*): (with friends present) You're the fattest, ugliest girl in the class.

   Shirley (*victim*): I'm the fattest, ugliest girl in this class.

   Judy: And you're stupid, dumb, and smelly.

   Shirley: (calmly) You're absolutely right: I'm stupid, dumb, and smelly.

   Judy: And the boys think you're even worse than we do.

   Shirley: You're absolutely right—the boys think I'm all of those things.

   Judy: And your mother's ugly, too.

   Shirley: And my mother is ugly, too.

This exchange continues for a few more minutes with Judy finally giving up and leaving. What she really wants is for Shirley to get angry and engage in a power struggle with her. By remaining calm and distant from Judy's attack, the message is "I'm stronger than you are and I won't let you feel powerful at my expense." Judy walks away to look for a more willing victim.

3. *Rechanneling negative energy.* Since the victimizer wants attention and power, it's a safe bet that deep down he/she feels lacking for each. One way of preventing put-downs is to rechannel this energy into more appropriate and less harmful outlets. The student who uses the put-down should be given responsible tasks that allow for the expression of power and fulfill the needs for attention. Making this person the teacher's helper, room monitor, nurse's helper, safety patrol monitor, and classroom aide for younger students are a few methods that can allow for safer expressions of one's needs for power and control. We suggest that you develop your own list of possible student responsibilities, and give choices of these to your students who are the most frequent victimizers of others.

4. *Acknowledging the put-down.* Develop a classroom rule (see discussion of social contracts) around the use of put-downs. One suggested consequence for the victimizer is to publicly state, after the put-down, the following: "I want to feel powerful right now and I'm doing it at (victim's) expense." While it's unlikely that this will lead to lasting personality change, it does serve the purpose of putting the victimizer up front before the class, and he/she may wish to avoid this consequence in the future. One follow-up to this may be "I want to feel powerful right now and I'm doing it at (victim's) expense. Other ways that I can feel powerful are _____

_____."

The latter gives the victimizer a chance to think through alternatives to his behavior which may help him to discover other behaviors by which to express his power. But if the student says this rotely or mechanically, it will serve as a punishment and will have some, but not much, lasting effect. Students who are asked to make public apologies rarely mean them, and do so only to avoid further punishment. The benefit of this activity derives from a skilled teacher who is more interested in acknowledging that the student has a need beyond hurting the victim and has a genuine concern and desire to assist in finding other ways to meet the need. Thus ridicule should not be a part of the teacher's behavior toward the victimizer. This would only serve to reinforce the idea that the more powerful can ridicule the less powerful.

APPRECIATIONS

Students who are discipline problems are often lacking in self-esteem. When a child feels uncared for and unappreciated, he learns not to care for himself and not to appreciate others. As another way of preventing discipline problems, particularly in the early elementary school years, it is important for all students to feel cared for and appreciated by both their teacher and their peer group. Students who don't get enough warmth will learn not to give any and will gradually distance themselves emotionally from others.

1. Place a picture of each of your students along with his/her name on a large sheet of newsprint. Explain to your students that each day one child's picture will be hanging on the bulletin board. Tell them that at any time during the day (free time or play time might be preferred to minimize distractions) any student may go to the poster and write a statement beginning with, "One thing I like about you is _____ ," or to draw a picture expressing their caring and appreciation of this student. No put-down statements are allowed. Prior to the end of the school day, take a few minutes to allow students to file past the poster and encourage them to read each statement or describe a drawing that they made on the poster. When you have finished doing this, ask if there are any further expressions of appreciation. When the process is completed, put the child's poster away until his/her turn comes up again.

   After two rounds, allow the student the option of taking home the poster or displaying it in school.

2. *Self-Appreciation.* We believe that one important desired outcome for students is to gradually shift their dependency on support from their environment to support within themselves. It's rare in our society for people to express genuine appreciation for each other, and unless one learns to value and appreciate his own worth, he'll often bitterly wander from person to person seeking a sense of security.

   This activity can be done once a day, once a week, or several times each day. Have the students complete the following aloud: "Something I did, felt, or said today that I'm proud is _____ ." "Something that I like about myself right now is _____ ."

3. *Expressing feelings through art.* Give the students crayons, paints, and/or thick pencils and tell them, "Right now I'd like you to draw or color in a way that expresses your feelings. If you feel sad, draw sad, if you feel angry, draw angry, if you feel happy, draw happy. These are your pictures and you may keep them when you're finished or show them to the class." Be sure to provide no more structure than this. The less structure you provide, the more likely the students are to express their feelings as they feel them.

FOLLOW-UP

Students may be given the option of displaying their work in the class-room. This can be done by having an "art gallery" in which all participating students hang up their work and then browse through the "gallery" to observe each other's work. Comments are encouraged by helping each commenting student to recognize his/her feelings. This is not a contest but rather an opportunity to facilitate a feeling discussion among the class. You might provide a little structure by suggesting that students say, "When I look at this drawing I feel (think, am reminded of, etc.) _____."

FANTASY DIALOGUE

For a quick three-step process for dealing with your feelings regarding disruptive students, try the following. This activity can be done with a colleague or other facilitator to guide you through the steps if you so desire.

STEP 1: Accept yourself as you are, not as you "should be." Ask yourself, "How do I feel about a specific disruptive student?" Most teachers who are honest with themselves find it difficult to like the student who is disruptive, and it is very important that as a first step they privately acknowledge this and any other feelings that they may have. It is okay not to like every student or like being with certain students at certain times. It is possible that they do not like being with you all the time.

STEP 2: Set up a fantasy dialogue with an identified student with whom you are having trouble. We recommend that you use an empty chair and imagine the presence of the student sitting in that chair. Let the student know exactly how you feel. Tell him all the things that he does that you resent and how you feel about them. Don't hold back. Let yourself scream, yell, shout, cry, be as unprofessional as you want to be. Remember, he's not really there. After you have finished expressing your resentments, make some demands. "I demand that you _____." And finally, share any appreciations you have for him and how you feel about these. When you have finished this process, switch chairs and become the student. As the student, tell the teacher your resentments, demands, and appreciations. Continue your fantasy dialogue until you feel a sense of completion. At the end of this process, most teachers report a lessening of tension and an increase in their feelings of being in control, although for some, several dialogues on different occasions are needed.

STEP 3: Consider what this student needs from you or your classroom for him/her to stop misbehaving. Use the brainstorming technique, perhaps with a colleague or support group, to invent a list of possible solutions to the problem.

We find that by using fantasy dialogues, teachers have dealt with many of their feelings safely with positive results. We are often asked, "After I express my feelings in this way, how can I begin to interact with students directly?" Many times, the need to share feelings directly is diminished after a fantasy dialogue, yet we are advocates of direct encounter with students. Because of the relationship in which the teacher has position power over students, fantasy dialogues can "clear out" many feelings so that direct encounter can be more positive. In the *resolution* dimension we describe various methods for positive student encounters.

STUDENT FANTASY

Just as it is important to understand the needs of your students, it is important for your students to understand and consider your needs.

Directions: Tell the students that you'd like them to imagine that they are now grown up, that they have completed their education and are teachers. Have them relax in the class either on the floor reclining or comfortably seated. Suggest that they close their eyes and make themselves comfortable. Have them do the following:

Silently tell your class of twenty-five students what kind of teacher you are. What you like about your job. What you dislike. How you are different from the teachers that you had when you were a student. How you are the same. Are there certain students who bug you? Tell these students what it is about them that makes teaching them difficult. Which students do you especially like? Tell them what you like about them. Tell them what you were like when you were a student. Tell the class how you were like them and different from them (I was like you _____ ; I was different from you _____). Now imagine that you could teach this class anything you wanted (like how to read; how to build the fastest paper airplane, etc.). It can be anything that you want. You have no restrictions.

Now become yourself as a student. What do you want to say to this teacher who you just imagined yourself to be. Silently tell your imaginary teacher anything that comes to mind. Now, when you are ready, I'd like you to open your eyes and return to this classroom as the student that you are.

Processing: Invite any willing student to share his/her fantasy either in part or whole. There must be no coercion, and any students who wish to keep their fantasies to themselves must be allowed to. You might wish to structure the feedback by asking such questions as: What joys or happiness did you experience as the teacher? What problems did you encounter? How did you feel being in front of twenty-five students? What do you imagine they thought about you? When you had the freedom to teach anything that you wanted, what did you choose?

Follow-Up: This activity can set the stage for students to contact their strengths through an identification with their imaginary teacher and what they'd teach. We believe that many school and classroom discipline problems involve youngsters who are generally in the role of being helped by somebody. By giving them an opportunity to be a helper, you may facilitate their development as people having worth and skills. For example, if the imaginary teacher taught students how to build the fastest paper airplane, then perhaps this student could from time to time teach others how to develop this skill. Maybe the student can be encouraged to further develop this skill and reading skills by doing an independent project on airplanes. Obviously, the need to place limits on the expression of some behavior is necessary, but keep in mind that when you legitimize previously unacceptable behavior, a student's needs to act out will diminish because he experiences you as someone from whom he doesn't have to hide. The teacher who's firm yet flexible can touch those students who have alienated themselves by allowing them to be both a helper of others as well as a person to be helped. It requires strength to accept help from somebody.

You may also follow up this activity by asking students to complete the following:

1. I can be a helper or help others when _____

2. I need or want help from others when _____

ROLE PLAYING

Role playing can be a highly effective method in developing empathy for others, trying out various problem-solving methods, and heightening awareness of thoughts, feelings, and actions. This gives children opportunities to understand others and to gain additional understanding of themselves. We offer the following vignettes to be role played by class members including the teacher.

DIRECTIONS

1. Explain the nature and purposes of role playing. Tell students that role playing means acting like somebody else or assuming the role of an-

other. Give a brief demonstration (particularly with younger children) by "making believe" that you're somebody else.

2. Ask for two volunteers.

3. Tell the rest of the class that they are to observe these two volunteers carefully because later on they will be asked to help solve a problem that they will see.

4. Tell the volunteers that they will each be asked to play a role. Tell one of them, "You'll be Brian and your role is to grab Bobby's pencil without asking for it." Tell the other volunteer, "You're Bobby and you are doing some written work when Brian grabs a pencil from your hand."

5. Have the role players sit in seats next to each other (preferably where the whole class can see).

6. Have the volunteers act out their roles. After Brian grabs Bobby's pencil, stop the role play and direct your attention to the class.

7. Ask the class, "What did you see?" "How do you think Bobby felt?" (sad, happy, annoyed, disappointed, angry) Younger children may need help in verbalizing their feelings, so provide them with possible feeling options. "What do you think Brian wanted?" "How did he feel before and after he got the pencil?" "What are some things that Bobby can do?" (Make a list on the blackboard of all suggested solutions.) "Now, of all these solutions, which do you think might be the best?" (Ask them to focus on what might happen to Bobby if he tried each solution.)

FOLLOW-UP

The following situations are merely a handful of possible role play options which can be modified as you see fit. Since role playing can be a difficult concept for younger children to understand, keep your explanations and demonstrations as simple as possible until you believe that the class has an adequate understanding. Role playing should progress from very *concrete* situations to more complex ones.

Role-playing vignettes:

1. Sally takes Susie's eraser.

2. Joey takes his pencil and makes a mess all over Jack's paper.

3. Lou comes late to class for the third straight day.

4. Jason's exam paper is marked in heavy red ink by the teacher. She tells Jason that he'd better study harder, even though Jason already spent hours upon hours preparing for the exam.

5. Three boys are playing ball during recess when Charlie comes to join them. They call him names and tell him that he can't play.

6. Jane goes to a party in which a lot of kids are drinking alcohol. Her two best friends bring her a drink, but she decides not to have it. Next day in school, her friends won't talk to her or sit near her.

7. Ben and Bernie want to use the same art supplies. After a minute or so, Ben pushes Bernie to the ground and says, "Now you leave the paints alone when I want to use them."

8. Dave is angry at his teacher who refused to let him go to physical education (his favorite period) because he didn't finish his homework. He's so angry that he calls the teacher names and runs out of the class.

9. Mrs. Karl notices that Johnny is out of his seat again. She says, "Johnny, go to the principal's office right now!" What she doesn't know is that Frankie just threw a spitball that landed right on Johnny's head.

10. Ellen brings her favorite doll to class to show the other children. She takes good care of it and puts it in her desk when she's finished showing it off. When she returns to her room after lunch, she discovers the doll missing. When the teacher (Mrs. Laramie) asks if anybody knows where Ellen's doll is, nobody speaks up. Mrs. Laramie searches the room and finds the doll in Charlotte's desk.

ROLE REVERSAL

1. Tell your students that for the next twenty minutes (adapt the actual time interval) we will each pretend to be the person whom we're sitting next to (Joe pretends to be Bill and Bill to be Joe.). Your first task is to imagine yourself as this other student. Consider what you like and dislike and how you feel in this classroom. Do you have any friends or do you feel alone? Who do you spend time with? Do you think the teacher likes you or not? What kind of student are you? Do you want to come to school or do you come because you have to? How do you feel? Are you happy, sad, worried, joyful, or angry most of the time? What are your interests? What are you good at? What do you need help with?

2. Now have each pair of students talk to each other and tell each other what it was like to be them. Suggest that they share the experience of being this other student by saying, "When I was Billy, I was (interested in, liked, disliked, felt about school . . .) _____." Each student makes one statement, then the other student makes a statement. This continues back and forth until each student feels finished.

3. Suggest to the class that they complete the following aloud: "Something I learned or discovered about myself is _____."

I'M SPECIAL

DIRECTIONS

Explain to your students that each of us is unique or special in different ways, and that we also are very much alike. All of us have eyes, ears, a nose, hands, and so forth, but some of us have blue eyes, others brown, some black, and others green. Just as we each have different physical features, so do we have different interests, different feelings at different times, different abilities, skills, likes, and dislikes. But sometimes, some of us feel that we are very much alone with our differences and this can make us feel weird, odd, and unacceptable to others. It is important that each of us learn to accept ourselves as we are, sometimes alike and other times different from others. When we can do this, then we usually feel happier and more fulfilled.

After these initial comments tell the students: "I'd like each of you to take out a pencil and three pieces of paper. On each paper I'd like you to write down one way in which you see yourself as special or different. I will do the same. I *don't* want you to write things like your name, birthday, parents' names, or street address. Each thing you write should be a feeling you have about yourself or others, a quality about yourself, a thought or interest you have. I'll be reading what you write after you've finished, but don't put your name on your paper. Nobody will ever know who wrote what."

(You might, if you want, set a limit and tell the students that you'll read no paper that has four-letter words. If you choose to do this, we suggest that you tell the students how you feel—that you would be offended or embarrassed. If at all possible, we advise you *not* to set this limit. Teachers who are willing to matter-of-factly read even an offensive remark can take the power of such language away from a student and make themselves difficult targets to test limits against in the future.)

After the students have had sufficient time to write down their special statements (and this must be done with no talking or peer consultation), collect one statement from each student. Inform them that the goal of the game is to get "out," whereby they learn that they're the only student in the class who is, in fact, special in a certain way. The teacher reads each statement aloud and tells the class that everybody who can identify with the statement is to raise their hand. The person who wrote the statement is *not* to raise his/her hand. If even one other student raises a hand, then this signifies that the person who wrote the statement is not special or different in this way.

After all first papers are read, tell the students who are not yet "out" to turn in a second statement or, if they wish, give them a few extra minutes to write a new one. Students who are "out" may choose to hand in another sentence. Go through the same procedure until the third round is completed.

FOLLOW-UP

Many students are surprised to discover that in most cases, many of their classmates see themselves in similar ways. It is very uncommon that any more than a handful of statements are, in fact, different or special. Since many similar interests, hobbies, and feelings are expressed, you can compile a list of student interests which can generate more interaction and new relationships. Several students are relieved to learn that they are not as odd or weird as they secretly thought.

This activity is particularly effective with the moderately alienated student who disrupts for attention. Such a student learns that he is not as alone or different as he imagined, and can experience his thoughts, feelings, and interests as being related to his peers.

8

THEORIES OF DISCIPLINE

Why do children misbehave? Many explanations have at one time or another been put forward as the primary causes of misbehavior: children wanting attention, being bored, feeling unfairly treated, not trusting adults or other kids, experiencing school failure, being treated like spoiled brats, wanting power or control over others, having to prove something to friends, fearing, feeling rejected and/or frustrated, having poor nutritional habits and biochemical or neurological disorders. Probably some or all of these reasons are valid in certain cases.

The three-dimensional approach pays relatively little attention to causes for the following reason. With all the accumulated research, the fact is that discipline problems have continued to increase at an alarming rate. When educators spend the bulk of their time in an analysis of what is causing Johnny to misbehave (as often happens), they can easily render themselves helpless by not engaging in direct action. Most theories expound the virtues of understanding the causes of misbehavior and pay too little attention to action that can improve the classroom atmosphere. We emphasize action. As we have discussed earlier, we believe that an awareness of yourself and your students, finding acceptable outlets to express feelings, and later developing and implementing social contracts makes a more positive difference than does general cognitive knowledge of models and theories. However, once teachers have developed these skills, they can choose either whole theories or relevant parts of theories to provide a wider range of alternatives. It is our premise that an integration of knowledge with your own values, attitudes, and needs can enable you to deal more effectively with disruptive youth in your classroom. In this chapter, it is our intent to present the work of others and to point out similarities and differences in approach. It is *not* our intent to provide a treatise, but rather to briefly familiarize you with a range of models and theories. Should you desire any additional information, we encourage you to explore any or all of these theorists in more depth (see Bibliography). We again wish to encourage you to adapt any theory or model so that it coincides with your own preferences. There is no right theory that is appropriate for everyone.

We would once again like to review our definition of discipline. As you recall, in Chapter 2 we gave you an impossible choice to make. We presented you with two extreme alternatives for eliminating discipline problems in your class or school. These choices were "there are no rules—anything goes" and "there are rules for everything in your classroom." We defined a discipline problem as a situation or event in which the needs of the group or authority conflict with the needs of the individual who is part of the group.

We believe that the work of most theorists can be viewed along a continuum ranging from those who favor a no control approach that tends to view the individual's needs as more important than that of the group or authority, to those who favor strict and complete control in which the needs of the group or authority are emphasized. Since the three-dimensional approach provides sufficient flexibility for you to pick and choose from alternatives, we trust that you will decide where you stand on this continuum, both before and after you read on.

In the survey that follows, we look at theories and models of behavior in terms of their primary focus; that is, are they concerned more with individual needs or group needs? We found it difficult to determine placement in many cases. Thus the continuum on page 79 represents our own somewhat arbitrary interpretation of the different theorists. It serves as a structure for examining the theorists only in terms of how *we* define discipline. It is not the only way of interpreting the theories.

If you tend to favor the individual's needs above those of the group/or authority, our hunch is that you will find those theories toward the "No Control" end of the continuum as more congruent with your own needs and values. Conversely, if you lean more toward favoring the group's or authority's needs you will likely feel more comfortable with

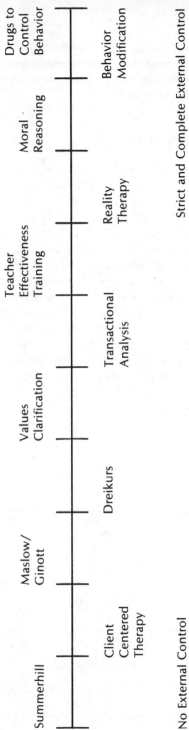

Summerhill

Maslow/
Ginott

Dreikurs

Values
Clarification

Transactional
Analysis

Teacher
Effectiveness
Training

Reality
Therapy

Moral ·
Reasoning

Behavior
Modification

Drugs to
Control
Behavior

Client
Centered
Therapy

No External Control

Individual More Important
Than Group or Authority

Strict and Complete External Control

Group or Authority More
Important Than Individual

those theories toward the "Strict and Complete Control" end. We will begin with the sharply contrasting views offered by the theorists at the polar ends of the continuum. The more moderate theories to be discussed later fall between these extreme positions.

No External Control/Summerhill

In A. S. Neill's Summerhill philosophy children are to work joyfully and find happiness. He believes that we should "make the school fit the child" and notes that "lessons are optional. Children can go to them or stay away from them—for years if they want to." He clearly places the needs of the individual above those of the group or authority and cautions against "imposed authority." [1] Expressed through the use of rewards and punishments, imposed authority is designed to force the individual to behave according to a set of behaviors that are determined by others. Healthy growth occurs when the child is allowed to have a wide range of experiences that are self-selected according to his/her preferences.

The seeds of this position can be traced as far back as Plato who discussed differences among individuals and recommended that steps be taken to discover each child's outstanding aptitudes so that education and training along the lines of his particular talents might begin early. Rousseau suggested that no great harm to the child or to society will result if the child grows with little adult supervision and direction. Much later on, John Dewey, a New England born philosopher, said that the child must have an opportunity to make his own choices, and then to try his choices for himself so that he can give them the only final test, that of action. This is the only way to learn which will lead to success and which to failure. Snygg and Combs see learning as a natural and normal activity which is not dependent on the stimulation of the teacher. It was their notion that adults actually interfere with much childhood learning through attempts to substitute their goals in place of the ones already possessed by the children. [2]

A brief analysis of these theorists suggests that the more the school attempts to coerce, manipulate, control, and shape the behavior of its students, the greater the likelihood of discipline problems. The cause of discipline problems is seen as a result of the school's interference in the natural growth process of the child. Since learning is viewed as intrinsically rewarding, outside interference with this process might stimulate the child to resist the efforts of others to shape him/her in a way that is not

---

[1] A. S. Neill, *Summerhill: A Radical Approach to Child Rearing* (New York: Hart, 1960), pp. 4–5.

[2] D. Syngg and A. W. Combs, *Individual Behavior* (New York: Harper, 1949).

natural. The role of the school is thereby limited to keeping in touch with each individual's needs and facilitating the growth potential inherent in each child. This philosophy also suggests that the more students believe that school is a pleasant place to be, the fewer discipline problems would occur. Somewhat simplistically, bad behavior is caused by an intrusive environment, and as the environment becomes less intrusive and more responsive to the needs of the individual, behavior improves.

Strict Control/Drug Therapy

A contrasting view asserts that the pleasantness of school is irrelevant and that schools should engage students in a mental toughening process which is of value in itself. In this view, the mind is strengthened through a series of difficult and frustrating experiences. Some argue that we live in an impersonal world which rewards the tough-minded, competitive spirit and in which the sensitive, caring individual is eaten alive. John Locke was committed to the ultimate rationality of man. He viewed education as a process to promote self-discipline, self-control, and the "power of denying ourselves the satisfaction of our own desires, where reason does not authorize them. From their very early cradles," he argues, "parents must begin instructing children in self-denial." [3]

This view set the stage for the more modern day theories of development and behavior offered by E. L. Thorndike, B. F. Skinner, and the learning by association theorists. Proponents of drug therapy in the schools would likely see impulsive youngsters who do not fit any acceptable norm as lacking "self-discipline," "self-control," and the power of self-denial. Whether for biochemical, neurological, or environmental reasons, the goal of drug therapy is to have the child fit within the socially acceptable norm. Its use is designed to control misbehavior that the individual either cannot or will not control. Recent estimates suggest that as many as 500,000 to 1,000,000 school age American children and adolescents are taking prescribed amphetamine-type drugs and other psychostimulants to control behavior. [4] But no one seems certain of these numbers. Oftentimes the child is symptom-free from a medical point of view, and is placed on medication after consultation among the physician, parent, teacher, and significant others in the child's life. The diagnosis that usually leads to drug therapy is based on parental or school complaints of distractibility, overactivity, inattentiveness, impulsivity, difficulty in disci-

[3] John Locke, *Some Thoughts Concerning Education* (London: Cambridge University Press, 1934), p. 25.
[4] Peter Schrag and Diane Divoky, "The Myth of the Hyperactive Child," Pantheon 12, 1975, p. xiii.

plining, poor social controls, and academic problems in school. These complaints, coupled with the physician's own clinical opinion, may lead to a prescription for psychoactive drugs.

One of the most widely prescribed psychoactive drugs is Ritalin. It is usually prescribed for children who are hyperactive, impulsive, distractible, and/or inattentive. Its effect is paradoxical in that while it is a direct stimulant drug, it has been found to have a calming effect on many of these children. Some studies indicate that hyperactive children are overaroused and stimulated and that amphetamines reduce this arousal, while others have found the opposite. One study showed that Ritalin significantly reduced the activity level of antisocial hyperactive boys while a placebo (a pill with no biochemical ingredient) had no effect; [5] Sprague showed that both Ritalin and a placebo reduced motor activity [6] while Millichap et al. suggested that motor activity actually was increased by Ritalin.[7] According to a review in the *New England Journal of Medicine*, stimulant drugs were found to improve performance on "repetitive, routinized tasks that require sustained attention. Reasoning, problem solving, and learning do not seem to be affected by Ritalin usage in adults or children." The most commonly reported side effects are height and weight suppression. Rare or uncommon side effects such as liver damage, crying fits, and psychotic-like symptoms (e.g., hallucinations) have been reported. Some research suggests that "the outlook for such children treated primarily through drugs is relatively poor. In their teens, these children were still having trouble with their families, often behaving antisocially and presenting academic and behavior problems." [8]

A recent follow-up study of the relationship of Ritalin to scholastic achievement showed that while Ritalin affects behavior, it does not enhance learning and may, in fact, mask academic problems. Even when behavior was significantly affected in the desired directions, there was no significant drug effect on academic achievement itself.[9]

Proponents of drug use claim that without drugs, the consequences to the hyperactive child are far worse and include school failure, a poor self-concept, and an inability to make an adequate adjustment to the

[5] L. Allen Stroufe, and Mark A. Stewart, "Treating Problem Children with Stimulant Drugs," *New England Journal of Medicine* 289, no. 8, pp. 407–412.

[6] R. L. Sprague et al., "Methylphenidate and Thioridizone: Learning Reaction Time, Activity and Classroom Behavior in Disturbed Children," *American Journal of Orthopsychiatry* 40 (July 1970), pp. 615–628.

[7] Millichap et al., "Hyperkinetic Behavior and Learning Disorders—III, Battery of Neuropsychological Tests in Controlled Trial of Methylphenidate," *American Journal of Diseases of Children* 116 (Sept. 1968), pp. 235–244.

[8] Stroufe and Stewart, "Treating Problem Children with Stimulant Drugs," *New England Journal of Medicine* 289 No. 8, pp. 410, 419.

[9] Rie et al., "Effects of Ritalin on Underachieving Children: A Replication," *American Journal Of Ortho Psychiatry* 46, no. 2 (April 1976), p. 313.

school routine. They point to the very rare deleterious side-effects, and the positive reports of behavioral and academic changes as reported by teachers and parents. Opponents emphasize the potentially serious side effects of drug use, as well as the coercive institutional intent of manipulating a child, through drugs, to improve his behavior. They also point to the danger that drugs may mask or keep buried the symptoms associated with hyperactivity that could be an outgrowth of emotional problems.

The outcome of most studies indicates that stimulant drugs are generally effective in making the child less distractible, more attentive, less active, and better behaved. Research has generally failed to show positive scholastic results with children who are medicated. Despite numerous studies which have attempted to identify a target population for whom drugs are particularly effective, outcomes suggest that both drug responders and drug nonresponders come from a heterogeneous population that cuts across socioeconomic status and psychiatric or medical diagnosis.

Although the relationship of the benefits to the dangers of drug therapy is debatable, there can be no question that the goal and purpose of such treatment is to improve the behavior of the child according to the standards of the child's environment. The primary problem is identified as coming from within the child, and the resolution is through the biochemical alteration of the child's inner environment.

Looking at the other end of the continuum, we find the work of Carl Rogers, Haim Ginott, Abraham Maslow, and Rudolph Dreikurs. We wish to explore how these theorists have contributed to our understanding of discipline.

Client-Centered Therapy

Carl Rogers is a nondirective, client-centered psychotherapist whose basic technique involves listening in a reflective way to a person's thoughts and feelings, and then feeding back the message that he has heard. The client then has the option of agreeing with the feedback if it fits, or clarifying for himself what it is he means. The key concept is that growth occurs in an acceptant, warm, empathic, nonjudgmental environment that allows people the freedom to explore their thoughts and feelings and to solve their own problems. The therapist needs to be trained in listening skills and must be able to understand the meaning of his client's message.

Ginott/Maslow

Haim Ginott's work extended that of Rogers through the introduction of the concept of limits. Ginott stated, "The essence of discipline is finding effective alternatives to punishment. To punish a child is to enrage him and make him uneducable. He becomes a hostage of hostility, a captive of rancor, a prisoner of vengeance. Suffused with rage and absorbed in grudges, a child has no time or mind for studying. In discipline, whatever generates *hate* must be avoided. Whatever creates self-esteem is to be fostered." [10] Ginott's model calls for firm limit setting on behavior but never on feelings. All feelings are to be accepted, no matter how heinous or destructive, and limits are to be placed on actions or behaviors that might result from such feelings. For example, let's assume that Joey has just punched Billy in the classroom. Based on Ginott's work, we could suggest that the teacher first reflect the feelings of the other to communicate understanding—"Joey, you probably feel angry." Next comes the setting of limits on the behavior or action such as, "but people are not for punching." Third provide a symbolic outlet for the feeling such as "but the punching bag in the back of the room is," and fourth communicate to the child that the symbolic outlet is not as good as the real thing—"I know that punching Bozo is not as good as punching Billy, but in this classroom people are not for punching."

Abraham Maslow constructed a hierarchy of human needs. This is a developmental model suggesting that growth occurs by having sufficient environmental support. The support gradually shifts in emphasis to an individual's ability to nourish and support himself within his environment (Fig. A).[11] At the base of the pyramid are the basic human needs for food, clothing, and shelter. Survival comes first. A child who comes to school hungry will spend most of his time thinking and dreaming about food, not math. In other words, this needs' hierarchy proposes that some needs must be met before others because they are more urgent and basic to our life function. People who have needs for security and safety must have these needs satisfied before they can move on to satisfy other needs. A child whose parents are frequently fighting and who threaten to divorce is often preoccupied with fantasies of abandonment. He is often motivated to seek security from others; if he becomes stuck in this pursuit, then much of his energy will be directed toward finding others to take care of him. The first two needs at the base of the pyramid are considered "outer needs" and are almost completely dependent upon being received from the environment outside. The next need is for love and belonging, and Bessell spells out four ways in which this need is met. They are *"attention"* (young people must be aware that others know they exist); *"acceptance"* (you have a right to be here); *"approval"* (I like this about you); and *"affection"* (I like you).[12]

[10] Haim Ginott, *Teacher and Child* (New York: Macmillan, 1972), pp. 147–8.

[11] Abraham Maslow, *Motivation and Personality* (New York: Harper Brothers, 1954).

[12] Harold Bessell, *Methods in Human Development: Theory Manual* (San Diego: Human Development Training Institute, 1970), pp. 77–79.

Harlow in his work with monkeys demonstrated in a laboratory set-ting that physical touching and warmth were necessary for the develop-ment of both physiological and psychological health.[13, 14] More recently, Abidin has discussed the importance of a person's feeling worthwhile, lovable, competent, and responsible in order to develop a positive self-concept.[15]

Figure A. Maslow's needs hierarchy

Factors that contribute to the needs for respect and self-esteem in-clude recognition from others, accomplishments, having goals or a sense of worth, gaining influence, independence, and self-control. Knowledge and understanding are important in order to help children make decisions which allow them to live their lives more effectively. The final human need is for beauty and self-actualization which is a need to experience the world directly and to be open to it. Maslow described self-actualized peo-ple as having their faults, but as perceiving reality more clearly. He views

[13] H. F. Harlow and R. R. Zimmerman. "Affectional Responses in the Infant Monkey." *Science*, no. 3373 (1959), pp. 421–432.
[14] H. Harlow and M. H. Harlow, "Learning to Love," *American Scientist*, no. 3 (1966), pp. 244–272.
[15] Richard R. Abidin, *Parenting Skills: Trainer's Manual* (New York: Human Sciences Press, 1976), for more information.

them as more creative, tolerant, and spontaneous. They accept themselves and others as they are.

We believe that few would argue that the primary goal, either explicit or implicit, of most typical schools is directed toward needs for knowledge and understanding. Schools are often expected to determine for the child what must be learned, rather than to use the child as a primary source for determining the curriculum. Maslow's point is that the needs for knowledge and understanding, as with all other needs, must be felt by the student. If there is a large gap between the student's view of relevant knowledge and the school's, then conflict, unrest, discipline problems, and disaffection often result. Thus, Maslow would likely see discipline problems as a result of a student being stuck at one need level (e.g., love and belonging) while the school requires that he value another (knowledge and understanding). Such a student would be more interested in feeling part of the group than in learning his multiplication tables. The more the teacher pushes such a youngster into doing his multiplication tables while ignoring his more basic needs, the greater the likelihood of the student becoming a discipline problem.

Dreikurs

Rudolph Dreikurs stated that misbehavior occurs because a child has developed faulty beliefs about himself which lead to his/her having goals which may lead to misbehavior.[16] His work has been extended by Dinkmeyer and others. The goals for misbehavior include attention, power, revenge, and display of inadequacy. A child seeks attention when he believes that he belongs only when he's being noticed or recognized. Such a child is often calling out answers in class, despite repeated admonitions, or cracking jokes which disturb the teacher or the other children. Parents sometimes say that their child won't do his homework unless they're right there. A student makes his needs for power felt through his faulty belief that he belongs only when he's in control or is the boss, or when he's proving that no one else can boss him. The child who refuses to do his homework because it's assigned by the teacher, or who is always in the middle of disputes and arguments with other students is showing his needs for power. A child wants revenge when he believes that he belongs only by hurting others as he feels hurt. Such a student often sees himself as unworthy and unlovable. The unruly student who is angry with others

---

[16] Discussion is summarized from Rudolf Dreikurs with Vicki Stoltz, *Children: The Challenge* (New York: Hawthorn Books, 1964).

that have repeatedly let him down may show his hurt through antisocial action. The delinquent population has often developed this belief about themselves. The final faulty belief discussed by Dreikurs is the child who believes that he belongs only by convincing others not to expect anything from him. This belief is frequently experienced by those who feel hopeless or helpless; by the student who is always at the teacher's desk asking for help and who is mostly pleading ignorance by convincing others that he is incapable or stupid. The goal here is the display of inadequacy.

Dreikurs suggests the use of natural or logical consequences for dealing with misbehavior and advises against engaging in power struggles with children. Simply stated, this amounts to making sure that the punishment fits the crime. If, for example, Sally intentionally broke Susie's pencil, then a logical consequence might be that Sally would not be allowed use of a pencil for a given time interval. Or Steve's lateness to class could be dealt with through the consequence that Steve misses the information presented while he was tardy (natural consequence). We have found that the application of logical and natural consequences to classroom misbehavior has considerable merit. It has the potential of enabling the teacher to avoid the traditional self-defeating roles of policeman and arbitrary judge, and instead calls for the child to suffer the natural or logical consequences of his own actions. The approach is limited in that the child still has to misbehave before he knows what the consequences are, and calls for the teacher to make judgments as to what constitutes a natural or logical consequence. Nevertheless, the guidelines are sound. In our social contract phase of the prevention dimension, we will show you how to adapt and extend the use of natural and logical consequences within a classroom setting.

Toward the middle of the continuum, we find some models which combine the needs of the individual with the needs of the group or group authority. These models include values clarification, transactional analysis, teacher effectiveness training, reality therapy, and moral reasoning.

Values Clarification

Values clarification is a process that helps youngsters answer some of their questions and build their own value system. It is based on an approach formulated by Louis Raths. His focus was on how people come to hold certain beliefs and establish certain behavior patterns. He looked at specific behavior problems related to students with unclear values.

RATHS' CHARACTERISTICS OF STUDENTS WITH UNCLEAR VALUES

1. Some are *apathetic*. They are listless and uninterested, willing to let the spinning world carry them along whichever way it will.
2. Others are *flighty*, interested in many things but only for fleeting moments. They often are involved in something with high spirit, but with equal spirit and in short order, they abandon it for another favorite.
3. Some are very *uncertain*, seemingly unable to make up their minds about the many choices with which the world continues to face them.
4. Then there are very *inconsistent* ones, persons involved in many things that are mutually inconsistent if not mutually destructive. Unlike their flighty compatriots, they have patterns in their lives, but the patterns tend to be incompatible.
5. Others might aptly be called *drifters*. For these persons there is a pattern of behavior characterized by planless and unenthusiastic drift from this to that, like humans without power or rudder in the sea of life.
6. A large number are *overconformers*. Not having a clear idea of what they want to do with their lives, many take the road of conformity, accommodating themselves the best way they can to what they perceive to be the dominant viewpoints of the moment. Other-directed with a passion are those in this subgroup.
7. Some are *overdissenters*, not occasional and reasoned dissenters, but chronic, nagging, and irrational dissenters.
8. Finally, we note a group of *poseurs* or *role players*, persons who cover their lack of clarity about what life is for by posturing in some role that is not more real for them than a made-up cardboard image.[17]

Raths believed that clear values can help change some of these behaviors. His early research supports the notion that value clarification helps improve discipline.

He claims that in order for something to be a value, it must involve the following processes:

- Prizing one's beliefs and behaviors
  1. Prizing and cherishing
  2. Publicly affirming
- Choosing one's beliefs and behaviors

[17] Raths, Harmon and Simon, *Values and Teaching* (Columbus, Ohio: Merrill, 1966), pp. 5–6.

3. Choosing from alternatives
4. Choosing after consideration of consequences
5. Choosing freely
- Acting on one's beliefs
6. Acting
7. Acting with a pattern; consistency and repetition [18]

Discipline problems, according to this model, are caused by two factors. Students with unclear values are often experiencing considerable inner turmoil which leads them to engage in a variety of behaviors in an effort to restore themselves to more fluid functioning. In the process of restoration, they may "try on" behaviors that may lead them to conflict with the prevailing school system. Consider for a moment the case of Jane, a fourteen-year-old girl with a history of shyness, bordering on withdrawal. When she entered junior high school, she began to throw food in the cafeteria, cut classes, and refused to turn in homework assignments. Upon careful examination, it was discovered that Jane was struggling to gain the acceptance of other students who would often dare Jane to behave in the above mentioned ways. In order for her to see herself as an accepted member of her peer group, she was forced to challenge the values of her school which led to her suspension. When Jane received peer group counseling, she began behaving in more appropriate ways. She began to accept herself more as she was without taking on the phony identity that her peer group demanded.

The second cause of discipline problems, as viewed through the values clarification model, occurs when both the identified misbehaving student and the school (teacher, administrator, etc.) have clear but different values and when either or both are unable to accept each other's differences. It is sometimes cultural differences that are responsible for such problems. Mrs. Jones was a first year fifth grade teacher who was teaching in an inner-city, predominantly black school. She was from a white, middle class background and had little previous experience with inner-city culture. She was easily intimidated by her class, and she became tyrannical in her verbal assaults as a response to her fears. She was particularly upset when she scolded a youngster and the youngster would say nothing to her, refusing to make eye contact. Little did she know that it is a sign of disrespect in the black inner-city culture for the child to make eye contact with an adult in authority. Her value system had taught her that when an adult speaks to a child, he/she looks the child squarely in the eye. For the child to avoid this eye contact is a sign of disrespect. Quite the opposite value was held by many of those in her class.

[18] Ibid, p. 30.

The importance of values clarification is its emphasis on communication in a nonjudgmental, acceptant atmosphere. All participants including the teacher are to be free to share their thoughts, values, and feelings and to learn the values of recognizing and accepting their differences. Some teachers have associated values clarification with freedom, permissiveness, and a "do your own thing" attitude. By contrast, we believe that allowing a person to become aware of his needs and values serves to develop trust, enhance involvement and help students become responsible for learning. Traditional school instruction often illustrates the difference between teaching by preconception (what those in authority think is relevant) and teaching by awareness (that which is seen as relevant by the students). We believe that all teachers have a right to show their students that what is being taught is important for them to learn. If, however, the prevailing attitudes or values of certain students, or in some cases most of the class, is at odds with those of the teacher, then we suggest that the teacher either be an extremely good salesman, or consider opening himself or herself up to accommodate the needs of the class. Sometimes teachers feel that if they were to abandon the curriculum in favor of values accommodation, then consequences such as disfavor from the principal, parents, colleagues, and students might result. We suggest that if you are limiting your creativity because of such fears, then make these fears public. Talk to your students and see if there are alternatives that you can find together to resolve such issues. Saying something like, "I'm required to teach you about the natural resources of China, but I find that every time we have social studies few of you pay attention. If I don't teach this subject, then I imagine that many of you will fail your final exams and I'll be called on the carpet by Mr. Paul. Now do any of you have a suggestion as to how we can solve this problem?"

The limitations of values clarification are that few people have developed in such a way as to be able to accept the views of others without judgment. The task of planning a curriculum based upon the unique needs and values of thirty people can be extremely arduous if not impossible. We do believe that values clarification has many advantages for those teachers who have the willingness and strength to struggle with differences and who believe that teaching by awareness is preferable to teaching by preconception.

Transactional Analysis

Transactional Analysis is concerned with analyzing transactions; analyzing, understanding, and paying attention to what goes on between two or more persons.[19] According to this model, each person has three existing ego states. Even young children have each ego state, although the degree of functioning or voice that each is given is dependent upon one's age, past experiences, and current situation. There is the Parent ego state which develops through the recordings of "all the admonitions and rules and laws that the child has heard and learned from his parents,"[20] parent surrogates, or other authority figures. The Parent ego state is subdivided into the Critical Parent which is righteous, judgmental, and moral, and the Nurturant Parent, which is giving, loving, and caring. The Child ego state relates to the feelings of the person and records the feelings of frustration, anger, and hurts in response to parental demands, as well as "creativity, curiosity, the desire to know and explore, and the urge to touch, feel, and experience."[21] Both of these ego states begin at birth. The third ego state is the Adult, which acts as a computer making rational decisions after considering information from the Parent, the Child, and the data which the Adult has accumulated. The Adult begins to emerge as people begin to control and manipulate objects in their environment. As the Adult develops, it begins to discard some of the messages from the Parent that are experienced as inapplicable. The Adult ego state, for example, learns to handle crossing the street despite parental protestation, and learns the ABC's despite the child's urge to play with the attractive doll house in the back of the classroom. The young child will eventually take the risk of crossing the street despite parental attempts to block such behavior. As people develop feelings of worth and competence, moral standards which were incorporated from parental and authority messages lose power. It is not only possible, but probable that some parental standards and urges from the Child will be rejected by the healthy Adult. He/she discovers that certain (Parent) standards no longer apply or that the consequences of acting on immediate needs or wants (Child) may be too severe. Personality develops through transactions between ego states of self and others.

Transactions can be of several kinds. When they are complementary, then communication proceeds in an uninterrupted way. Complementary transactions that involve Adult-Adult communication rarely lead to discipline problems. For example, consider the following transaction:

Transaction A:

Student: "I forgot if Russia is located in Europe or Asia."
Teacher: "Russia is in Europe."

[19] Thomas A Harris, *I'm OK—You're OK* (New York: Harper & Row, 1967), p. 42.
[20] Ibid, p. 49.
[21] Discussion is summarized from: Eric Berne, *Games People Play* (New York: Grove Press, 1964).

Diagramatically, transaction A looks like this.

The student shared information from his Adult and the teacher responded from his Adult. Thus, no conflict.

Now consider how this statement by another student who is out to get the teacher leads to a whole different series of events which culminate in conflict. This student's tone of voice conveys rebelliousness and the real message is "What you're teaching is silly and unimportant."

Transaction B:

> *Student:* (with tone of voice and body posture suggesting defiance) I forgot if Russia is located in Europe or Asia.
>
> *Teacher:* If you'd done your homework assignment like you were supposed to, you'd know.

Diagrammatically, transaction B looks like this:

The above is an example of a crossed transaction at one level with an ulterior complementary transaction at another level. The words of the student convey an Adult-Adult transaction, but the feeling, tone, and bodily gestures convey a message of anger and rebelliousness. This latter message "hooks" the teacher's Parent who responds in a judgmental, critical way. This transaction has the potential power of continuing uninterrupted and escalating a power struggle with conflict; a discipline problem is the result. The dialogue may proceed as follows:

> *Student:* (angrily) You're always picking on me. Leave me alone.
>
> *Teacher:* If you don't quiet down, you'll receive a zero for today's class.
>
> *Student:* I don't care what you do. You'll give me a zero anyway.
>
> *Teacher:* If you paid more attention to your work and less time fooling around, you'd know a lot more.
>
> *Student:* Bug off. Leave me alone.

Teacher: That's enough. Go to the principal's office right now. You're not to talk to me with disrespect ever again.

At this point, the transaction ends with the student leaving the classroom. The teacher has "won" the immediate battle of will at the expense of feeding this student more food for his already strong feelings of defiance and rebelliousness. All game players continue their games because it is the method that they've learned to get the strokes and the attention that they want. It is likely that the student will resort to more subtle, yet equally provocative negative transactions in the future as a way of hooking the teacher into battle.

Proponents of transactional analysis would probably suggest that the way to stop or avoid destructive game playing is for teachers to stay in their Adult mode. An antithesis to the above described game might go as follows.

Student: (angrily) You're always picking on me. Leave me alone.

Teacher: You see me as unfair. I'll have a few minutes after class to discuss this with you if you wish.

Student: (still baiting teacher) I don't care what you do. You'll give me a zero anyway.

Teacher: Right now, I'd like to continue our discussion of Russia.

Student: You never listen to me.

Teacher: I can see that you're hurt, upset, and angry with me. And I'd like to discuss this with you after class. Now who can tell me the names of the Russian port cities?

In the above example, the teacher was able to stay in his Adult by briefly reflecting the student's thoughts and feelings, by paying no immediate attention to the accusations, by providing the student with another alternative, and by continuing with the lesson. The transactional analysts are *not* suggesting that a teacher stay always in his Adult, as this would lead to monotonous, boring discussions in the classroom. However, staying in the Adult when challenged and threatened by game-playing students serves to decrease the likelihood that the game will continue.

OTHER EXAMPLES OF SCHOOL TRANSACTIONS

COMPLEMENTARY TRANSACTION

1. *Student:* I'm really worried about Friday's exam (Child).

   Teacher: You can come to class after school, and I'll be happy to help you (Nurturing Parent).

2. *Student:* (jokingly) Let's put a pin on Mrs. Lewis' (teacher's) seat so we can let her hot air out.

   Student 2: Yeah, we'll do it right after recess.

CROSSED TRANSACTION

3. *Student:* (wanting extra help) This work is too hard. I don't understand it.

   Teacher: This is the fourth time I've told you to get your work done. If you don't start listening and getting your work done, I'll call your parents!

Most children, especially younger ones, will go back to their seats fearing the teacher will follow through on the threat. So while the immediate transaction has ended, the student is left without getting what he wants (teacher's help) and begins to collect resentment stamps. Should this type of interaction continue, it's a safe bet that one day this student will find ways to hook the teacher into disruptive game playing which will lead to more of a payoff for him/her.

ULTERIOR TRANSACTION

4. *Parent:* How's Johnny behaving now? (Ulterior—Johnny has never had any behavior problems before and you're to blame for them.)

   Teacher: I've done everything I can, and still he gets into fights almost every day in the class. (Ulterior—"I've had it with him. I can't stand him.")

   Parent: (annoyed) He didn't have these behavior problems last year in Mr. C's class.

Teacher: (hooked and guilty) I just don't know what to do with him. He doesn't listen and just. . . . I'll keep on trying.

According to the view of transactional analysis (T.A.), discipline problems are to be viewed in terms of the transactions that occur between people. Discipline problems can be avoided by understanding how a teacher gets hooked into playing a game with a disruptive student, and by being sensitive to his/her own ego state and that of the student at any given moment.

Most transactional analysts would likely advise teachers of the necessity of their staying in the Adult ego state, particularly when confronted with students who have problems with authority. Since the Adult is the rational, thinking computer which reflects upon information from the Parent and Child, it is best able to resolve daily hassles which occur in all classrooms. The T.A. model considers both the student and his environment as responsible for discipline problems, as well as the interaction of environmental factors. We believe that while T.A. has much to offer the teacher, it's main strength is for those who are already aware of their own needs, and who have developed the emotional strength to observe, identify, and deal with the resentments and games of others without becoming hooked into the game. We recommend Ernst's Book, *Games Students Play*, for a more comprehensive treatment of transactional analysis in the classroom.

The fact is that children and adults need and want strokes through recognition, and they will attempt to get them in whatever way they can. They prefer to get them negatively rather than not at all. Rollo May, an existential philosopher and theorist has said:

The mood of the anonymous person is, if I cannot affect or touch anybody, I can at least shock you into some feeling, force you into some passion through wounds and pain; I shall at least make sure we both feel something, and I shall force you to see me and know that I am also here! Many a child or adolescent has forced the group to take cognizance of him by destructive behavior, and though he is condemned, at least the community notices him. To be actively hated is almost as good as being actively liked; it breaks down the utterly unbearable situation of anonymity and aloneness.[22]

[22] Rollo May, *Love and Will* (New York: W. W. Norton, 1969), p. 31.

This is a fitting description for many children who are identified by teachers and others as "discipline problems."

Teacher Effectiveness Training

Thomas Gordon's approach to discipline places the focus upon communication as being of primary importance. Gordon considers his method to be democratic. He suggests that the primary reason that teachers spend so much classroom time with discipline is because of the emphasis on "repressive and power-based methods." These methods include "threats of punishment, actual punishment and verbal shaming and blaming." He claims that these methods invite "resistance, retaliation and rebellion" [23] in students. His alternative is to provide teachers with a model of communication that includes "active listening," "I-messages," "problem ownership," and "negotiation."

Active listening is a process that involves one person listening carefully to what another has expressed (including nonverbal communication), and then feeding back the message to convey understanding. This approach is utilized by a teacher when a student "owns" the problem. For example, student-owned problems include one student breaking another's pencil, two students arguing, an upset child who has just failed an exam, a student who believes the teacher does not like him, the child who is scapegoated, and many others. Generally, when a student is upset, disappointed, or angry, this problem is *his*, or to put it another way, *he owns* the problem. The teacher is instructed to feed back to the child in a way that is quite similar to the communication models of Rogers and Ginott. The emphasis is placed upon reflecting the students' feeling rather than the content. For example, Sally just received a D on her test, and Mrs. Willoughby assumes from her tears that she is sad and upset. Mrs. Willoughby's Active Listening statement to Sally is "You're sad and upset about your grade." The goal of Active Listening is to convey empathy and understanding to a student who's experiencing a problem, and through this process, to help the student to find her own solutions.

Gordon suggests that when the student's behavior has a real, "concrete and tangible" [24] effect upon the teacher's ability to function, then the teacher owns the problem. Teacher-owned problems are to be dealt with through the use of I-Messages. Some guidelines to forming an effective "I-message" include a description of the student's behavior that is causing

---

[23] Thomas Gordon, *Teacher Effectiveness Training* (New York: Wyden, 1974), p. 16.
[24] Ibid, p. 39.

the teacher to have a problem; what the tangible or concrete effect upon the teacher is; and how this makes the teacher feel. The characteristics of an effective "I-message" according to Gordon are:

1. They have high probability of promoting a willingness to change.
2. They contain minimal negative evaluation.
3. They do not injure the relationship.[25]

An effective I-message involves the willingness of the teacher to share her real feelings. Some teachers feel vulnerable giving I-messages because they expose themselves to their students. One example of a teacher-owned problem was Billy, who was always tardy returning to class from lunch. The teacher chose to spend time away from teaching to track Billy down almost daily. An effective I-message might be, "When you don't return to class on time (describing behavior), I have to stop the lesson to look for you (tangible concrete effect) and this makes me feel frustrated and disappointed (feelings)."

Sometimes both the teacher and the student own the problem, and conflicts emerge. An example might be a bored student (student's problem is boredom) who disrupts the class (talks out of turn) and creates a problem for the teacher ("I can't teach my class when she talks out of turn."). Gordon suggests that power and authority destructively influence the teacher-student relationship. His methods call for negotiation and problem solving rather than winning and losing. His belief is that by giving all classroom members a voice in the classroom rules, they come to feel more connected with what goes on in the classroom. Consequently, his approach suggests that discipline problems are lessened, because autocratic decision making is eliminated.

As noted earlier, Gordon's approach shares similarities with those of Ginott and Rogers, in that communication, understanding, and acceptance are emphasized. It is somewhat unique in its democratic emphasis which calls for a process of negotiation and problem solving in the establishment of classroom rules. In this way, it shares some similarity with our concept of social contract setting in the classroom. This approach has value in the notion of problem ownership, which leaves the primary responsibility of problem solving to the one with the problem. In this way, it is possible for the teacher to avoid involvement with every petty conflict and dispute that develops, and to spend more time with nonproblematic events.

We differ with Gordon in that we encourage teachers to use "I-messages" even when there isn't such a high willingness for change in the student. All too often, those espousing a humanistic orientation have led us

[25] Ibid, p. 140.

to believe that problems would be solved by sharing feelings. While this is true in some cases, we believe this to be a dangerous and naive expectation. Teachers should be prepared to express I-messages without expecting that anything will change in their students. If they really believe in the value of stating feelings, then this in itself is a valuable learning experience for students. Teachers are still important role models despite their shrinking popularity. If you only express yourself when change is probable, then students learn that openness is to be valued only when they can get something they want. Openness then becomes a tool of manipulation rather than a direct statement about oneself. The risk of openness is the possibility of rejection.

Gordon also lists the types of messages which he terms the "language of unacceptance." [26] These messages "block communication" and can therefore lead to problems in classroom management. He advises the teacher to avoid using these statements, and instead to concentrate on active listening, I-mesages, and problem solving.

THE LANGUAGE OF UNACCEPTANCE: THE TWELVE ROADBLOCKS TO COMMUNICATION

Solution Messages
1. Ordering, commanding, directing. Example: "You stop complaining and get your work done."
2. Warning, threatening. Example: "You'd better get on the ball if you expect to get a good grade in this class."
3. Moralizing, preaching, giving "shoulds" and "oughts." Example: "You know it's your job to study when you come to school. You should leave your personal problems at home where they belong."
4. Advising, offering solutions or suggestions. Example: "The thing for you to do is to work out a better time schedule. Then you'll be able to get all your work done."
5. Teaching, lecturing, giving logical arguments. Example: "Let's look at the facts. You better remember there are only thirty-four more days of school to complete that assignment."

Put-Down/Judgment Messages
6. Judging, criticizing, disagreeing, blaming. Example: "You're just plain lazy or you're a big procrastinator."
7. Name calling, stereotyping, labeling. Example: "You're acting like a fourth grader, not like someone almost ready for high school."

[26] Ibid, pp. 48–49.

8. Interpreting, analyzing, diagnosing. Example: "You're just trying to get out of doing that assignment."

Denial/Deflection Messages

9. Praising, agreeing, giving positive evaluations. Example: "You're really a very competent young man. I'm sure you'll figure out how to get it done somehow."

10. Reassuring, sympathizing, consoling, supporting. Example: "You're not the only one who ever felt like this. I've felt that way about tough assignments, too. Besides, it won't seem hard when you get into it."

11. Withdrawing, distracting, being sarcastic, humoring, diverting. Examples: "Come on, let's talk about something more pleasant." "Now isn't the time." "Let's get back to our lesson." "Seems like someone got up on the wrong side of the bed this morning."

Probing Messages

12. Questioning, probing, interrogating, cross-examining. Examples: "Do you think the assignment was too hard?" "How much time did you spend on it?" "Why did you wait so long to ask for help?" "How many hours have you put in on it?"

Reality Therapy

Glasser believes that students misbehave as a result of a lack of involvement in the school process. School failure is the cornerstone of his theory of student misbehavior. Disruptive events occur when students lack involvement with the school, when they feel like failures, and when they don't take responsibility for their own actions. It is his belief that schools must eliminate failure and increase involvement, relevance and thinking.[27] He notes that the development of responsibility, which is an antidote to failure and misbehavior, is achieved only through a strong, positive, emotional involvement with a responsible person. Glasser feels that carefully understood and firmly enforced rules are proof to the child that he/she is cared for enough to become responsible: he further suggests that the child will interpret this care as love.

His principles of reality therapy[28] include guidelines such as *be personal*, which calls for spending some time each day reinforcing involve-

[27] See William Glasser, *Schools without Failure* (New York: Harper & Row, 1969), for more information.

[28] From "Schools without Failure," a course offered by the Education Training Center, Los Angeles, to the Rush-Henrietta Schools in Rochester, N.Y.

ment. He emphasizes focusing on *present behavior*, by asking the student, "What are you doing right now?" He suggests an awareness of current behavior and avoidance of references to the past with an emphasis on present behavior, not feelings. His next principle is to ask the student to evaluate his own behavior by making his own *value judgment* ("Is what you're doing helping you?"). Glasser cautions that it must be the student's decision to do something better than what he's doing now. His next step is to develop a *plan* with the student. This calls for working with the student to formulate an alternative. The plan should be simple, short, and success oriented. We imagine that this plan would call for new student behaviors to be developed in small increments. The final principle is to obtain a *commitment* from the student, which "seals" the plan and may be a verbal or written agreement. It's considered of utmost importance that the student accept some responsibility for the plan.

Glasser stresses the importance of success experiences. He believes that a child forms his self-concept of being a success or a failure between the ages of five and ten. To encourage success experiences, Glasser believes that the school staff must be positively involved with each other, have a cooperative working relationship, care about each other, and work and plan together in the best interests of the child. He stresses the importance of classroom meetings around a variety of topics in which the teacher acts as a nonjudgmental facilitator rather than a dispenser of information or judge of what's right and wrong. During such meetings children are encouraged to share their opinions, views, preferences, and feelings openly, without the concern of being judged negatively by the teacher or classmates. He believes that classroom meetings help children to be involved in their own education. Classroom meetings can consist of "open-ended" meetings in which the child is helped to think and communicate knowledge about a given subject. "Educational-diagnostic" meetings are designed to provide feedback to the teacher on how well a particular concept is being received by the students. "Problem solving" meetings are geared to helping the children both individually and collectively to learn to solve the problems of living in a sometimes "hostile and mysterious" world.

Glasser's theoretical orientation suggests that our world has undergone a major shift since the end of the World War II.[29] He claims that affluence, political ideologies, the television industry, and the advertising industry have played a major role in causing this shift. The emphasis on survival in a goal-directed society which focused on achieving a socially sanctioned goal has shifted to self-discovery and exploration and to people (knowing yourself and what you want) being more important than a

[29] Summarized from William Glasser, *The Identity Society* (New York: Harper & Row, 1972).

job or other external events. He calls the current society the "Identity Society" and his book of the same title explores its origins in depth.

His notion is that schools need to reflect this major cultural shift and change from an "external locus of control" (do what the teacher says because he/she knows best), to an "internal locus of control" (involvement in the planning and direction of school by its students). Delinquency and other antisocial acts are caused by students who believe they are not worthwhile and view themselves as failures. Schools must emphasize success and be a place in which students can experience happiness, comfort, and safety—a place in which all students feel loved and worthwhile.

In summary, Glasser's plan for dealing with misbehavior includes an emphasis on behavior rather than on feelings. His approach is a rational, cognitive one which encourages problem solving by the student and elicits a plan for behavioral change that encourages a commitment from the student. He believes it necessary to reinforce appropriate behavior when the student is being successful. The teacher is advised to have clear rules which are firmly enforced and which are nonpunitive in that blaming and threatening are eliminated. Teachers need to provide students with a friendly greeting and classroom tasks that show the teachers' belief in their (students') ability to be responsible.

Glasser's approach shows some similarity to those of the behaviorists who emphasize "behavior" and the use of positive reinforcement. His approach is also humanistic; that is, value is placed on providing success experiences that are based on involvement with the student and helping him to become responsible.

Consider the following example that demonstrates some of Glasser's principles:

Mike is pushing Sam in the back of the classroom near the art table. The teacher approaches the boys and directs her comments to Mike.

> *Teacher:* What are you doing right now (present behavior)?
>
> *Mike:* He won't let me have the box of colored crayons.
>
> *Teacher:* That's what he's doing, but what are *you* doing right now (return to present behavior)?
>
> *Mike:* I pushed him.
>
> *Teacher:* I'm glad to see that you know what you did (positive reinforcement). Is pushing Sam helping you (value judgment)?
>
> *Mike:* Well, he won't let me have the crayons.
>
> *Teacher:* Let's see if there are other things that you could have done to get the crayons without pushing Sam (plan). In this classroom we don't solve problems by pushing (rule).

Mike: I tried to talk to him but he wouldn't listen.

Teacher: I'd like to suggest (plan) that you tell Sam that you'd like to share the crayons with him, and if he refuses, then let me know. Do you have any other ideas?

Mike: No, that's okay with me (commitment).

Teacher: So, the next time you don't get what you want, you'll tell Sam or any other classmate that you'd like to share the materials with them, and if they refuse, then you'll tell me (restating plan).

Mike: Yes, I'll do that (seals the plan).

Moral Reasoning

Lawrence Kohlberg has made a major contribution to the understanding of "moral development." His model is based on cognitive-developmental theory which suggests that moral reasoning progresses in stages.[30] Kohlberg studied the moral reasoning of children over a wide age range by presenting children with hypothetical moral dilemmas. He then probed in depth how they solved each dilemma. For example, he asked a child in one of his situations, "Is it better to save the life of one important person or of a lot of unimportant people?"[31] In another, he told the child, "A man's wife is dying of cancer and urgently needs a drug; the man tries all possible legal means to obtain it but fails; he eventually steals it"; then he asked the child for his opinion of the man's behavior and how he arrived at his opinion. Kohlberg pays some attention to affective factors such as guilt and sympathy in decision making, but emphasizes that moral decisions are cognitively developed by the judging individual. Consequently, intelligence and the individual's ability to reason abstractly are important factors in the attainment of an advanced morality. Interestingly, Kohlberg minimizes the importance of such issues as religious training, types of child rearing, amount of punishment or love, or homes with a single parent or two parents. These issues have been emphasized to one degree or another by most other theorists as being of utmost importance in the healthy development of children. Kohlberg instead emphasizes the degree and variety of social experience, and the ability of the child to understand the effects of his behavior on other people. The child's ability to assume different roles is important and as Sara Sanborn, in her review of Kohl-

[30] Summarized from L. Kohlberg's "The Child as a Moral Philosopher," *Psychology Today* 7 (1968), pp. 25–30.

[31] Sara Sanbom, "Means and Ends: Moral Development and Moral Education," Annual Editions Readings in Human Development, pp. 163–166. Reprinted from The Harvard Graduate School of Education Bulletin, Fall 1971.

berg, says, "to encounter other perspectives." [32] Moral development depends a great deal on your ability to "put yourself in the place of others."

Kohlberg defines moral development as occurring and progressing through six stages. Stage 1 is a morality based on an orientation to punishment or reward and to physical and material power. At this stage, the individual behaves according to those who have the power to punish or to reward. Stage 2 is defined as "social contract orientation" which involves an exchange of favors between people. This morality is that if you do something for me, then I'll do something for you. The orientation is, therefore, "You scratch my back and I'll scratch yours." For example, Billy says to Bobby, "If you give me the answers from the math test, then I'll let you ride my bicycle whenever you want."

The first two stages are considered "Pre-conventional" in that decisions are made on the basis of self-interest and/or material considerations.

The third and fourth stages are defined as "conventional" and most of the adult population operates at this level. Stage 3 is called the "good boy" orientation, in which the individual's actions are geared to pleasing others and thereby gaining acceptance from them. Behavior is emitted because it's the right thing to do and because others will accept you for behaving in a certain way. This stage is illustrated by those children who are constantly telling the teacher about other students' misbehavior with the hope of being seen as a "good boy" or a "good girl" for being morally righteous. Students who function primarily at this stage rarely misbehave. Their moral value is based on meeting expectations that others have set for them. Stage 4 is a morality based upon the respect for those in authority. Behavior is governed by the dictums of the church, the home, the school, and other institutions which are trusted with moral authority at this stage. Students who do not deviate from the rules out of fear of incurring the wrath of those in authority are functioning at a Stage 4 morality. These students have internalized the moral norms of those in authority, and behavior that is incongruent with these norms is likely to result in feelings of guilt and shame.

The highest levels of moral development occur at Stages 5 and 6. These are referred to as the "post-conventional" level. At this level the individual moves from conforming to the expectations of those in authority, to the development of individual judgments that will at times vary from prevailing social opinion. At Stage 5, the individual is motivated through the recognition that all individuals have rights, and that each individual has a right to exist regardless of his social orientation, status, role, sex, race, or importance. The morality of the American Constitution is a stage

[32] Ibid.

five morality. The individual transcends those expectations in his immediate environment to a morality which extends beyond the prevailing socially acceptable attitude. The most advanced morality, Stage 6, is the "morality of individual principles of conscience" which have "logical comprehensiveness and universality." The highest value is placed on human life, equality, or dignity.

We believe that institutional relationships such as those within a school tend to be based more on authority than on ideas of justice. The school atmosphere is generally a mix of Stage 1 (punishment morality), Stage 3 (good boy orientation), and Stage 4 (law and order morality). If all kids were operating at one of these three stages, then we hypothesize that no discipline problems would exist. But if a student is at Stage 2 and trades his math paper with another student for the other student's English assignment, then a conflict occurs between the institutional moral norm and that of the individual. Telling the child that it's bad for him to cheat because cheating is against the school rules (Stage 4), or punishing him for the cheating (Stage 1) will not solve the problem. A Stage 4 explanation won't work because it's beyond the child's ability to reason at this level, and a Stage 1 solution won't work because the child believes that the exchange of favors is more important than an orientation to punishment. The refusal of one student to report another to the teacher for misbehavior is often an example of Stage 2 morality. Telling the class that they will be punished unless those responsible for cheating on the exam admit to it is almost never successful in getting one student to tell on another. Since nearly all students will engage in cheating at one time or another during their school career, violating the Stage 2 morality of "You scratch my back and I'll scratch yours" leaves any student vulnerable to being identified as a cheat at some other time. Consequently, nobody says anything. Stages of morality are assessed not by the actions of students, but rather by the motives which underlie a student's behavior. Two students may behave the same, but be at different moral stages. Moral emphasis is placed on how a person thinks rather than on what a person does.

We believe that most school discipline problems can generally be viewed as a conflict between the schools' Stage 1, Stage 3, and/or Stage 4 morality and the student's Stage 2 morality. Less frequently, the student's Stages 5 and 6 morality can also lead to conflict for him.

Consider the following conflict:

Principal: This is the fourth time I've spoken to you about your verbal disagreements with Mrs. Rosen. Now are you just a disagreeable sort or do you enjoy talking back to those in authority? (Stage 4).

Larry: I've only been honest with her. I've told her that I'm not interested in her subject, and I've asked for permission several times to study in the library. She's refused to allow me to do this each time. I also don't like the way she talks down to the students. I'm a person and I should be respected also (Stage 5).

Principal: That's no excuse for being disobedient (Stage 4). Now the next time you're sent here, you'll get a good paddling (Stage 1).

Larry: That would be a violation of my basic human rights (Stage 5 or 6).

This example illustrates the lack of adequate communication because each person's statements are based upon different levels of morality. The principal talks to Larry at Stages 1 and 4, while Larry is operating at Stage 5. So there are potentially negative consequences associated for an individual who is operating above or below the moral norm (Stages 4 or 5). Many war resisters whose basic morality centered on the value of human life have suffered the consequences of opposing the basic social order ("When the government tells you to fight, then you must fight"). Others were at a lower stage and simply refused to fight because they did not want to.

A key principle of Kohlberg's theory of moral development is that of justice. He defines justice as a primary regard for the value and equality of all human beings and for reciprocity in human relations. Kohlberg has developed a moral education curriculum which consists of moral dilemmas such as those mentioned earlier. The students and instructor discuss each dilemma and there are no right or wrong answers. The emphasis is placed on how children think rather than telling them what to think. He maintains that a child tends to prefer the highest stage of reasoning which he can comprehend, which is usually one stage higher than his own. He's found that when a child is regularly exposed to the one higher stage, he/she will incorporate it into his thinking.

In summary, Kohlberg minimizes factors such as love-oriented methods versus threat-oriented methods that have loomed large in the theories of others. He sees moral development as a congitive skill, associated with one's general intelligence and capacity for abstract thinking, which involves making judgments and which progresses through stages. Children can learn to think at higher moral levels when they are exposed to a series of moral dilemmas and are provided an opportunity to examine their decision-making process.

We view Kohlberg's work as being very attentive to the conflict that may be generated between the differences in group versus individual needs. A student who consistently functions either above or below a Stage 3 or 4 morality is likely to encounter adjustment problems within a school setting. Kohlberg's work was one of the most difficult to place on our continuum because of its shift in emphasis from earlier stages which are more group oriented to the later stages which are more oriented toward the individual. Of greater consequence is the fact that his work has important theoretical implications regarding the causes of discipline problems in school settings.

Behavior Modification

Behavior modification is among the most widely known and extensively researched approaches to classroom management. The basic tenet of behavior modification is that learning depends on events that occur after a certain behavior. E. L. Thorndike, a pioneer learning theorist, developed his *Law of Effect* which states that "Any act which in a given situation produces satisfaction becomes associated with that situation, so that when the situation reoccurs, the act is more likely than ever before to reoccur also. Conversely, any act which in a given situation produces discomfort becomes disassociated from the situation so that when the situation reoccurs, the act is less likely than before to reoccur." [33] In other words, if a student has had a satisfying experience, chances are that under similar conditions, he will tend to behave similarly and have another satisfying experience. Conversely, if being in a classroom is associated with discomfort, then he will remove himself either physically or psychologically from the situation (classroom) that is causing him discomfort.

Later on, B. F. Skinner developed extensive principles of operant conditioning which state that the events which follow a given behavior either strengthen or weaken that behavior. He used the term "reinforcement" to mean those events that follow a behavior and cause that behavior to increase in frequency. Skinner's theory suggests that all behavior is learned and it is the outside environment that either strengthens or weakens a given behavior. In his paradigm, punishment describes a procedure in which a behavior is followed by an aversive or unpleasant event.

A classroom reinforcer can take several different forms such as a concrete reward (piece of candy, money, a small toy), an activity reward (ten minutes of free time for completed work), or a social reward (teacher praise, classroom monitor, etc.); or it can take a negative form such as the removal of an unpleasant stimulus (the teacher who stops yelling, a loud interfering noise that stops, or the removal from the classroom of a child who hates the class). The latter example (removal of the child) is illustrative of how a teacher can unwittingly reinforce (or reward) a child's behavior that she intends to extinguish (reduce the frequency of occurrence).

---

[33] E. L. Thorndike, *The Elements of Psychology* (New York: Seiler, 1905), p. 202.

What may be viewed as punishing by the teacher (removal from class), can be viewed as rewarding by the student ("I finally acted up enough to get out of this miserable class."). In such a case, the student misbehavior may actually increase. It is important to know what is perceived as reinforcing to a given student, and to arrange the classroom environment so that in-classroom time is viewed as rewarding by the student.

According to this view, misbehavior occurs because it is reinforced by the environment. The antithesis is to change the child's behavior through a manipulation of his environment which reinforces or rewards "good" or socially appropriate behavior. This shaping process occurs through rewarding successive approximations (behaviors which gradually come closer to the desired outcome) of the target behavior. Reinforcement is contingent upon the student emitting behaviors that are closer to those desired by the teacher. Reinforcement can be given continously (for each and every appropriate student response) or periodically. Periodic reinforcement can be given on a fixed schedule (i.e., after every fifth appropriate response or after each five-minute interval of appropriate behavior) or on a variable schedule (i.e., after *approximately* every fifth appropriate response or approximately five-minute interval). Research has shown that in the initial phase of behavior shaping, continuous reinforcement is needed until the student gradually progresses to one of the variable schedules, which appears to ultimately have the strongest effect.

Carl, a third grade student, was observed to be spending most of his time out of his seat. Despite repeated reprimands from Mrs. Fuller, this behavior not only continued, but worsened. After gathering some data from Mrs. Fuller, it became clear that she was most concerned about Carl during reading groups, when she'd work with one group and expect the others to work quietly and independently. She also noted that Carl loved his physical education period and was extremely well coordinated physically. Carl was placed on a points system so that for every two-minute interval in which Carl was seated, he would earn one point. For every five points that he earned, he received two extra minutes during his next gym period. Ten points was rewarded with five minutes of classroom free time.

And for fifteen points or more, a letter would be sent home to his parents, informing them of how well he was doing. Gradually, Carl's behavior showed improvement, and rewards were given less frequently. He gradually had to behave appropriately for longer time intervals to earn a reward. Mrs. Fuller was shaping Carl's behavior through successive approximations to the desired outcome (a full period of Carl's being in-seat).

Proponents of behavior modification suggest the reinforcement of behavior that's incompatible with the student's misbehavior. A person cannot be behaving well and misbehaving at the same time, and by rewarding good behavior, the probability of that behavior occurring again increases.

Let's look at a child who believes that he belongs only when he's the boss. His goals are to feel powerful and to gain attention.

Teacher: Stop fighting this instant, Johnny!

Johnny: I don't have to if I don't want to.

Teacher: Fighting is not allowed here.

Johnny: Well, he started it, and I'll beat his brains in.

Teacher: Johnny, this is the third time today I've had to talk to you about this.

Johnny: I don't care. You always pick on me anyway.

Teacher: That's not true, Johnny. Fighting is not allowed for anybody.

Johnny: He started it.

This exchange goes on for five minutes before Johnny is finally sent to the principal's office for using abusive language to the teacher.

In this example, Johnny received five minutes of exclusive attention from the teacher in front of his peers which, in fact, strengthened the whole series of events leading to his being sent to the office. Because he needs this attention and feels that he must have the power to acquire it, it is likely that he will fight again after a brief nonfighting period. In this example, to reinforce behavior that's incompatible with fighting, the teacher might have attended to Johnny when he was talking, doing his class assignment, or verbally disagreeing with another classmate. She could have said at these times, "Johnny and Pam are disagreeing with each other. Let's listen to see how they talk out their differences" (attention for more acceptable behavior). The teacher might also have chosen to reward Johnny for each day of nonfighting by sending home a nice note, giving a concrete reinforcer, or some other positive reward. Yet another alternative could be to administer a punishment which involves presenting aversive consequences such as taking time away from a desired activity or a spanking. We will examine the pros and cons of punishment later.

The final technique of behavior modification that we wish to explore is that of praise. Praise is the most commonly used social reinforcer. It is often given to a student with the intention of making him feel good about something and to get him to repeat this good behavior again. Teachers are usually taught to use praise frequently through such words and phrases as "good job," "good work," "Sally had the best math paper," "You're doing just fine," and so forth. While praise can be an effective technique, it can also have some deleterious effects. Many teachers and parents have discovered that praise can in fact lead to a worsening of behavior. There are some children, adolescents, and adults who do not believe themselves to be praiseworthy people, for many different reasons. Generally, these are people with low self-esteem, who rarely trust others. They experience praise as manipulative, and their behavior actually deteriorates as they try to maintain whatever control they do have over other people and themselves. Praise can also have some harmful effects on those students who are well motivated.

Greene and Lepper [34] demonstrated with preschool children that when praise is given to children who are intrinsically motivated (turned on by the task), it actually makes them less motivated toward that task than they were prior to being praised. They suggest that those who lack intrinsic motivation are probably the best population to benefit from praise.

Imagine the plight of the child who is ready to go out with his friends to play ball, when his mother demands that he mow the lawn. He finally consents under duress to do the job, and when he finishes, his mother comes to him and says, "You're such a good, helpful boy! Mother loves you."

Now, it's possible that Mother's praise will reinforce the job done and increase the likelihood of the child's mowing the lawn again. However, it's probable that this child experienced a lot of anger toward his mother for blocking his ball playing. Mother's praise is far more likely to elicit guilt in this child, which will ultimately lead to anxiety or anger.

Another danger of praise is that it can serve to set up unrealistic standards which ultimately lead to feelings of failure. We recall the case of David, a very talented violinist who received lavish praise from his parents and teachers for his musical exploits. All was well until David auditioned for a high level musical group and was rejected. Since his self-concept had been strongly tied to his musical ability, and had been strongly reinforced through praise, his rejection from the group led to a series of events which culminated in David's rejecting the violin and his own musical talents.

We believe that if you use praise, use it descriptively and praise the behavior, not the person. Also, take responsibility for your own feelings of praise. It's one thing to say, "I loved your short story and this is what I especially liked about it . . ." and quite another to say, "You're the most talented writer in the class." The former is a statement of feeling with specifics, while the latter is a judgment that sets up an expectation that may be impossible for the student to reach. Nobody is the best at anything all the time!

PUNISHMENT

We define punishment as the intent of those in authority to change the behavior of others through unpleasant or aversive consequences. Consequences such as verbal threats, removing children from activities

---

[34] David Green and Mark R. Lepper, "Intrinsic Motivation: How to Turn Play into Work," *Psychology Today.* Sept 1974. Vol. 8, no. 4, p. 49.

they enjoy, giving zeros, suggesting that parents remove privileges at home, making children stay after school, and paddling are a few behaviors that meet the requirements of being a punishment. Punishment can be an effective means of behavior control as long as it's coupled with a message of caring that gets through to the child. Punishment has the effect of stopping a child's misbehavior for a short interval of time, but does not effect lasting behavioral change. It only suppresses temporarily the punished action. Another important effect of punishment is that it teaches a child how to be better at misbehaving so as to avoid or escape the consequences of the punisher. There are many everyday examples of this both in and out of school. A child who's caught cheating on an exam and who's punished by getting a zero on the test will temporarily stop cheating until he discovers a better, less obvious method to cheat. A man who's caught cheating on his I.R.S. forms will keep better records to support his cheating the following year. A child who's paddled for abusive language will discover other more clandestine or sophisticated methods to let the teacher know he's angry. The point is that punishment alone is rarely an effective method of changing a person's behavior. Physical punishment shows or models aggressiveness as a problem-solving model, and children learn that when they're in control, it is appropriate to act in punishing ways. Bandura's and Walter's research in the area of social learning suggest that young children in particular learn primarily through imitation and modeling.[35] In essence, aggression breeds aggression.

Wesley Becker, a behavior modification proponent, has suggested the following guidelines, which he call "rules to remember." [36]

1. Effective punishment is given immediately.
2. Effective punishment relies on taking away reinforcers and provides a clear-cut method for earning them back.
3. Effective punishment makes use of a warning signal, usually words ("No," "Stop that," etc.) prior to punishment.
4. Effective punishment is carried out in a calm, matter-of-fact way.
5. Effective punishment is given along with such reinforcement for behaviors incompatible with the punished behavior.
6. Effective punishment is consistent. Reinforcement is not given for the punished behavior.

Punishment should be used selectively and cautiously. For those who see benefits in punishment we offer Becker's guidelines to help you

[35] A. Bandura and R. H. Walters, *Social Learning and Personality Development* (New York: Holt, Rinehart and Winston, 1963), for more information.

[36] Wesley C. Becker, *Parents Are Teachers* (Illinois: Research Press, 1971), p. 127.

maximize the effect of this approach, while minimizing the potential of deleterious side effects.

CONCLUSION

It is simply impossible to examine the total field of research and to include everybody's work. It is also not our intent to provide you with a complete overview, but rather to show you that you can adapt other approaches and methods within the three-dimensional framework which can help you to become a more congruent, effective classroom manager. One teacher may wish to include some principles of behavior modification in setting up a preventive classroom environment, while another may be more comfortable with one of the humanistic theories. Your choice of method depends upon who you are, what you believe, and what you want. The limitation in each of the theories is the narrowness of scope. Each would have you believe that theirs is the best, and if only you behaved according to its guidelines, then you would no longer have to worry about discipline problems in the classroom. The approaches obviously differ: there are those which call for the role of the teacher as a facilitator who presents the students with options and choices, and those which endow the teacher with the authority for determining what consitutes acceptable behavior and to manipulate the student into behaving accordingly. Some call for training the cognitive skills of the individual while others call for an emphasis on affective development. We feel far more comfortable in advising you to be what you are, and to adapt theories to your own preferences. Our primary focus is *awareness*, and *action* based upon this awareness.

9

ESTABLISHING SOCIAL CONTRACTS

The heart of the prevention dimension is the establishment and implementation of social contracts. As we have stated before, discipline problems occur when the needs of the teacher, the needs of the individual student, and the needs of the class come into conflict. We have found that the use of social contracts, when developed according to the basic principles described in this chapter, can eliminate many of these conflicts and establish a procedure for resolving them once they do occur.

The classroom social contract is comprised of those rules and consequences which set the standards for the acceptable behavior of the teacher and each student in the classroom. Expected behavior is defined, and consequences for unacceptable behavior is also defined. The process for establishing social contracts involves these steps.

1. The teacher develops rules and consequences regarding student behavior.
2. The students develop rules and consequences regarding the teacher's behavior.

3. The students develop rules and consequences regarding each other's behavior.

After all of the *proposed* rules and consequences have been developed, the class uses a specified decision-making procedure to determine which rules and consequences become the social contract. After the classroom social contract has been completed, a test is administered to ensure that everyone knows the content of the contract. Mechanisms for feedback are built into the social contract, so that everyone knows how well it is working. The feedback component involves a transition from the prevention dimension to the action dimension. We will discuss this in greater detail later.

The remainder of this chapter is a guidebook that outlines a step by step procedure for establishing social contracts. You may follow the steps as listed or modify them to meet your unique circumstances.

Step One: Teacher Develops Rules for Students

The first step in the development process is for you, the teacher, to develop a comprehensive list of rules. These rules will not constitute the social contract, but become part of the raw material from which the contract will be developed. In order to develop your set of rules, it is usually helpful to follow these guidelines:

1. Brainstorm as many rules as you can without censoring yourself. Try to have a rule to meet every one of your needs as a teacher, and one to meet what you think are the needs of the class as a whole (e.g., students will be on time for class; students will be recognized only when they raise their hands; and so forth).
2. If you are using rules in your classroom now, include any that you wish to continue to use.
3. Test the completeness of your list by imagining situations in which you are angry with your class for doing something wrong. If their behavior is not covered by a rule, then add one to the list.
4. Eliminate any rules from your list that violate a school rule, or a class rule dictated by the school (unless you are willing to accept the personal consequences). If you do include a rule for your class which violates a school rule, you may ask permission to deviate from school policy before going ahead. No food in class and no gum chewing are common examples of school rules from which some teachers choose to vary from school policy.
5. Eliminate any rule that violates a local, state, or federal law. While

this step might seem unnecessary, later it becomes a central part of the development process. We suggest that you take a quick look at your rules to see if any need to be eliminated for this reason.

6. Rules usually fall under three general categories:

   a. Classroom behavior—all the behaviors that students display while in your classroom; for example, fighting, throwing paper airplanes, talking back, swearing.

   b. Study habits—the manner in which learning activities are carried out; for example, handing homework in on time, neatness, including all the steps used to solve math problems, cheating.

   c. Achievement—behaviors or results of evaluations that indicate what a student has learned; for example, scoring 90 percent on a test, knowing all of the vocabulary, building a perfect bookcase.

   We believe that there should not be rules for achievement in a successful discipline program. Eliminate any rule that regulates how much a student learns or how well he performs on a test or learning task. Effective rules should cover only classroom behavior and study habits.

7. This step is difficult, but one of the most important. Make sure that each rule is specific; that is, there should be no doubt whether or not the rule has been broken. Many teachers boast that they only have one or two rules, but these rules are vague catch-alls that are continually being broken by students who do not understand what the real limits are. Some examples of vague rules are: "Students must be respectful of me and each other." Unless the teacher specifies what constitutes respectful and disrespectful behavior, there is little likelihood this rule will be effective. Another example of a rule that is too general is, "Students must try their best." It is impossible for a teacher to ever know whether a student is trying or not, other than guessing or assuming. We are not saying you will always know if a rule was broken or by whom. There may be times when a student breaks a rule and you are not aware of it; for example, when a student steals from another student. You may not have seen the behavior that broke the rule, but if you had seen it, there would be no confusion that the rule was broken.

8. Rule making can be and is a powerful experience when the rules are stated positively. Most rules specify what is unacceptable, such as "no fighting" or "no food throwing." Setting up an effective social contract requires that acceptable behaviors be given at least as much attention as those that are unacceptable. For example, instead of "no fighting," a more effective rule is, "arguments and disputes are to be settled through talking rather than fighting."

TO SUMMARIZE

A good rule
1. is clear and specific. You can always tell whether or not it was broken and the students can also tell whether it was broken.
2. does not violate a school, local, state or federal law.
3. says what behaviors are acceptable as well as what behaviors are not acceptable.

    Example: No fighting. Differences can be settled through discussion. If you are angry you can tell how you feel. If you must let off steam, you can write angry thoughts on a piece of paper and rip it up.
4. does not relate to academics. It can relate to study habits such as: all homework must be in on time, or cheating is not allowed in this classroom.[1]

Directions. List your rules for students. Write every rule so it is specific, clear, and if possible, state what behaviors are acceptable.

1. _____
2. _____
3. _____
4. _____
5. _____
6. _____
7. _____
8. _____
9. _____
10. _____
11. _____
12. _____
13. _____
14. _____
15. _____
16. _____
17. _____
18. _____
19. _____
20. _____

[1] Richard Curwin and Allen Mendler. "Three-Dimensional Discipline: A New Approach to an Old Problem." *American Middle School Education.* (Athens, Ga.: Vol. I, No. 4. Spring, 1979).

You must implement a consequence whenever the contract is broken. Consistency helps the students learn that their actions will result in a consequence whenever the contract is broken (providing their actions are detected). There are circumstances which can affect your willingness to implement a consequence. For example, you might find that you have a student who never breaks a rule, suddenly doing just that because of understandable reasons. Mary forgets her homework the first time, or John is overly active and pushes another student after coming back from three days in bed. It becomes very easy in these instances to tell the students that you understand and that you will not hold them responsible for their actions. Yet the other students, as well as those involved, learn that they can get away with rule breaking if their excuse is good enough and the circumstances can be made to be sympathetic for them. It is this learning that promotes creativity in excuse thinking and the whining, "I didn't mean it," that teachers of young children have grown to dread.

The students will learn another negative outcome if you implement a harsh consequence regardless of the situation. If Mary got a zero for forgetting her homework, she may have negative feelings about the heartless teacher she has. Her behavior later may reflect her desire to get even or to show the teacher that she also has power. The same may be true for John if he must spend the rest of the day alone. Getting even (need for power) is a common catalyst for future discipline problems and can be expressed overtly or passively. Neither is desirable.

Our solution to this dilemma is to avoid harsh consequences when they are not justified, while *always* implementing a consequence for a violation of the rule. We feel that a range of alternatives, with at least one that falls in the warning and stop and think category, and one that is stronger, will resolve the problem. (In essence you become a judge, as you must, when dealing with discipline. And once it has been determined that the law was broken, to use your powers of discretion to find the best sentence for rehabilitation given the circumstances of the crime.)

Step Two: Teacher Develops Consequences for Students

Each of the rules previously listed must have consequences for students who break them. This is critically important to the success of the social contract. The consequences should reflect the following principles:

1. Consequences are not punishments. Remember from the research cited in Chapter 8 that punishments do not produce long-term changes in behavior. The purpose of the consequence is to teach the students that misbehavior produces effects which are both desired

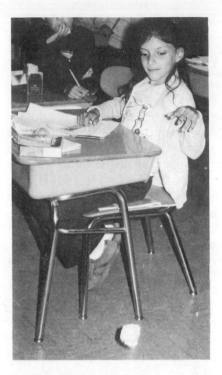

Sue throws paper on the floor.

(the reason for breaking the rule) and not desired (the reason there is a rule against that behavior). Punishments are designed to get even and hurt. The more closely related the consequence is to the rule the less likely it is to be a punishment. Note the following example:

Sue throws paper on the floor.

Punishments:
a. Stay after school and write on the board, "I will not throw paper on the floor," one hundred times.
b. Detention.
c. Going to the principal's office.

Consequences:
a. Picking up the paper off the floor.
b. Cleaning the room.
c. Apologizing to the teacher and/or class for disturbing them.

Students may perceive consequences as punishments. When the contract is implemented, you must carefully explain the difference between consequences and punishments, so that the students clearly understand the difference.

2. There needs to be a range of options for the teacher within the consequence. This can be either a set number of consequences available to the teacher, any one of which can be implemented for rule violation at the discretion of the teacher, *or* a hierarchy of consequences which make clear what will happen each time the rule is violated. Consider the difference between the two:

   a. Set number of consequences available:
      Rule: Students will arrive for class on time.
      Consequences: (what will happen if the rule is violated)

      - Student will attend class after school to make up time.
      - Student will be penalized one point from report card grade for every two times late to class.
      - Students who are on time will earn one point. Any student who earns five consecutive points will earn one point toward his/her final grade (positive consequence).
      - Parents will be contacted for a student-teacher-parent conference to discuss class tardiness.

   Any one of these consequences may be implemented at the discretion of the teacher.

   b. Graduated series of consequences:
      Rule: Students will arrive for class on time.
      Consequences:

      - First infraction results in teacher-student conference.
      - Second infraction results in student attending after school class to make up lost time.
      - Third infraction results in parent-student-teacher conference to find ways that student can get to class on time.
      - Fourth infraction results in the loss of one point toward final grade.
      - Students will earn one point toward final grade for each five consecutive days that they come to class on time (positive consequence).

With a hierarchical system of options each rule violation has a specific consequence that everybody in the class knows about. The teacher has less discretion, but the consequences are uniform as everybody knows in advance what specifically will happen each time a rule is violated.

3. Each consequence must be clear and understandable to the student.
4. The consequence should be implemented as soon after the violation of the social contract as possible.

TO SUMMARIZE

A good consequence

1. is clear and specific. Students know what will happen when they break a rule.
2. has a range of alternatives so that the teacher can always implement a consequence and still pay attention to individual needs.
3. is not designed to punish, but to help students learn "cause and effect" in relation to rule violations.
4. relates as directly to the rules as possible.[2]

Directions. Write a set of consequences for each of the rules you listed in step one.

Rule 1.
Range of consequences:
    a. _____
    b. _____
    c. _____
Rule 2.
Range of consequences:
    a. _____
    b. _____
    c. _____
Rule 3.
Range of consequences:
    a. _____
    b. _____
    c. _____

[2] *Ibid.*

Rule 4.
Range of consequences:

    a. _____

    b. _____

    c. _____

Rule 5.
Range of consequences:

    a. _____

    b. _____

    c. _____

Rule 6.
Range of consequences:

    a. _____

    b. _____

    c. _____

Rule 7.
Range of consequences:

    a. _____

    b. _____

    c. _____

Rule 8.
Range of consequences:

    a. _____

    b. _____

    c. _____

Rule 9.
Range of consequences:

    a. _____

    b. _____

    c. _____

Rule 10.
Range of consequences:

    a. _____

    b. _____

    c. _____

POSITIVE CONSEQUENCES

So far, we have described a process for developing consequences for those instances when students break the rules. There are situations in which it may be helpful to have positive consequences (i.e., consequences that are desirable such as free time, preferred activities, reduced homework) for those students who consistently follow the rules. Some teachers feel that it is inappropriate to reward expected behavior, fearing that this practice sets up an environment in which good behavior must be bought by the teacher. Opponents of the behavior modification school of thought see other harmful effects and are reluctant to use positive consequences. Yet there is another side to this question. Providing positive consequences can prevent good students from developing the attitude that "the only way to get attention is to act out." Also, for many students, the potential of rewards is enough to help them follow the rules.

The use of rewards has both positive and negative effects. We believe that each teacher must make up his/her own mind on this issue, and it has been our experience that the use of rewards works best for those teachers who believe in them; they do not work well for teachers who do not believe in them. If you decide to include positive rewards as part of your social contract we offer the following guidelines:

1. You can have positive consequences for each rule or for students who do not break any rule. For example: any student who does not interrupt the class for one week can have ten minutes of free time (a consequence for a given rule); any student who does not break any rule for three days receives a weekend with no homework (an all rules consequence). We think either method can be effective although it is easier for the students if the positive consequences are related to each rule. This is especially true if you have a problem with a specific rule and want to enforce it more than the others. The problem with individual consequences for each rule is that it requires more record keeping on the part of the teacher, and if it gets too complex, it can become a burden that might not be worth the effort.

2. The consequences should be attainable. If the rewards are only received after an effort that the students feel is too difficult, they will give up and not try to get them.

3. The criteria for positive consequences must be clearly spelled out, so that there is no doubt when they are earned and what the rewards are. This is true for negative rules and consequences as well.

4. The rewards should be personally meaningful to the students. Giving reading time to students who hate to read will not be very helpful.

5. The guidelines for establishing negative consequences apply for positive consequences as well, including the development of a range of alternatives.

Step Three: Students Develop Rules for Teacher

In the previous steps you developed rules and consequences for your students. These were designed to meet your needs and the needs of the class as you perceived them. In this step (and the next three) your students will be given the opportunity to meet their individual needs as they relate to living in your/their classroom. The first step in this process is for them to think of rules for you, the teacher. These rules are intended to give the students a chance to let you know what their limits are regarding your behaviors. This gives them an opportunity to feel that what happens in the classroom is at least partly determined by them.

By gaining some control in developing classroom rules and consequences, the necessity to break rules as a means of being heard diminishes. After all, the students are being heard and listened to before a rule has been implemented or broken. Participation in this process is especially important for the youngsters who frequently misbehave. Such students typically feel alienated and at their core, unimportant. This process is a way of involving them in a decision-making procedure in which their voice is as equally important as any other.

The basic principles of rule development as previously discussed apply to the development of these rules. Now the notion of having rules that do not violate federal, state, local, or school rules has an important function. These become your safeguards against the listing and potential adoption of such rules as, "All students can smoke (cigarettes or marijuana) in class whenever they want." It will be easier for your students to understand and accept this limit on their rule development, if you can show them that your rules for them follow the same guideline. This is why we suggested that you follow this guideline earlier and make sure your rules fit. It is also helpful to recall that at this stage of the development process, the students are only generating a list of rules to use as raw material for the social contract. *Not every rule will necessarily be adopted.* It is okay for them to list any rule, regardless of how silly or impractical as long as it meets the guidelines previously discussed.

STRATEGIES FOR DEVELOPMENT OF STUDENT RULES

There are a number of ways to have the students develop a list of rules for the teacher, depending on the students' ages and grade levels. Here are some suggestions:

1. On the first day you implement the three-dimensional approach, tell the class that you have developed some possible rules and consequences for them. Carefully explain each one and why you want it

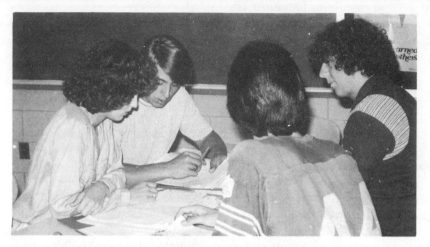

These students are developing a list of rules for the teacher.

implemented (e.g., your desire for a supportive, productive classroom environment). Then tell them that they will have the chance to think of some rules for you and provide them with two or three examples. Finally, present the guidelines for rule development.

2. Ask the class to think of a list of rules they would like you to follow to be a fair and supportive classroom teacher. Provide the guidelines and examples. After they present their list, you can present your list for them.

3. For older students, as a homework assignment, you may have each student think of two rules for you and them combine all the rules, eliminating any duplicates.

4. Have a class brainstorming activity suggesting any rules they can think of, and later eliminate any from the list that do not meet the guidelines.

5. Divide the class into groups and have each group think of three or four rules and eliminate any duplicates.

6. For younger students, think of rules that you imagine they may like- for you and let them choose the ones they like best. Give them an opportunity to add to the list if they can think of any others (e.g., "If I was a student in this class, I'd like the teacher to _____ ").

Directions. List the student rules for teacher.

1. _____

2. _____

3. _____

4. _____

5. _____

6. _____

7. _____

8. _____

9. _____

Step Four: Students Develop Consequences for Teacher

There must be consequences for you, the teacher, should you violate any of these rules, if adopted. Teach your students the definition of a consequence and provide the) guidelines mentioned above for the development of your consequences for them. You can use any of the suggested ways for rule development as an instruction strategy, although it may be best for the students to combine both steps at the same time and develop a list of rules and consequences together.

Here are some examples of rules and consequences which were developed by students for teachers.

1. The teacher must give all homework for the upcoming week on the Friday before, so that students may plan their weekly work schedule.
   Consequences:
   a. Teacher can only give four days of homework, none on the weekend.
   b. Teacher cannot give any homework that week.
   c. All homework is optional for extra credit.
   d. The students can choose their own homework assignments for that week.
2. The teacher can only call on students who raise their hand to avoid embarrassing those students who do not know the answers.
   Consequences:
   a. Teacher cannot ask any questions for ten minutes.
   b. The student does not have to answer.
   c. The students can spend five minutes of class time asking the teacher questions.
   d. The student called upon has the right to confer with another student of his choice before answering.
3. The teacher must call on all students by name. The students will

wear name tags to help the teacher learn the names of students. (If a student is not wearing his/her name tag, there are no consequences for not following the rule).

Consequences:

a. The student does not have to respond.

b. The teacher must apologize.

c. The student can call the teacher, "Hey, you."

d. The teacher must learn that student's name within two days.

4. The teacher must meet with each student at least once a month for ten minutes to discuss how things are going in the class.

Consequences:

a. No grades can be given until the meetings have occurred.

b. Students may withhold homework until they have had their last month's meeting.

c. Students may use class time for their meetings.

5. Teacher must allow students to work in groups with students of their choice at least half the time for reading groups.

Consequences:

a. Students can warn the teacher when they notice they haven't been allowed to form their own groups.

b. Students do not have to do reading workbook assignments until they are given a chance to form their own groups.

c. Students can form their own groups for three weeks.

6. Teacher must bring in a show and tell object from his/her home and explain it.

Consequences:

a. The students do not have to bring in a show and tell object if the teacher does not.

b. The students can choose a category of show and tell for the teacher to bring in (for example, clothes, favorite hobby, a prepared food).

7. The teacher cannot embarrass a student in front of the class.

Consequences:

a. Warning.

b. An apology.

c. Five minutes free time for entire class.

8. If the teacher accuses a student of stealing, the teacher must give the student a chance to give his/her side of the story.

Consequences:

a. No consequence can be given to the student until he/she has his/her say.
b. The teacher must apologize to the student publicly (in the presence of the whole class).
c. The student can complain to the principal during class time.

Now list the student consequences of student rules for teacher if they were not developed in step three.

Step Five: Students Develop Rules for Each Other

Now it is time for your students to develop a series of rules for each other. Using the same process and methods discussed previously, have your students develop a list of rules that will define acceptable and unacceptable behaviors for each other. Step six centers on the development of a series of consequences for these rules, and you may wish to combine these two steps.

Directions. List students' rules for each other.

1. _____
2. _____
3. _____
4. _____
5. _____
6. _____
7. _____
8. _____
9. _____
10. _____
11. _____
12. _____
13. _____
14. _____
15. _____
16. _____
17. _____
18. _____
19. _____
20. _____

Step Six: Students Develop Consequences For Each Other

If you have not already done so, have your students develop a series of consequences for each of their rules. Some examples of student rules and consequences for each other follow:

1. Name calling or use of four-letter words or use of put-downs are not allowed.

   Consequences:

   a. Public apology.

   b. Written letter of apology.

   c. The student who is the name caller must call himself the same name (the same for put-downs).

2. Permission must be asked of others and granted by them before borrowing items that belong to them.

   Consequences:

   a. Student must return borrowed item.

   b. The borrower must loan the student something of the student's choice for one day.

   c. The borrower must pay rent; no more than twenty-five cents a day is allowed.

3. Fighting is not permitted; students may tell each other that they are angry.

   Consequences:

   a. Loss of all privileges for one week.

   b. One day school suspension; student will be permitted to class only if accompanied by his parent.

   c. Writing a poem about why fighting is bad and performing it before the class.

4. Other students' books are not for writing on or damaging in any way.

   Consequences:

   a. Clean book.

   b. Replace book.

5. Students can ask each other for help on homework assignments and class assignments.

   Consequences:

   a. The student who asks for help receives recognition by others for being brave enough to admit that he does not know something.

Step Seven: Implicit Teacher Rules for Students

This step is one of the most difficult to complete. Implicit rules are those rules that you expect your students to follow, but you never state them. These are the rules that seem to "come from nowhere" or to be made up on the spot. To help you think of implicit rules, imagine your classroom running perfectly for about five minutes. Write down some of the observable behaviors that both you and your students exhibit. Then imagine the students behaving in as many ways as you can think of that would make you angry enough to ask them to stop or to admonish them. Write each of these behaviors down. Make a rule to account for any behavior, not already covered in your first list, that you wish to limit.[3]

Here are some examples of one teacher's implicit rules. *Note:* For you, these rules might be explicit, and you may have an entirely different set of implicit rules.

1. Forgetting materials, such as pens, books, or supplies, is not acceptable. All items necessary for class must be brought on time.
2. No student can take more than five minutes to go to the lavatory unless that student is sick.
3. No swearing is allowed.
4. Gum chewing is allowed. All gum must be wrapped in paper and thrown in the waste basket when finished. No gum is allowed on furniture or other students' property.
5. Students must come to class on time and be ready to work within three minutes of the bell.

List your implicit rules here.

1. _____
2. _____
3. _____
4. _____
5. _____
6. _____
7. _____
8. _____
9. _____

[3] This step may be unnecessary for some. Many teachers feel no need to add more rules to their list developed in Step 1. However, Step 7 gives you another opportunity to make sure that all the student behaviors that you want a rule for are covered.

10. _____
11. _____
12. _____
13. _____
14. _____
15. _____
16. _____
17. _____
18. _____
19. _____
20. _____

Step Eight: Teacher Develops Consequences for Implicit Rules

Using the same guidelines and methods just described develop a series of consequences for each of your once implicit, but now explicit rules.

You now have generated, with the help of your students, four lists of rules and consequences; one list of teacher rules for students, one list of student rules for teacher, one list of student rules for each other, and one list of implicit teacher rules for students. These lists can be combined into one master list, which is the raw material from which the social contract will be developed. Note the following example of a partial list of rules and consequences actually developed in a fifth grade class. A complete list of rules and consequences is generally much more extensive than the example which follows.

PARTIAL LIST OF CLASS RULES AND CONSEQUENCES

1. Only one person may speak at a time.
   Consequences:
   a. The teacher will remind any student who speaks to wait when another student is talking.
   b. The teacher will give a stern warning.
   c. The teacher will send the violator to a timeout corner for five minutes.
   d. The teacher will not allow the violator to have a turn to speak for five minutes.
2. No one may fight (physically) in the classroom.
   Consequences:

a. The teacher will send the violators to the timeout area for fifteen minutes.

b. The teacher will have a conference after school with each violator (either individually or together).

c. The teacher will have a conference with student and his/her parents.

3. Each student has the right to his/her own belongings. The teacher may not take the belongings of any student without permission.

Consequences:

a. The student will give the teacher a warning.

b. the student will have permission to examine the contents of the teacher's desk.

c. The student may ask for a public apology.

4. Desks and other school property are not for carving on, writing on, or destroying in any other manner.

Consequences:

a. The student violator will clean up.

b. The student will repair any damages.

c. The student will pay for replacement of item.

d. There will be a parent-teacher-student conference.

5. Students and teacher cannot use abusive language in class. No put-downs are allowed.

Consequences:

a. A bulletin board will be kept and after any put-down is heard by the teacher or a student, a picture (a hostile picture of guns, war machinery, and the like) will be put on the board. A day without any new pictures will remove one picture already posted. For every week with no pictures, a class period will be given to the students for their own use.

b. Any teacher picture on the board for more than three days results in a class period for the students' own use.

Step Nine: Class Discussion of Rules and Consequences

Now that you and your class have developed a list of rules and consequences, a decision must be reached to determine which of these will become the social contract. The first task is to make sure each student understands the implications for each of the rules and consequences and how they will affect classroom life. The following suggestions will help you and your students better understand these implications.

1. Role play each rule violation with your students observing.
2. Have the students role play rule violations.
3. Implement some sample consequences, in a role play, after demonstrating rule violations.
4. Have your students take turns role playing the teacher giving consequences.
5. Use the following questions to process the role play, or just as a basis for class discussion.
    a. Are there any rules you do not understand?
    b. Are there any consequences that you do not understand? (Role play can be used for any rule or consequence that is not understood.)
    c. Does anyone have a strong feeling about any rule or consequence, either to be included or excluded from the social contract? Why?
    d. Imagine what our class would be like if everyone followed each of the rules listed, and each consequence was implemented for each violation. Take some time imagining.
    e. What comments or observations can you make (from your imagination)?

Step Ten: Adoption of Rules and Consequences

The social contract is made up of those rules and consequences that are agreed to by the class. In the following guidelines we consider the class, "a group." As the teacher you have a choice to be the "authority" or an equal group member. We feel it is beneficial to assume the role of a group member, while maintaining control to see that the decision-making process works effectively. However, you will ultimately have to live by the contract and be responsible for its implementation. If there are some rules and consequences that you cannot accept, make this clear from the outset during the class discussion. You *can* give yourself the power of veto, particularly for those rules and consequences which are not acceptable to you and which you are expected to enforce. However, as a way of avoiding mistrust, we encourage you to go along with as many rules and consequences as possible which are agreed to by the class. The contract is "on trial" for a month or so and modifications and changes can occur at that time. So veto only those with which you absolutely cannot live. After a month of trying a rule or consequence that you had believed was unacceptable, you may find that it is not as bad as you imagined. Maybe the catastrophe that you had thought the rule or consequence would bring never materialized, or because you accepted it, your students were more willing to follow the contract. Or if the rule does not work out, you can explain to your class why it will be eliminated based on real data after the trial period. To summarize, eliminate before the decision-making process any rule or consequence that you cannot accept, but stretch your limits and give as many rules and consequences as possible a chance.

According to Edgar Schein, there are five basic ways that group decisions are reached. Note the following methods that Schein patterned after the work of Robert Blake:[4]

1. Authority rule.
2. Minority rule (handclasp).
3. Majority rule (voting and polling).
4. Consensus (everyone agrees to follow a decision, although some group members feel a different decision may be better).
5. Unanimous consensus (the decision is everyone's first choice).

In *authority rule* one person takes on the responsibility for making the decision. In *minority rule* or *"handclasp"* the power of decision making is deferred to a few esteemed (or vocal) people, and the remainder of the group simply goes along with what they have decided. A typical school example of *minority rule* is when a few articulate students say, "We, the senior class, believe that we should be allowed more privileges." In fact, the majority might disagree, but the outspoken few have made a decision for the group. *Majority rule* is the familiar way of deciding things in a democratic society where 51 percent agreement is needed. In a *consensus*, there is generally lively discussion and disagreement, but when a decision is reached, everybody agrees to follow the decision although some group members may feel that a different decision would be better. In *unanimous consensus* everybody gets what they want since the decision is everybody's first choice.

We suggest you use this decision-making model when reaching agreement on the social contract. Note that decisions are more easily reached at the top of the list and become progressively more difficult toward the bottom. Yet decisions will be followed more consistently beginning at the bottom, and be followed less at the top. Therefore agreement on the social contract can be made using the following procedure:

1. Attempt to reach unanimous consensus. Some rules and consequences will be readily agreed to by the group the first time through. Go through the entire list. All rules and consequences that reach unanimous consensus will be included in the social contract.

[4] Edgar Schein, *Process Consultation: Its Role in Organizational Development* (Reading, Mass.: Addison-Wesley, 1969), pp. 53–57.

2. On all rules left, try for consensus. Through debate and discussion, many more rules and consequences will be reached this way. Your guide to a consensus decision is that when discussion appears to ebb, and when differences in perception appear minimal, you may say, "I can see that most of you want this rule and I am wondering if anybody who does not would really object to trying it for about a month to see what happens."

We have found it useful to ask each member of the class who votes against the rule or consequence to propose any changes in its wording or language that would make it more acceptable. After each proposed change, survey the rest of the class to see if the rule will now meet with unanimous consensus. For example, notice the following rule change:

Teacher: How many can accept this rule: All homework will be handed in on time? Raise your hands.

Teacher: (*noticing all but two students raise their hands*) Steve, can you reword that rule so you can agree?

Steve: All homework assigned more than three days in advance will be handed in on time.

Teacher: Can we all agree on this change? If so, raise your hands.

Teacher: (*noticing one hand is still not raised*) Chris, can you reword the rule so you can agree?

Chris: All homework assigned more than three days in advance will be handed in on time, unless there are good reasons such as the necessary books are unavailable from the teacher, the library, or bookstore in time to do the assignment.

Teacher: I can agree with this rule. Is there still someone who cannot? (*Seeing no hands.*) Okay. This is now part of the social contract.

If strong objections persist, then consensus is *not* possible. Stay with this process until there are some rules that cannot be agreed to, except by vote.

3. Use a vote to determine inclusion or exclusion of remaining rules. We suggest that you model your procedure on the Senate (treaty ratification) or House of Representatives (impeachment vote) and use either ⅔ or ¾ majority to ensure more commitment from most of the students to accept the rule or consequence.

4. It is our belief that either minority or authority rule is not effective for the three-dimensional approach because the class needs to feel ownership of the contract for it to be successful.

These students are voting on rules for a social contract.

Step Eleven: Testing for Comprehension

Some of the prime reasons that students break rules is that they do not know they exist, they do not understand them, or they "play ignorant" (they know the rule, but claim to be ignorant of it). Before the contract was finalized, you spent some time making sure that each student understood all the rules and consequences so that they could make an intelligent, informed choice. We think one additional step can ensure that real or "play" ignorance is not a cause for discipline problems. We suggest you develop a test which will measure whether or not your students understand the social contract. Your test, like any test, should match the age and abilities of your students. Either a perfect score or near perfect score is required to pass the test.

    We have found that some students prefer not to pass the test, so that they have an acceptable excuse for breaking the rules. One way to avoid this phenomenon is to tie all class privileges to successful passing of the test. If a student does not pass, he/she should be given instruction for those items missed and an opportunity to take the test over as many times as necessary until he/she passes. This "rule" should be made clear before the test is administered. We compare this test to that of a driver's test: one that earns privileges and can be taken as many times as desired without penalty. Notice the following example of an eighth grade test.

SAMPLE TEST FOR SOCIAL CONTRACT COMPREHENSION

In 8-310 we have established a series of rules. Please answer the questions about the rules as best you can.

1. When must homework be handed in? _____

2. Fooling around is permitted during class time. Yes _____ No _____

3. When someone else is speaking and you want to speak, you must _____ .

4. Put-downs in class are strictly _____ .

5. Students can never throw things in class. True _____ False _____

6. When can you break other students' property? Often _____ Sometimes _____ Rarely _____ Never _____

7. The teacher can assign homework whenever she wants. True _____ False _____

8. The teacher can use put-downs in class because of the rights all teachers have. Yes _____ No _____

9. No student can ever tell the teacher he or she is bored. True _____ False _____

10. When can the teacher give detention? _____

11. How many chances do you get do explain why you did something wrong?
    0 _____ 1 _____ 2 _____ 3 _____ 4 _____ 5 _____

12. Name three things you must never forget to bring to class. _____ _____ _____

13. How much time do you have to go to the lavatory? _____ _____

14. How often can you swear in class? _____ _____

15. If you chew gum, what must you do with the gum when you are finished? _____

16. Who is allowed to fight in class? _____

17. When is cheating allowed? _____

18. Can you write in other students' books without their permission? Yes _____ No _____

19. What can you steal in class? _____

20. Is it okay to make or encourage other students to smoke? _____

21. Each of the above questions refers to a rule. List the consequences for breaking each rule mentioned above.

Step Twelve: Displaying the Social Contract

The final step in the social contract phase of the prevention dimension is to design and display a poster or bulletin board which clearly states each

This class social contract is displayed on the blackboard.

rule and consequence. If you have more than one class you may have more than one contract which can be put up just before class time. It is often fun for students to take responsibility for designing the contract.

PRINCIPLES OF SOCIAL CONTRACT SETTING

By developing the social contract in the manner described in this chapter you will have implemented a process which will go a long way toward the prevention of discipline problems. The basic principles upon which the process is based are:

1. All parties who must follow the contract had the opportunity to contribute to its development.
2. All parties who will follow the contract have had the opportunity to have at least some of their needs met.
3. All parties who will follow the contract will have the opportunity to govern and be governed by it.

4. Each party has ownership of the agreement.
5. Everyone understands and knows the rules.
6. The contract is integrated into the everyday normal classroom functioning.

This contract will help prevent discipline problems, but they will still occur. When they do, the *action dimension* will help you to implement the social contract in ways which will stop most classroom misbehavior.

10

THE ACTION DIMENSION

Despite all your efforts (and those of your students) to prevent discipline problems from happening, conflicts will inevitably occur in any setting in which twenty to thirty people are expected to be together over an extended period of time. The purpose of the action dimension is twofold. When a discipline problem occurs, somebody (usually the teacher) needs to do something to stop the problem as quickly as possible. This requires action. The first step is to implement the consequence associated with a rule violation, as stated in the social contract. However, there is more to implementing consequences than saying, "Nancy, there is no gum chewing in this class and because you are chewing gum, you must stay after school and clean all the desks. Don't argue. You agreed with this rule and consequence last September." The method of implementation is at least as important as the presentation of the consequence. *How* the consequence is implemented is as important as the consequence itself. Simply implementing consequences as rules are broken can become mechanistic and dehumanize the whole three-dimensional approach. For simple violations of rules, consequences can be implemented quickly and without a great deal of fuss. Nevertheless, rule violations provide the teacher and students a chance to interact in positive ways. By terminating the conflict using the consequences and positive interaction, your class can realize its full energy and aliveness.

The second purpose of the action dimension involves the monitoring of the effectiveness of your class' social contract. The social contract is *not* to be seen as fixed, inflexible sequences, but rather as rules and consequences that govern classroom or school behavior at any given time. This means that contract modification and rewriting can and should occur if the current social contract is not effective. For example, if you notice that one of the rules is being violated with considerable frequency by a number of students, then it may be helpful to consult with your class and possibly rewrite this part of the social contract. Use the same procedure as detailed in our discussion of the social contract setting. (See pages 133–134.)

TYPICAL INEFFECTIVE METHODS OF IMPLEMENTING CLASSROOM CONSEQUENCES

The following activity is adapted from Dr. Fitzhugh Dodson's *How to Discipline with Love*.[1] Dr. Dodson analyzes some of the types of punishment used with children, but analyzes them as if they were being used on adults. His book focuses primarily on parent-child issues in discipline, but certainly the significance to classroom issues is clear and unmistakable.

He notes that scolding, lecturing, taking away privileges, sending a child to his/her room, and spanking are some typical methods of parent discipline. By analyzing these methods as if they were being used on adults, he points out the negative consequences of using such methods with children. We have adapted Dodson's examples to a school setting.

We wish to reiterate what others before us have suggested. Although many children are often unable to *think* at an adult's level of abstraction, their *feelings* are no less sensitive than an adult's. We encourage you to be particularly aware of this as you proceed.

Read the following examples and let yourself react to each.

1. *Scolding:* The head teacher or principal visits your classroom and observes your lesson. When you've finished, he tells you, "How many times do I have to tell you to sharpen up your math skills? These kids did not know what you were talking about and if you don't improve,

[1] Fitzhugh, Dodson, *How to Discipline with Love* (New York: Rawson Associates, 1977), pp. 43–45.

I'll have to get a kid from the high school to come in here to help you out. Now, do you understand? Do I make myself clear?"

QUESTION: Would you like to be on the receiving end of such criticism? Does it motivate you to change your behavior in the future?

2. *Lecturing:* After the third fight that Billy, a chronic disruptive student, has had today, you send him to the office. An hour later, the Vice-Principal, tells you, "Billy has had a very difficult home situation, and I expect you to be more understanding of him. I told you last week that I didn't want to see him in the office. Now, do you have a hearing impairment or are you just learning disabled? I don't want to have to speak to you again."

QUESTION: Are you going to be any more understanding of Billy? Maybe you'll stop sending him to the office, but most likely you will find other ways to punish him—ways that satisfy your own needs.

3. *Taking away privileges:* Your principal says, "You have not handed in adequate lesson plans for two weeks. You will be allowed no field trips until they are done correctly. And you will stay after school today to do them correctly.

QUESTION: How does this make you feel? If you do stay after school, how much energy and excitement will you have for the task? Is it worth doing?

4. *Sending to office or room:* You are eating your lunch in the faculty room and you overhear your colleagues sarcastically discussing a student who you particularly like. You voice your dissatisfaction to your colleagues. For speaking out of turn, you're told to leave and informed that you'll have to eat your lunch in your room for one week by yourself.

QUESTION: How does this punishment motivate you? Does lunch become more enjoyable?

5. *Spanking:* The principal discovers that you've been teaching reading by using magazines and not the basal reader. He orders you into the office, closes the door, takes out his paddle, puts you over his knee, and spanks you. When he's finished, he says, "I trust that this will be a good lesson to you. Now get busy teaching reading the right way."

QUESTION: Think this is bizarre? How do you suppose kids are helped or motivated to change with this method?

Suggestion: To help you enlarge your awareness of your use of these methods we suggest that you keep a personal log. Each time you scold, lecture, take away privileges, send to office, or spank, make a notation of this event. Our hope is that as you become more familiar with three-dimensional discipline, the frequency of your need to resort to such methods of conflict resolution will diminish. Place a three-by-five-inch card on your desk designed like the one below. Use it for a two-week period.

	Mon.	Tues.	Wed.	Thurs.	Fri.	Mon.	Tues.	Wed.	Thurs.	Fri.
ɔld										
ɔture										
moval of vileges										
fice										
ank										

In the remainder of this chapter we look at more effective methods of implementing consequences.

Methods of Implementation

Action, Not Lecturing.   When the contract has been broken by a student, action is needed. Be clear, concise and parsimonious when you implement the consequence. We suggest, particularly with elementary school children that you *calmly* walk over to where they are, lean down, and make direct eye contact with them as you implement the consequence. If the child looks away, move yourself so that you can make eye contact (even if this means looking at the child's eyes from under his chin). Tell him firmly and quietly, "You hit Sally with your pencil. This is your warning. If I have to speak with you about this again, there'll be five minutes of time-out. Do you understand?" It's important that you not smile or in any way lead the child to think that you are not serious. On the other hand, don't be overly serious so that you are perceived as hostile and/or aggressive. Shouting, lecturing, moralizing, or sounding hurt only confuse and interfere with the process.

Notice the non-verbal messages in the body language of the teachers in the photographs on pages 143 and 144.

Do Not Bargain.   Many students will try to find an excuse or blame another student for getting him/her into trouble. When a rule has been broken, this is *not* the time for negotiation, problem solving, discussion, or bargaining. It is a time to show that you're serious about implementing the social contract as agreed to by the class; not because it is now written in stone, but rather because you believe in it. When the student starts to explain away his misbehavior, tell him that this is not the time for discussion

The teacher is keeping physically distant and does not make eye contact with the student. Her body language communicates uncertainty.

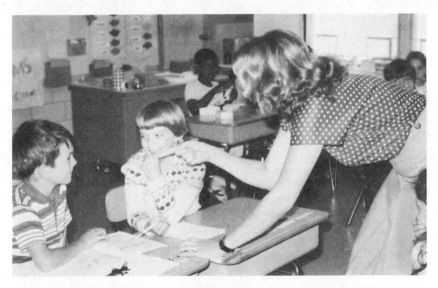

The teacher is clearly communicating hostility and anger. Her finger is pointing like a weapon and her body appears ready to attack.

Through close physical proximity, direct eye contact, and her calm expression, the teacher is effectively implementing a consequence.

or excuse making, but give him the option of discussing the matter at some other time. The following sequence may help to illustrate this point.

1. Johnny hits Sally on the head with a pencil.
2. The teacher slowly and with authority approaches the student, makes direct eye contact, and says, "You hit Sally with your pencil. I'm here to warn you, and if I see this happen again today, you'll be sent to the timeout area. Do you understand?"
3. Johnny the Student says, "But she wrote on my paper."
4. The teacher replies in a quietly firm manner: "I won't discuss this with you. Heads are not for hitting. If Sally is bothering you, we can discuss this after lunch. Do you understand?"
5. Johnny begins to protest, "But she _____."
6. The teacher slowly removes himself/herself from contact with Johnny and walks away.

Use of Proximity Control.   This technique can be used as a way of both preventing and resolving minor classroom annoyances that may not be covered in the social contract. By arranging your classroom in a manner that affords you close proximity to your students, you can make more frequent contact with them. Students with an underdeveloped system of behavior control are often in need of more structuring from their environment. We suggest that you arrange your classroom in a U shape, so that you can walk or cruise around at ease and be in close physical proximity to your students. Dr. Frederic Jones, formerly of the University of Rochester, has demonstrated the effectiveness of such an approach in lessening the frequency of behavior problems.[1] When students feel that you are in contact with them, there is less of an opportunity for acting out to occur.

State the Rules and Consequences (particularly with older students).   Junior high school and high school youth who misbehave are often very sensitive to hearing criticism and blame as a response from adults to their misbehavior. This criticism actually refuels their resentments and confirms their belief that adults are "unfair and out to get me." While there are some students who will tenaciously cling to this belief despite overwhelming evidence to the contrary (and in spite of anything you might say or do), most will take responsibility for their misbehavior when confronted in a nonblaming way. After all, the social contract system was developed with their input and therefore has a high probability of effectiveness. We encourage the teacher to simply state in a straightforward manner *what* the violated rule is, and *what* the consequence is. We urge you to avoid blaming, lecturing, or debating with a student. If possible, we suggest that you avoid making a scene. Confront the student with a firm yet calm tone of voice that avoids embarrassment of the student in front of his/her peers. Then your statement should be quiet enough so that no other student can hear your conversation with the student. If the student persists in denying responsibility and refuses to accept the consequence, then simply walk away and get back to the student after class. The resolution dimension provides strategies for working with such youngsters. Remember, adolescents have a strong need to *save face*, particularly in the presence of their peers; if you escalate the conflict at that moment, you will either win the battle at the expense of the students' accumulating resentments, or run the risk of being seen as weak and submissive. Students who refuse the consequence (and this is rare) will need to be dealt with by using the principles outlined in the resolution dimension.

The following examples deal with common classroom disruptions. Contrast and compare each example. What do you imagine would be the effect and outcome of each method of implementation? Rather than providing a critique for you, you be the judge.

1. *Rule:* All students must be quiet during a test or examination.
   Consequences:
   a. Warning.

[1] We wish to thank Dr. Jones for teaching us this approach through his workshop demonstration.

b. Test paper will be removed and exam will be scored on the basis of performance prior to talking.

c. Seat will be changed during time of exam.

d. Students will stay after school and take another exam.

Method of Implementation/Example A:

Teacher: Connie and Paul, both of you stop bickering right now. The rule is that students cannot talk during a test, and if you do not stop, you will both stay after school.

Connie: It's his fault. He tried to steal my pencil, and I just told him to give it back. Then he started yelling at me.

Paul: That's not true. I asked her nicely to borrow a pencil, and she started yelling at me and calling me names.

Teacher: Do not tell me, Paul. You are always causing problems. Judging from past performance, my guess is that you are at fault.

Paul: I am not. You always take her side. This time she started it.

Teacher: Don't argue with me, Paul. If you behaved better in class more often, then I wouldn't always suspect you, but I always find you fooling around. Now stop arguing with me or stay after school.

Method of Implementation/Example B:

Teacher: Connie and Paul, I see you both bickering and I want you both to stop. The rule here is "no talking during a test." This is your warning.

Connie: Paul started it. He tried to steal my pencil and I just told him to give it back. Then he started yelling at me.

Paul: That's not true. I asked her nicely to borrow a pencil and she started yelling at me and calling me names.

Teacher: It doesn't matter who started it. The rule in this room is no talking during a test. I want both of you to get started on your tests right now with no talking. If I see or hear you talking anymore, your exam papers will be removed. Paul, if you need a pencil for the test, raise your hand and you can tell me.

2. *Rule:* When other students are working during quiet time, nobody is allowed to speak.

   Consequences:

   a. First infraction during quiet time is a reminder.

   b. Second infraction during quiet time is the loss of five minutes of privileged classroom time.

c. Third infraction during quiet time results in five minutes of timeout.

d. Fourth infraction during quiet time results in parent conference.

Method of Implementation/Example A:

Teacher: (loudly and with pointed finger) Judy, if I have to speak to you one more time, I will go crazy. Don't you know that you are bothering the whole class. Don't you care about how others feel? In this class we must respect each other and I don't think you respect any of your classmates or your teacher. Isn't that true?

Judy: I respect you, but I . . .

Teacher: Don't talk back to me, that proves you have no respect. If I have to speak with you again, you will be given a consequence, and it won't be just a warning. Do you understand?

Method of Implementation/Example B:

Teacher: (matter of factly in a low voice in close physical proximity) Judy, this is your reminder. There is to be no talking when other students are working. If I have to speak to you again, five minutes of free time will be lost. Do you understand?

3. *Rule:* Each person's belongings on his/her desk are not to be taken by another.
   Consequences:
   a. Warning.
   b. Personal apology to the student.
   c. Returning belongings.
   d. Staying after school for an extra assignment.

Method of Implementation/Example A:

Teacher: Mack, did you just take that book from Fred's desk?

Mack: No, it was mine, and I just took it back. He took it from me first.

Teacher: Mack, I told you to leave things that are on other peoples' desks alone. I want you to stay after school and discuss this with me.

Mack: It was mine. It's not fair that I have to stay after school when I just took my own book.

Teacher: Okay, this time you don't have to stay after if you promise not to bother Fred again.

Method of Implementation/Example B:

Teacher: Mack, I saw you take a book off Fred's desk. I want you to return it now, and do not take anything off another student's desk again. This is your warning.

Mack: It was my book and I was just taking it back. He took it from me first.

Teacher: I saw you take the book off Fred's desk. In this class there is no taking things from students' desks. (To Fred and Mack.) Now in thirty seconds I expect the book to be returned to the person who owns it. If either of you should take something that doesn't belong to you again this week, then I'll see you after school.

4. *Rule:* Permission to leave your seat for pencil sharpening is required; raise your hand to be recognized by the teacher.

   Consequences:
   a. First daily infraction—warning.
   b. Second daily infraction—a written explanation: Why I left my seat without permission.
   c. Third daily infraction—loss of your pencil for the rest of the morning or afternoon.

Method of Implementation/Example A:

Teacher: Ken, why are you sharpening your pencil? You know that the rule in this class is you can't leave your seat without permission. Sit down right this minute.

Ken: That's not fair. I didn't know that before.

Teacher: Yes you did. We talked about it before.

Ken: No, I didn't.

Teacher: Yes you did; look on the board. The rule says no leaving your seat without permission.

Ken: But I thought it was okay to sharpen a pencil. Mine broke.

Teacher: You knew the rule. It doesn't say that you can leave without permission to sharpen pencils. You are always making trouble.

Ken: I didn't know I couldn't sharpen my pencil. I thought that it was okay to do that.

Teacher: I don't think you are telling the truth. You are just testing me to see what you can get away with.

Ken: But my pencil's broken. See, look for yourself.

Method of Implementation/Example B:

Teacher: (slowly and firmly approaches Ken at the pencil sharpener) Ken, this is the second time today you have left your seat without permission. I want your written explanation before lunch. If I have to speak with you again, I'll remove your pencil for this afternoon's work. Is that clear?

Ken: But . . .

Teacher: (slowly walks away as she maintains eye contact with Ken)

Choosing the Best Alternative Consequence

In the social contract, you have developed a series of alternative consequences for each rule. One of the most important decisions for you is to pick the best alternative consequence for each situation in which the social contract has been broken. Having alternative consequences gives you the ability to treat each situation individually and provides you with a mechanism for being consistent. It is difficult for us to give directions for choosing the best alternative consequence, because each situation is unique and only you, the teacher, can consider all the factors involved in making the best choice. However, we present the following guidelines to help you choose from among your alternatives:

1. Use your smaller consequences first. Save your "heavy artillery" until later. For example, consider the following rule: A student is required to raise his/her hand to ask the teacher's permission to leave his/her seat. The alternative consequences for failure to observe this rule are as follows:

   a. Reminder.

   b. Warning.

   c. Student must stay in seat for fifteen minutes.

   d. Student must come after school for a conference.

   If Susan breaks the rule for the first time, it might be appropriate to remind her to return to her seat. However, if Susan has broken this rule six times in the last two weeks, it might be better to use the third or fourth consequence. If Susan broke the rule for the first time, but three other students have broken it before during the same day, a reminder may be too weak. A strong warning is more appropriate with an announcement for the whole class that the next violation will result in a fifteen-minute timeout period in which that student may not leave his seat or there will be a conference after school.

Some teachers and students are more comfortable with sequential consequences which spell out specifically what will happen each time a rule is violated during a given time period. This leaves less room for teacher discretion since the social contract lets everybody know what happens for a first infraction, a second infraction, and so forth. If you and your students opt for sequencing of consequences and you also want some discretion, then you may choose to have two or three possible consequences per infraction, out of which one can be selected based upon your own needs and the circumstances. For example, failure to observe the rule that requires a student to seek the teacher's permission before leaving his/her seat, may result in the following choice of consequences per infraction.

a. First daily infraction—reminder or warning or loss of privilege.

b. Second daily infraction—student must stay in seat for 15 minutes or student-teacher conference or loss of preferred activity.

c. Third daily infraction—parent notified or student spends half-hour after school.

2. Do not continually choose a consequence which is ineffective with any one student. Move on to another consequence.

3. There may be times when it is best that a student choose his/her own consequences from the contract.

4. Remember, consequences are not designed to punish.

5. Consequences are designed to manage misbehavior when it occurs. Tomorrow is a new day, and any consequence you implement is for today's misbehavior. Start fresh each day.

Monitoring

The purpose of monitoring your social contracts is to discover which rules and consequences are effective and which are not, and which students are having difficulty in following one or more of the rules. It also serves to demonstrate to individual students and to the class as a whole that everybody can have a voice in determining which rules and/or consequences need modification and which do not. The following steps describe a formal sequence of record keeping and data collection, and we suggest that you use this as prescribed. We are keenly aware of teacher resistance to keeping yet another set of records, but we strongly believe that at least in the beginning of the development of the social contract that having formal records will make your job easier later on.

DATA COLLECTION

1. Record each time you discipline or want to discipline a student for behavior not covered in the social contract. If a behavior problem recurs with more than one student, a new contract might be needed for that behavior.
2. Keep a record of every rule that is broken by students and teacher. Note whether or not the consequence was followed as described in the social contract. Modify any rules that are broken continuously by many students by restating them or finding better consequences. Determine a percentage of the number of times the consequences were followed. If this figure is under 85 percent, be more consistent following them. Try to know why you had trouble and redesign any consequence accordingly.
3. Do you have some students who are chronic rule breakers? (Check data.) Establish individual contract for any chronic rule breakers (see Chapter 11). A pre-post analysis might be necessary for this step.
4. Use the data to make your social contracts work by meeting your needs and your students' needs. Change must be built into the social contract system.

Notice the example data collection chart on page 152 for Mrs. Tillson's class. Without explaining the meaning of each of the rules and consequences, it is evident that most of the rules were effective, and there was a high degree of consistency between "times broken" and "consequences" applied; that is, nearly each time that a rule was broken, the consequence was applied. One rule that was frequently broken by all students was "No fooling around in class." The data collected suggests both a high frequency of rule violation and low consistency of consequence implementation. This feedback to Mrs. Tillson and the class set the stage for both the rule and the consequence to be modified. Mrs. Tillson noted that the rule was too vague and stated negatively. The rule was rewritten in more specific and positive terms. Since the "fooling around" behavior was mostly occurring during nonteacher instruction time, it was suggested to Mrs. Tillson that she develop some high interest activities that students could choose after they completed an independent, seatwork task. She did this by her asking students what interesting activities they'd like to do in the classroom which would keep noise to a minimum. She collected their suggestions, put a free time activity cookbook (see p. 56) together, and modified the rule. The modified rule was: "Following completed work, each student may choose one of the suggestions from the book or may remain quietly seated at his desk." The consequences were: "One warning during each seatwork period; the second infraction results in the student's personal apology to each student in the class."

The following is the data collection sheet of Mrs. Tillson's eighth grade class after the first month of social contract implementation. Their sheet is based on the contract described in the example text on page 136.

Rules	Times Broken	By Whom	Consequences
1. All homework handed in on time.	16	Sam 1, Earl 10, Billy 1, Greg 2, Mary 2	6 (Earl was sick)
2. No fooling around in class.	35	everyone	10
3. No speaking when someone else is speaking.	3	Mrs. Tillson 1, Greg 2	3
4. No put-downs	2	Susan 1, Mark 1	2
5. No throwing things.	0	no one	0
6. No breaking others' property.	1	Susan 1	1
7. Teacher cannot give homework without week's notice	0	no one	0
8. No teacher put-downs.	0	no one	0
9. Students can tell if bored.	3	no answer	2
10. Teacher must give options for detention day.	0	no one	0
11. Each student can explain why he did something wrong.	1	Mrs. Tillson 1	1
12. No forgetting materials.	6	Allison 1, Earl 3, Greg 2	4
13. Five minutes to go to lavatory.	0	no one	0
14. No swearing in class.	0	no one	0
15. Gum must be wrapped in paper and thrown in basket.	0	no one	0
16. No fighting in class.	1	Billy and Greg	1
17. No cheating is allowed.	0	no one	0
18. No writing in books of others.	0	no one	0
19. No stealing in class.	0	no one	0
20. No forcing others to smoke.	0	no one	0

While Mrs. Tillson's list of rules and consequences appears at times to be somewhat ambiguous, the point is that they worked for her and her class. It is up to the judgment of each teacher and class to arrive at rules and consequences that fit the unique makeup of that group of people. Your rules and consequences should reflect your environment. A teacher of inner-city children and one with rural farm children may need to have a set of rules and consequences that are very different.

USING A FEEDBACK FORM

A feedback form is used in the analysis of social contracts. It is for your own personal use but can also help students to tell you how they perceive the effect of each rule on the total class environment. You can then utilize this feedback to alter, modify, or simply discuss the effect of the rules with your class(es).

A SAMPLE FEEDBACK FORM FOR ANALYSIS OF SOCIAL CONTRACTS

Atmosphere	Communication with Students	Communication with Teacher	Learning	Average (for teacher use)
1.				
2.				
3.				
4.				
5.				

Score each rule according to its ability to help communication, learning, and class-room atmosphere. *Very good* (5), *good* (4), *neutral* (3), *negative* (2), *very negative* (1). For younger students, faces can be drawn with various expressions such as

(5) ☺ (4) ☺ (3) ☺ (2) ☹ (1) ☹

The action dimension guide which follows includes in more detail the principles and procedures necessary for monitoring your class' social contract.

ACTION DIMENSION GUIDE

Step 1: Keep a record of all the times you discipline either the class or a student for misbehavior that is not covered by a rule, or times that you *want to discipline them but do not.*

1. _____
2. _____
3. _____
4. _____
5. _____
6. _____
7. _____
8. _____
9. _____
10. _____
11. _____
12. _____
13. _____
14. _____
15. _____
16. _____
17. _____
18. _____
19. _____
20. _____

Make up a rule and consequence to govern any incident that occurs over four times and bring it up before the class for a vote to add to the list of rules.

Step 2: Keep a list of every rule that is broken both by students and teachers each month. (You can also do this weekly or bimonthly, especially at the outset.)

Rules	Times Broken	By Whom	Were Consequences Applied?	Which Ones
1.				
2.				

Rules	Times Broken	By Whom	Were Consequences Applied?	Which Ones
3.				
4.				
5.				
6.				
7.				
8.				
9.				
10.				
11.				
12.				
13.				
14.				
15.				
16.				
17.				
18.				
19.				
20.				

Step 3: Keep your first two lists as feedback for yourself to see which students are breaking what rules. These lists can be used as a basis for comparison later on.

Step 4: List two optional rules or consequences (for those rules or consequences which aren't working) to meet the same need of the originals.

1. _____

2. _____

Discuss and reconsider with your class the value of the old rule and/or consequences and the new ones proposed. Use the same method (vote) for approval as outlined in the prevention dimension.

Step 5: Examine whether or not you enforced the consequences that you stated. What is the percentage? _____ (Divide number of broken rules into number of times the consequences were enforced.) If the figure is less than 85 percent, what inference can you make? Write a short paragraph.

_____

_____

Step 6: Rewrite any consequences that in your view were not enforced often enough for your satisfaction (perhaps less than 85 percent).

Step 7: Consider your data: Are there some individuals who seem to have trouble following all rules or some who have trouble following certain rules? Has individual and/or group behavior improved weekly or monthly according to your data? Look at your first few lists and make an assessment.

Step 8: If behavior has improved (e.g., during month #1, Billy broke a rule twenty times; during month #2, fifteen times, and month #3, nine times), then you might conclude that the contract is slowly taking effect for him. If not, then do not despair. The resolution dimension may be the answer (see Chapter 11).

Step 9: Consider your own or your students' need to change a rule if it's not working for a significant number of your students.

Step 10: Each quarter, get feedback from your students on which rules help and which hinder the following:

1. Classroom atmosphere.
2. Communication with students.
3. Communication with teacher.
4. Learning.

See page 153 for an example feedback form.

Step 11: Discuss with the class the possibility of alternatives to any rules with an average of less than three.

11

THE RESOLUTION DIMENSION

The resolution dimension is a process for establishing individual contracts with students when the social contract fails to work. Generally, there are three types of situations that require the use of individual contracts.

1. A student does not accept a consequence established in the social contract.

   Example: Susan throws an eraser at Tony, and Mrs. Tyler tells her to go to the timeout area for five minutes. Susan refuses and begins to call Tony dirty names.

2. A student breaks a number of different rules and is a constant source of disruption.

   Example: Billy always seems to be doing something which violates the social contract. One day he will talk out of turn, later he will engage in a private conversation about his girlfriend with a friend in class. He will occasionally come to class late and twice a week he will forget his homework, his pencil, or his books. None of these incidents is a serious problem alone, but they add up to a significant drain on his teacher.

3. A student refuses to follow a specific rule of the social contract.

     Example: Sandy threatens to beat up a couple of students she doesn't like. Her threats are taken seriously by the other students and a potentially volatile situation builds up.

We find that most teachers who have taken preventive measures and have consistently applied consequences to rule breaking have little need for individual negotiation. Yet all teachers will face situations where they will need to develop individual contracts with specific students. Before we explain how to set up individual contracts, we wish to discuss some of the main concerns that teachers have expressed to us in regard to the resolution dimension.

1. *Is it a good idea to negotiate individual contracts with special students which are not available for the entire class? Is it not better to use the same contracts, rules, and consequences for everyone?*

The reason that you are considering using individual contracts is that for some students the social contract is not working. In simple pragmatic terms, the use of individual contracts is necessary. The individual or resolution dimension contract is a process of negotiation between the teacher and the chronic rule breaker to determine what the student needs or wants from the classroom that he/she's not getting. We believe that a major cause of disruptive classroom behavior is that the student views either the whole classroom or parts of it with dissatisfaction. In effect, he/she sees the class as not meeting his/her needs for attention, power, connectedness, or achievement and resorts to unacceptable behavior to meet these needs. Thus, the goal of the resolution dimension is to help the student to identify what he/she needs or wants from the class and how he/she can go about getting it without resorting to disruptive actions that violate the classroom social contract. The purpose, therefore, is to find ways by which the student can accept and live by the classroom social contract. It is *not* a new set of rules and consequences for the student but rather an agreed upon system (between the teacher and student) to increase the probability of the student's following the class social contract. It may seem more fair philosophically to have the same contract for all students, but in reality, if a student is demanding a large portion of the teacher's time and energy, by acting out or misbehaving, the rest of the students are not being treated equally. The issue is not whether or not a student should receive special attention. It is in determining the type of special attention he will get. We believe that a systematic attempt to work with the disruptive student to help him adjust to class life in positive ways is better than continually battling him on a daily basis.

2. *Schools have been compared to the "real world."* [1] *Educators and parents want schools to reflect the way things will be when the children finish school. In the real world contracts cannot be renegotiated if they are continually broken. Shouldn't students learn to live within the system no matter what?*

We disagree with these sentiments. Schools differ from the real world in many ways. First of all, school is mandatory for all students, and no other institution in our society (except penal institutions) makes this demand. People can change jobs, move, choose their friends, but students cannot choose to leave school. Secondly, the role of the school is to educate, which requires a different perspective in many ways than, say, a job in which the employee is expected to function with already acquired skills and knowledge. In the same way that we do not teach driving by allowing students to operate a car under actual road conditions, we must establish gradual steps for some students who have trouble with their behavior. We give the resolution dimension its name because we conceive of individual negotiation as a very effective method of resolving problems of misbehavior. No social contract can meet the needs of all children, just as no curriculum can. Courses and programs are modified to meet individual needs all the time and we feel that modification of the social contract for specific students is just as desirable.

3. *Is it a good idea to reward students who are disruptive with special contracts when most students who are not disruptive are not rewarded with special contracts? Won't the "good" students try bad behavior when they see that they can get special attention for doing so?*

   a. We do not suggest that teachers give students whatever they want in the resolution dimension contract. We do not encourage in teachers the attitude, "I'll give you whatever you want if you don't give me any trouble." The purpose of the resolution dimension is to work with the disruptive students so that they can behave in appropriate ways. Bribery and extortion are not a part of the process. The process of negotiation is to help the student, the teacher, and the class as a whole.

   b. Students misbehave because they have significant needs which are not being met. It is very rare that a student will scheme to be disruptive just to see what special privileges he can get. If a teacher does think this is occurring, he can set limits when working with the student individually. It is our belief that most students want to follow the rules and if they do not then either they don't know how or they are hindered by special circumstances.

[1] School is a real world, although it is different from the world apart from school. We think it would be better for teachers and students if a school was thought of as having a reality of its own for the people who live and work there.

The resolution dimension is designed to remove the obstacles and teach students ways to accept the social contract.

c. Students are not all the same and do not have the same advantages. Not every student needs the same advantages. Just as a family may have different responsibilities and privileges for children of different ages, a classroom can have different contracts for certain individuals.

d. If the teacher wants to ensure that the "good" children, those who follow the social contract, are rewarded, we suggest the use of positive consequences as described in Chapter 9.

The resolution dimension is designed to help individual student(s) and the teacher develop a contract to meet the needs of both parties. It is not a plan in which the teacher bribes or begs the student to follow the rules. The more effective the implementation of the prevention and action dimensions the less need there will be for individual negotiation. Individual negotiation is reserved for those students who cannot or will not live by any plan that does not meet their individual needs. We do not envision great numbers of students fitting this category. However, there are some classrooms for which no social contract can work, unless several students have an opportunity to discuss and negotiate ways in which they can accept themselves and the social contract.

Unlike the prevention dimension and the action dimension, the resolution dimension cannot be implemented in a clearly defined step by step procedure. During the heat of dealing with a disruptive student, it is close to impossible to review the steps and execute them as described in this book. Thus we suggest you read through all of the steps before trying any of them. You might practice some of them with colleagues or even by yourself, so that you can use them without having to think through each point while dealing with a student. (This practice is similar to any crisis intervention system. For example, it is not helpful to learn fire evacuation procedures while the house is burning down.) In actual practice you may wish to change the order of the steps, or blend them in any way that feels right for you.

Steps of the Resolution Dimension

Step 1.   Identify those students who are having trouble following the social contract. These may be students who are having trouble following rules or accepting consequences. Most of these students will be easily identifiable because you will be dealing with them in direct confrontations. There may be one or two students, though, who are not noticeable at first glance. It may be helpful to review the information collected in the data-collecting stage of the action dimension to see if any student may need help with an individual contract.

Step 2.   Once you have identified a student who needs to work with you on an individual basis, it is important to "clear the deck"; that is, before you actually confront the student, you get in touch with your feelings for him/her. You might use the fantasy dialogue activity described earlier or some other of the activities described in the awareness of self or expression of feelings sections of this book. Maybe you can just list the words that accurately describe your feelings for the student. It is important for you to experience (without inhibition) both your positive and negative feelings. Remember, it is okay to have any and all feelings and to express them any way you want in safety and privacy. This step is important because whether you acknowledge your feelings or not, they will be with you when you meet the student. There will be less chance of them spilling over unexpectedly and hindering your work with the student. We find that the clearer you can be about your feelings, the more effective you will be in a face to face meeting with him/her.

Step 3.   Arrange a time that is mutually convenient for both of you. Allow enough time to finish your work together, if you so desire. (You may wish to end the conference in an incomplete state if a dead end has been temporarily reached.) The conference might take place after school, but usually it is better to arrange it during school time, so the student does not react as if the meeting were a punishment. You may find someone to cover your class for a period or time segment, or perhaps your principal will hire a substitute for an hour or so. It might be possible to arrange a time when you both are free during the day.

Step 4.   When you meet, explain the purposes of your meeting. It is important that from the beginning you be honest and forthright in your response to the student and that you be as specific as possible. Having close access to your records from the action dimension could be helpful in demonstrating to the student the frequency with which he's broken the social contract. For example: "Steve, we are meeting today to see if we can work out a plan that we can both agree will help us get along better in the class." If there are any limits such as time constraints, clarify them at the beginning: "I know that lately we seem to be having trouble relating to each other. I want to spend the next thirty minutes talking with you to see if we can work something out."

Step 5. Show the student that you are not perfect and that perhaps you or your class are lacking in certain ways as perceived by this student. For example: "Steve, for the last week you've broken the homework assignment rule five times. I'm quite sure that at times the homework is boring and not interesting and I imagine that there are other things that you would prefer to do with your time. How do you spend your time after school?"

Step 6. Return to the conflict (broken contract). "What I'd like to do is to find out what you need from me or from the others in this class that would make it more possible for you to turn in your assignments."

Step 7. If the student is unresponsive, then tell him to think about the discussion and that you and he can plan a time tomorrow for further discussion or negotiation. You can suggest that as part of his assignment for class, that he make a list of all of his resentments or dislikes that he has for you and/or the class.

Step 8. If after three attempts at individual contract negotiation, you and the student are unable to agree upon a common solution, then we suggest that you enlist the aid of an independent third party to help with negotiation. You might say, "Steve, I can see that we're not going to be able to solve this problem by ourselves. Is there somebody that you can suggest who you trust that can help us? I'd prefer that this person not be a friend or associate of either of us." You are also free to suggest others who you feel might be of help. If you can't even agree on the third person, then perhaps each of you can choose an advocate to attend another meeting.

Step 9. Follow the process as detailed in "Positive Student Confrontation" which suggests other methods of negotiation that you can use or that can be used by an intermediary or third person.

Positive Student Confrontation

In relating to our students we must be careful not to permit small irritations to accumulate "under our skin," build into resentments, and become potential sources of hostility. Feelings of hostility can have a very negative effect in our relations with individuals and classes as a whole.[2] To prevent

[2] Our discussion of positive student confrontation is adapted from Richard Curwin and Barbara Fuhrmann, *Discovering Your Teaching Self: Humanistic Approaches to Effective Teaching* (Englewood Cliffs, N.J.: Prentice-Hall), pp. 91–95.

stockpiling of resentments it is helpful to deal with the irritating incidents as they occur by sharing our feelings with the students who are causing us to feel uncomfortable.

In actual classroom situations it very often seems difficult to deal with problems openly and positively. The pressures of the situation and the presence of the other students sometimes seem to mitigate against dealing spontaneously with feelings; and we are tempted to either ignore the situations and let resentments slowly build into hostility or to attack the students by putting them down in some way. While either of these practices might alleviate the situation for a time, they usually do little to solve the problem in the long run. Positive student confrontation can, however, lead to open communication between you and your students so that negotiation and compromise can be used to solve relationship conflicts.

Confronting students positively takes practice because, for most of us, it is an unfamiliar behavior. The following activity is to be used as practice so that you can develop the skills necessary to transfer this positive behavior into your classroom. We have found that this method of confrontation is effective with students at all grade levels.

PRACTICING POSITIVE STUDENT CONFRONTATION

DIRECTIONS

To practice positive student confrontation we suggest two methods, depending upon the number of people present.

Method A: To practice this method you need a group of six or more people, preferably about ten. One person volunteers to be "teacher," one person volunteers to be "coach," and the rest are "students." Each member of the group should have a chance to be teacher, coach, and student, at some time in further rounds. The teacher separates from the students and prepares a ten-minute lesson in any subject for any age group. The students, meanwhile, plan to role play different "student types." The types can include a bored student, a troublemaker, an arrogant student, a brown noser, any student stereotype that might be found in a classroom. (Note: in role playing students, it is helpful not to get so locked into the role that you do not react normally to stimuli from the teacher or other students. The quiet student, for example, should speak if he has something to say. The troublemaker should behave if the teacher effectively does something to cause him to settle down.) The coach at this time need not prepare anything.

When everyone is ready the teacher begins the lesson with the students role playing the age suggested by the teacher, slightly exaggerating their roles to make the experience more enriching. The coach is an observer at this time. Once the lesson is completed, the teacher chooses one student who made him the most uncomfortable, and the two, teacher and student, sit face to face, and engage in positive confrontation as described below. Now the coach plays an important role keeping the confrontation positive by not allowing destructive statements (personal attacks), by keeping the participants on the subject, and by making sure that each participant has equal opportunity to speak.

Method B: This method requires at least two people and preferably three. One person volunteers to be "teacher," one person volunteers to be "coach," and one person volunteers to be "student." If only two people are present, then one person is both teacher and coach, and the other is student. When everybody is ready, the teacher describes some real or imagined problem that he/she has with a student who chronically misbehaves. The teacher should specify the problem student's age and any other characteristics that would help the volunteer assume the role. The teacher and student then sit face to face and engage in positive confrontation as described below. Now the coach plays an important role, keeping the confrontation positive by not allowing destructive statements (personal attacks), by keeping the participants on the subject, and by making sure that each participant has equal opportunity to speak. When the confrontation has completed and after a period of discussion, participants are encouraged to switch so that each has an opportunity to experience all three roles.

These teachers are practicing positive student confrontation.

THE CONFRONTATION

The teacher states what he resented in the student by using a sentence similar to the following, "When you . . . I resented it because . . ." The student responds by stating a resentment to the teacher using a similar sentence. Both resentments must be stated clearly so that teacher and student understand exactly what the other means. In sharing feelings avoid placing blame or guilt on the students, for this will only create defensiveness and block open communication. Statements that begin with, "I feel . . ." or "When you . . . I feel . . ." often are the most constructive.[3] The teacher's and student's resentments should be restated by rewording them to indicate understanding. The next step is for both parties to state and restate any appreciations they have for each other. Next the teacher makes a demand of the student, and the student responds with a demand of the teacher. Once the demands are clearly stated and restated the two participants negotiate until both have agreed to do something they are comfortable with, something that helps remove or reduce the cause for resentment. Repeat the process as many times as necessary to deal with all the resentments between the teacher and student.

QUESTIONS

1. What did you learn about yourself in the role of teacher?
2. What did you learn about yourself in the role of student?
3. What difficulties did you encounter in positive confrontation?
4. What did you learn about the person you confronted?
5. How can you best use positive student confrontation with your own students?

FOLLOW-UP

Once you have mastered the techniques of positive student confrontation you may develop your own style for use in the classroom. When you are ready, make a list of specific resentments that you feel in your classes. Rank the completed list, numbering the most important −1, the second most important −2, and so on. After each resentment think of something within that presented behavior that you can appreciate (see pages 166–167 and 169 for examples). Then make a demand of your class or the student to remove or reduce the cause of that resentment. Start with the top of your list and try to resolve your problem by working a compromise with your students, making your demand in a positive way, and asking for a return demand.

---

[3] See Hiam Ginott, *Teacher and Child* (New York: Macmillan, 1972) for further examples.

EXAMPLE OF POSITIVE STUDENT CONFRONTATION

This example is taken from a student confrontation activity with college students role playing a high school teacher and students.

Teacher: Dan, I've asked Mr. Reed to be here today to help me find some way to get you to stop talking in class. I'm tired of seeing you break this rule repeatedly. During the last week, you've violated this rule ten times.

Coach: I'd like you to tell Dan exactly what he does that you resent or dislike.

Teacher: I resent you when you interrupt me while I'm teaching. I resent how you get up and walk around the classroom whenever you feel like it.

Coach: Is that all you resent?

Teacher: Yes.

Coach: Dan, I'd like to make sure that you understand what your teacher resents. In a few minutes, you'll have a chance to tell her what you resent in her, but for now, tell her what you've just heard her say.

Dan (student): You resent me when I walk around in class and when I call out an answer. But this class is boring.

Coach (to teacher): Does Dan understand what you resent?

Teacher: Well, not just when you call out an answer, also when you start talking loudly to another student during class time.

Coach: Dan, would you tell her again what she resents?

Dan: You resent me when I walk around in class and when I interrupt and when I talk to other students.

Coach: Does Dan now understand what you resent?

Teacher: Yes.

Coach: Okay, Dan, now it's your turn. Tell Mrs. P. what you resent or dislike that she does.

Dan: I resent all the homework that I have to do and how boring this class is. And I resent that you always pick on me even when others are talking also.

Coach: Mrs. P., tell Dan what he resents that you do.

Teacher: You resent my picking on you, how boring this class is, and all of the homework that I give.

Dan: Yeah.

Coach: Okay. Mrs. P., although this may be hard, I'd like you to tell Dan what you appreciate or like about his interruptions and wandering in the classroom. Or you can tell him other things that you like that he does.

Teacher: I appreciate your sense of humor and your ability to make friends easily.

Coach: What does Mrs. P. like about you?

Dan: You think I'm funny and that I have a lot of friends.

Coach: Dan, now tell Mrs. P. anything that you can think of that you like about her.

Dan: I like the way that you talk to some of the kids after class. That's all.

Teacher: You like that I talk with some kids after class. Would you like me to talk more often with you?

Dan: Sometimes.

Coach: Mrs. P., tell Dan what you want Dan to do that will solve your problem with him.

Teacher: I want you to raise your hand and be acknowledged by me before you talk in class and I want you to stay seated during class time unless I give you permission to get up.

Coach: What demands is Mrs. P. making of you?

Dan: You want me to sit in class and not speak out unless my hand is raised.

Teacher: (nods head approvingly)

Coach: Dan, tell Mrs. P. what you want to do that will solve your problems of boredom and being picked on.

Dan: I don't want to do the homework all the time. I want to do things that I like. I want to read books that I enjoy and I want to leave the class when I'm bored. And I want to talk to my friends.

Coach: Now I'd like the two of you to keep talking to see if you can reach a compromise agreement that you can each live with.

Teacher: I can't let you talk to your friends because it will disturb others, and besides, the information might be important to the unit. I'd be willing to allow you to leave class so long as you tell me before the class begins that you don't want to be there. I will however, hold you responsible for the material that you have chosen to miss. What things or interests would you like to pursue in class?

Dan: I like sports and I'd rather study the history of sports than have to do that term paper on the life of Sun Yat-sen.

Teacher: If you'd like, I'll accept a paper from you on a topic that relates to the history of sports. In return, I expect you to sit quietly in class and not cause a disturbance.

Dan: Okay.

Coach: Are you both satisfied with this resolution?

Student and Teacher: Yes.

> *Coach:* Each of you restate your solutions and what you're willing to do.
>
> *Dan:* I won't talk to my friends or walk around the room and you'll let me do a paper on the history of sports. And if I don't want to come to class then I don't have to, but I'm responsible for the work that's been assigned.
>
> *Teacher:* That sounds good, except I want you to go to study hall or the library if you choose to miss class.
>
> *Dan:* Fine.

Notice in this example that neither the student nor the teacher attacked the other, and that both maintained a high level of honesty and openness. Each considered the other's demand and reacted to it as a real possibility. In the end they reached a compromise solution that was comfortable for each of them, one which might never have been considered without the confrontation.

Guidelines for Positive Student Confrontation

WITH COACH

1. Coach sets tone for meeting by describing the problem, the process of positive student confrontation, and his role.
2. The coach asks the teacher to share his feelings of resentment, anger, or frustration with the student ("I resent you [student] when _____" or "I dislike you [student] when _____").

3. The coach asks the student to repeat or paraphrase the teacher's statement. If the teacher feels the student did not understand, the coach may ask the student to try again and/or ask the teacher to repeat his statement.

4. The coach asks the student to share his feelings of resentment, anger, or frustration with the teacher ("I resent you [teacher] when _____" or "I dislike you [teacher] when _____").

5. The coach asks the teacher to repeat or paraphrase the student's statement. If the student feels that the teacher did not understand, the coach may ask the teacher to try again and/or the student to repeat his statement.

6. The coach asks the teacher to share with the student any feelings of appreciation ("I appreciate you when _____," or "I like you when _____."

   We believe that if something is resented, it can also be appreciated. If possible, encourage the teacher to express an appreciation about the same behavior that she resents. For example, the teacher may have stated, "I resent you when you fight in class." Try to get her to appreciate something in this behavior such as, "I appreciate that you're able to express your angry feelings." When a student feels appreciated, behavioral change is more likely.

7. The coach asks the student to repeat the teacher's statement.

8. The coach asks the student to share any appreciations with the teacher (use same guidelines as in 6).

9. The coach asks the teacher to repeat the student's statement.

10. The coach asks the teacher to make his demands of the student. These demands are what the teacher wants the student to do or not do, to solve the original problem.

11. The coach asks the student to repeat the teacher's demands.

12. The coach asks the student to make his demands of the teacher. These demands are what the student wants from the teacher to meet his/her needs.

13. The coach asks the teacher to repeat the student's demands.

14. The coach asks teacher and student to negotiate ("If I do this for you, will you do this for me").

15. After both parties seem to have made an agreement the coach asks the teacher to state what he will do for the student and what he expects the student to do for him.

16. The coach asks the student to state what he will do for the teacher and what he expects the teacher will do for him.

17. An agreement is reached which may be signed or clearly stated verbally. The coach might sum up what happened in the meeting. A meeting time in the near future is set to discuss how well the "individual contract is working."

WITHOUT COACH

Each of the above steps are done in the same way except that the teacher plays both the role of the coach and the teacher. It is more difficult for the teacher to have these dual functions, but the process still can be effective. It is usually helpful for the teacher to explain to the student that because they are working alone, he will be doing two things at once, so that the student understands how the process will work.

Resolution Dimension Examples

The following examples of resolution dimension negotiation represent actual events and have been shortened for the sake of brevity.

Example 1.   A resolution dimension conference between Mrs. Hilliard and one of her third grade students, Ralph.

> *Mrs. Hilliard:* Ralph, people are not for punching, and in the last two days I've seen you fighting with three of the children in class.

Ralph: They call me names and bother me.

Mrs. Hilliard: I'm sure that it upsets you when they do this, and I still won't allow fighting in our class. What can we do to help you to not fight with the other children?

Ralph: I don't know.

Mrs. Hilliard: I'd like to suggest something. When the other children call you names, I'd like you to agree with everything they say. For example, if they call you an ugly, smelly fool, I want you to look directly at them and without raising your voice, tell them, "Yes, I'm an ugly, smelly fool." In this way, I believe that before long, they'll stop doing this, because they'll see that you won't play their little game. I know that this is very difficult to do, but after all, what they really want is to make you mad, and when they do, they've won and you've lost.

Ralph: (with puzzled look) Just tell them not to bug me.

Mrs. Hilliard: You'd like me to tell the others to leave you alone.

Ralph: (nods his head)

Mrs. Hilliard: I'm willing to do this, and I wonder if we can discuss your need for a "no name calling" rule with the class.

Ralph: I don't want to do that.

Mrs. Hilliard: Okay, you'd be willing to stop fighting in class if I told the other children to stop calling you bad names. Is there anything else you need?

Ralph: I don't know.

Mrs. Hilliard: Well, Ralph, I think that it would be wise for you to learn how to agree with them rather than to fight them. I really believe that they'll stop bugging you when you learn how to do this.

Ralph: (reluctantly agrees).

Mrs. Hilliard then spent fifteen to twenty minutes with Ralph in teaching him through role playing the Dodson technique of learning to agree with uncomplimentary comments. Following this, Mrs. Hilliard wrote up the resolution dimension contract. She explained that a contract is when two people agree to do something, and when each person signs the contract, then that means that they will both do what they say they're going to do.

RESOLUTION DIMENSION CONTRACT

1. Ralph agrees not to fight with students in the class.
2. Mrs. Hilliard agrees to talk to the class about calling others bad names.

3. Mrs. Hilliard agrees to propose a rule to the class regarding calling others bad names.

4. Ralph agrees to use the bad names technique that he has learned.

5. Mrs. Hilliard agrees to listen to Ralph's upset feelings when he's called bad names.

6. Mrs. Hilliard and Ralph agree to meet again in one week to see how things are going.

Mrs. Hilliard

Mrs. Hilliard

Ralph

Ralph

*one copy for Mrs. Hilliard and one copy for Ralph

Example 2. The following resolution dimension contract was developed between Dale, a sixteen-year-old high school student and his principal, Mr. Katzner, to deal with Dale's chronic class cutting. The conference took place in Mr. Katzner's office.

Mr. Katzner: Dale, I see that according to the records, you've cut each of your classes many times. This tells me that you're unhappy with or disinterested in school. Is that right?

Dale: I'm always being picked on by the teachers and by you. There are plenty of other students who do worse things than me, and they never get into trouble.

Mr. Katzner: How are we all being unfair to you?

Dale: I don't do nothing. Just leave me alone.

Mr. Katzner: Dale, the rule is that you're allowed three class cuts before you're suspended from the class. You've exceeded those cuts in all of your classes, and my choice is to either suspend you from school or to find some ways to make life more tolerable for you in this school. Now, what do you need in order to go to class and to stop cutting?

Dale: I want to choose my own teachers and my schedule.

Mr. Katzner: So, if you choose your own teachers and your schedule of classes, then you believe you'd go to class.

Dale: Yes.

Mr. Katzner: That puts me in a tough spot. I'd like to give you permission to do this, but I'm afraid that other students would see this as very unfair. After all, they don't get to have this choice.

Dale: Well, then, I guess we have nothing more to talk about.

Mr. Katzner: I also see in your record that you've been sent to the vice-principal for disciplinary reasons in between classes. I will agree to allow you to choose your teachers and your schedule, but with one condition. I want you to have your classes scheduled so that *no* free periods exist. And after you finish your classes, I will arrange for you to leave school on the early bus. Now, to the degree that your choices match the schedule that I am proposing, I will allow you to pick your teachers and scheduled class times. Is this acceptable to you?

Dale: Yeah, I'll give it a try.

Mr. Katzner: I want more than just trying from you. Will you do it or not!

Dale: Okay, I'll do it.

RESOLUTION DIMENSION CONTRACT

1. Dale agrees to attend his classes regularly. If he feels that he's being unfairly treated by the teacher(s) then he can arrange an appointment with Mr. Katzner to discuss his problem.

2. Mr. Katzner agrees to allow Dale to choose his teachers and his schedule with the stipulation that his schedule can be arranged in such a way as to allow for back to back classes.

3. Dale agrees to leave school after his regularly scheduled classes.

4. Mr. Katzner and Dale agree that upon the first incidence of class cutting Dale's parents will be contacted and a conference will be arranged.

5. Mr. Katzner and Dale agree to meet at least once every two weeks to discuss Dale's school progress.

Mr. Katzner

Dale

In both examples, the adults responded without defensiveness and with a genuine desire to help the student rather than to administer punishments. A system for monitoring the effects of the resolution dimension contract (such as building in future conferences) was also used, and we see this as critical to the success of the contract. The actual method of negotiation that you use will depend upon who you are. If you approach a resolution dimension contract with a willingness to be open to yourself and your feelings with the student, then you increase the chances of a successful outcome. We offer the following as a resolution dimension review.

Resolution Dimension Review

1. Identify students who are chronic contract breakers (see discussion of data collection).
2. Identify your feelings regarding the contract breakers.
3. Set aside a meeting time for you and the student which is convenient for both of you.
4. Develop an individual plan in which both the teacher and student express their needs and both sets of needs are built into the new contract.
5. With some students, it might help to put the individual contract in writing.
6. If the contract does not work (after the same data collection has occurred as previously described), repeat the above steps.
7. Provide any instruction, educational experience, or whatever resources are necessary to help group or individual students follow the social contract.
8. For those students who cannot follow a contract, after two or three tries, seek outside help from administration, parents, school psychologist, or any other support personnel. Use your data to help the others understand the exact nature of the problem. Perhaps try to develop a third individualized contract with input from significant others.

12

THE
OUT-OF-CONTROL
STUDENT

Traditional and Extreme Approaches

Successful implementation of the three-dimensional approach will prevent and resolve most discipline problems which occur in classrooms. Yet there are a number of discipline problems that are beyond the ability of any teacher or program. The resolution dimension will work with the marginally out-of-control student, but teachers are often faced with students who will not respond to any rational approach. These students are truly "out-of-control." They might repeatedly negotiate resolution dimension contracts with a teacher or administrator, yet fail to follow through on commitments. Some may refuse to negotiate at all. Authority figures often find themselves hooked into power struggles for control with such children or adolescents. To these students, control is often the primary issue involved in their struggle to perceive themselves as separate and independent people. This is the central need in the life of these students. Most people experience anxiety when their sense of control is threatened. They find comfort in the rules and consequences of their social system because these provide a structure which may help to reduce anxiety. But anti-authority students usually have little long-term regard for consequences because their anti-authority behavior serves the purpose of reducing inner anxiety that is created when their sense of control is threatened. Such students have often become immune to their feelings because of a number of hurts that their environment has inflicted upon them, and they refuse to be troubled for fear of feeling their pain. As a way of protecting themselves from their hostile world, they usually respond with condemnation, defensiveness, and occasionally violence, even to those who wish to make positive contact with them. The use of drugs is often sought as an avenue to avoid any feelings which may remind them of how hurt they really are. The specific events which cause antiauthority behavior are as varied as the individuals themselves, but in most cases these students have not received sufficient affirmation from significant others in their lives. They often have a history of school failures, parental abuse or neglect, and an inability to believe that they have much to gain by internalizing the prevalent attitudes and values of society. Often, such students live in a subculture that serves to support their anti-authority values. Since they cannot gain the recognition that they so desperately want (because they believe themselves to be incapable and lacking worth), they turn to extreme forms of behavior as a way of ensuring that their environment will attend to them. The difficulty in working with such students is that most of them are out of touch with their feelings, and respond to their world with out-of-control behavior. Efforts by others to make contact with them are usually met with mistrust and anger. We hypothesize that anti-authority behavior is more powerful for them than positive or negative consequences (even severe ones), because of its tendency to reduce anxiety. This leaves the teacher (or authority) who works with such youngsters in a seemingly impossible dilemma. If the teacher takes on a traditional authority role and opposes such behavior, then the student sees the teacher as another enemy trying to rob him/her of identity and independence. Since the anti-authority student is so preoccupied with affirming his own separateness, he responds to others' attempts to change him with even stronger resentments and subsequent efforts to undermine these perceived enemies. Although these behaviors are often self-destructive, the student rejects any awareness of this dynamic, particularly when it is pointed out by "authority." The very fact that an "authority" suggests such a possibility is reason enough for its rejection.

Another equally futile option is to ignore the misbehavior. Ignoring only challenges the student to try harder to "get the teacher," especially if the student is trying to publicly win the battle or get attention. Further, ignoring serious student misbehavior is a tacit or subtle way of endorsing such activities, which is then perceived by the student as permission to continue misbehaving. The student can then manipulate the teacher at will because he is in control. The teacher who is at the mercy of the anti-authority student is soon looking for a job outside the teaching profession or is at least wanting to. Most major school discipline problems are primarily functions of the anti-authority student who interacts with a social system that either ignores him or wants to change him.

Many of these students are referred by the teacher for special help which may include a psychological or psychiatric assessment and intervention, home contacts through the social worker, administrative referral and/or placement in a special school, class, or program. There is often little emotional support in the student's home and even when there is, the parents are often experiencing similar battles for control with their child. While family intervention is often indicated, factors such as limited parental support, feelings of helplessness to correct the home situation (either by the parent, professional, or both), limited financial resources, or the time-consuming therapy that is often needed to change deeply entrenched patterns that contribute to the student's antagonisms, leave the teacher with little immediate relief.

The passage of the Educational Law for the Handicapped (PL94:142) which guarantees each child aged five to twenty-one a free and *appropriate* education at public expense, is cause for encouragement and guarded optimism that more anti-authority youth will have programs to meet more of their needs.

Although numerous special schools, classes, and programs already exist, such programs are often costly and have limited enrollment. Many social agencies and special schools for the emotionally disturbed are confronted with overcrowded conditions, long waiting lists, or selective admissions standards. More financial assistance may partially correct this situation.

This state of affairs leaves many classroom teachers and administrators with school age youngsters who do not benefit from instruction, and who instead turn to dangerous mischief or violence. Many school boards have abandoned the old-fashioned methods of paddling, suspension, or expulsion with such youngsters primarily because such methods have repeatedly failed to effect the desired behavioral outcome.[1] The spirit of humanism has also moved many schools away from punitive methods and towards the philosophy of accommodating all students.

[1] We are aware that corporal punishment is still being used in many schools, and some schools have recently begun using it after the Supreme Court ruling that corporal punishment is legal. Our point is not to make social predictions concerning the use of corporal punishment, but rather to point out that it is not effective with out-of-control students.

While these more modern approaches have worked well with mildly or moderately troubled youngsters, they have generally failed with the anti-authority student.

It is not our purpose to argue here for the virtues of one approach or another. As educators, our obvious hope is that sufficient funding and resources for a variety of in-school or alternative school programs will materialize; and theoretically all students will get what they need. Since many of these youngsters will continue in a public school setting (at least until the process of referral to an alternative program is completed), certain things must be done to minimize the negative impact that they may have on others. The public schools exist for the public, and it is the schools' responsibility to protect the public from those students who are too unruly and unmanageable and whose behavior is or can be dangerous or injurious to others.

We first wish to remind you how necessary it is to deal with your feelings regarding these students. It is of the utmost importance that you take good emotional care of yourself. Some of the activities described in Chapter 7 will help. Further, we are well aware of the demoralizing effect that disruptive youth can have on an individual teacher or on a total school staff. It takes only one anti-authority child to have a significant negative impact upon a total classroom. The teacher's attitude in the classroom can strongly influence attitudes of peers toward the out-of-control student. Teacher support groups which encourage feeling expression, and a sharing of experiences can have a cathartic effect that may lead to group or individual problem solving.

Aside from expressing feelings and finding support, other steps are needed. We find that it takes extreme steps to deal with extreme students. Some of the following ideas are extreme and may not be useful to all teachers, but for the brave at heart they may prove effective in working with severe out-of-control students.

BEHAVING PARADOXICALLY

Viktor Frankl has described a therapeutic approach that he calls *paradoxical intention.*[2] The use of this technique involves purposely instructing patients not to change. The basic assumption underlying this approach is that people resist changing even when they wish to do so. The insomniac continues to resist sleep even when he/she wants to sleep. The person who fears riding on elevators resists them even when he would

[2] Viktor E. Frankl, *Man's Search for Meaning: An Introduction to Logotherapy* (New York: Pocket Books, 1963).

prefer to avoid walking up hundreds of steps. It seems that phobic people, just as anti-authority students, resist change and help by others for fear of losing control. As long as they maintain their fear, they keep their anxiety tolerable.

Instead of suggesting change, the person is instructed not to change. The insomniac is instructed to pay attention to not falling asleep. The elevator phobic individual may be told to avoid elevators at all costs, and to try hard not to even look at one when one is nearby. In effect, the therapist is siding with the patient's resistance, and instead of demanding change, demands no change.

When you exhaust yourself by *trying* to do exactly what you have been *doing,* the opposite effect may occur. A sense of humor and a willingness to side with a person's resistances seem to be two important variables in the use of this approach.

Behaving paradoxically can be a very effective method with anti-authority students. The message of the teacher is firmly, "I want you (student) to try to keep behaving exactly as you have been. You are just being yourself! This is in contrast to, "The way you are behaving is unacceptable and I expect or demand you to change." The former paradoxical message may have the effect of eliciting a challenge to the student who may then defy the teacher and behave in a desirable way. Consider the following typical and paradoxical messages:

1. *Typical:* "This is the third day that you have not done your homework. The consequence is that you will have to remain after school."
   Paradoxical: "This is the third day that you have not done your homework. That is terrific! (genuine) Your assignment for tonight is to try hard to forget your homework tomorrow."
2. *Typical:* "Larry, stop throwing erasers! That will be five minutes of timeout for you."
   Paradoxical: "Gee, Larry, you have a great jump shot with that eraser. You ought to try using it more often because I know that you cannot talk out your problems when you are throwing erasers."
3. *Typical:* "Jane, I will tolerate no more swearing in this class. If you use those words again, you will not come with us on the field trip."
   Paradoxical: "Jane, you said, '_____.' Tell me how you are defining that right now and I will write the definition on the blackboard."

The contrasting styles are probably obvious to the reader. The *typical* responses will work with most students who respect the voice of authority. They do not work for anti-authority kids. The paradoxical message sets up a challenge to the student whose behavioral mode of functioning is contradictory to the message. If a student does the homework assignment in defiance of your instructions to him to forget it, then you have motivated him to do a valued school task. If he forgets it, then he has behaved appropriately according to your wishes. Either way, you win! The same can be said for Larry. As an anti-authority youngster, the five minutes, or for that matter, five hours of timeout will make no impact on his undesirable behavior. By acknowledging his ability to throw erasers as a strength, you have taken away this weapon of control and have challenged him to learn to talk as well as throw things. By telling him that he cannot talk, you have potentially motivated him to prove to you and himself that he can. After all, "If that lousy authority figure thinks I cannot talk, well then, I will just have to show him/her that I can talk as well as throw things." The process involves setting up a situation where the student has to behave more appropriately as a way of defying your authority.

There are situations in which we would not advise this technique in a school setting. The most obvious is fighting or hard hitting (as opposed to the camaraderie showing that most junior high school students use to express the combination of friendship and manhood). Obviously it is too dangerous for a teacher to encourage a student to hurt another student.

Sometimes, the other students will feel threatened and angry by the use of this technique. They may perceive their "out-of-control" peer as receiving preferential treatment and will experience more hostility toward the student and the teacher. It is often helpful to have a class discussion (when the identified student is not present) to explain the purpose of this "preferential treatment" to the class members. This can also be a good time to enlist the support of students (particularly those who are not intimidated by the out-of-control student) to help you (the teacher) with your program.

BROAD BASE OF SUPPORT

A teacher must have the support and approval of the principal in working with the anti-authority student. Dealing with Jane in the example previously discussed, might get the teacher into deep trouble unless the principal has a thorough understanding of the child and is flexible enough to allow the teacher to use such an approach. The administrator must also be willing to take some "heat" from members of the community who might be appalled at a teacher's acknowledgement and possible use of four-letter words.

It may be particularly helpful to use the resource team (i.e., out-of-classroom school specialists including the principal and the teacher) to have frequent "staffings." At the staffing, the teacher and specialists may discuss some possible strategies that may be workable with a given student. We suggest that you thoroughly discuss any creative strategies before implementation. In this way, you can assess how much support there is from others, what the possible consequences of your actions may be, and what commitments others are willing to make to help you out. Remember, the teacher who alone is working with the anti-authority student may feel doomed (and often is)!

DESENSITIZATION

Although you may be an effective teacher, sensitive to your needs and those of the students, you are in trouble if you are easily offended by put-downs and antagonistic comments that anti-authority students use to excess. These behaviors are aimed at goading you into losing control of yourself and the class. Through the process of desensitization, feelings of anxiety, fear, or anger that are elicited in you as a result of misbehavior can be interrupted.

Desensitization is another technique that you can learn which may help to toughen you to the barrage of upsetting behaviors emitted by some students. The following technique is adapted from the work of Wolpe and

This teacher is practicing desensitization.

others who use it in their clinical work.[3] We believe it to be applicable for overstressed teachers who are working in difficult settings.

DESENSITIZATION TECHNIQUE

1. List all the behaviors that students emit in your class(es) that make you feel fearful, angry, agitated, or upset. These should include only those behaviors that result in your (or your students) approximate or actual loss of control.

   _____

   _____

   _____

   _____

2. Now rank order each behavior and place a 1 next to the behavior that upsets you the most, a 2 next to that which upsets you next to the most. Continue this until you have ranked each behavior from most to least upsetting.

3. Now, in a quiet environment, assume a comfortable position, either seated or reclining on the floor. Imagine yourself in a situation that you have experienced in the past that made you feel relaxed, peaceful, and pleasant. It might be a place you have visited, an activity you enjoy, a person you know, a fantasy you have had, and so forth. Let yourself go with wherever you are or whatever you are doing. After you have allowed yourself some time in your peaceful setting, silently think of the item that is ranked first on your list. When you begin to have unpleasant feelings, return to your peaceful fantasy. Stay with your fantasy until you have again relaxed, and then silently think again of that situation that makes you feel unpleasant. Continue this process until you feel relaxed even when you silently think of that problem situation.

   Follow the same procedure for each ranked behavior. We advise you to work on no more than one or two situations at any given time. It takes some people several weeks or months to continue feeling relaxed even when they are working on a behavior that was ranked low, so do not despair if the results are not immediate.

   One alternative method is to work with somebody (that you trust) and have them read each item while you are relaxing. Should you start feeling anxious, fearful, angry, or upset, raise your finger to cue your reader of these feelings. This cue tells the reader to stop, and for you to take some time to return to your peaceful experience. Take some time to discuss procedure with this person. When you are again

[3] Joseph Wolpe and A. Lazarus, _Behavior Therapy Techniques_ (Oxford: Pergamon Press, 1966).

at peace, signal the reader (lightly tapping your finger or in some other way) to repeat the same item. Continue this process until you no longer feel upset by the behavior.

4. The goal of desensitization for the teacher is to increase his/her immunity to student behaviors which negatively affect you. Just as one is vaccinated for smallpox, desensitization can be your vaccine against the negativism of some youngsters.

STRENGTH TRAINING

Strength training is based on the notion that if a teacher is faced with the worst possible conditions and survives, that teacher will build great inner strength which can help in dealing with the out-of-control student. The basic format of strength training is role playing with colleagues.[4]

Role playing with colleagues is a form of strength training.

STRENGTH TRAINING TECHNIQUE

1. Arrange a meeting of at least five to ten colleagues who are willing to role play. Usually each participant has a chance to role play a teacher and a student on different occasions.

[4] We are indebted to Joe Samuels, from the School of Education at The University of Massachusetts, who taught us this technique, and the "direct contact technique."

2. The "teacher" for each role play describes the age and general background of his/her real class to the role-playing students, so they can accurately play their roles. If there are one or two out-of-control students in the real class, the teacher can describe what he/she/they are like.

3. The teacher tries to teach a typical lesson while the rest of the role-playing students try to prevent the teacher from teaching. The behaviors of the students can be as difficult as the students wish, but they cannot be beyond the limits of the age and type of students who make up the real class. For example, third graders cannot go out for a smoke, nor can high schoolers cry like first graders. A class with passive students might be overly passive, but violence should not break out. One member of the group may have the task of note taker. The note taker does not role play, but observes the class and takes notes to share with the teacher upon the conclusion of the role play.

4. The teacher tries everything possible to gain control of the class (Note: Most teachers rarely succeed, and this is not the goal. Each participant should be aware of the built-in "failure" of teaching the lesson.)

5. Because of the role play situation, certain teacher behaviors which may work in a real classroom may not be effective. For example, detention has no power in a typical role play, because no real detention can be given. Letters to parents have the same useless effect. The student role players should try to respond the same way to these teacher controls as the students in a real class.

6. Once the role play has ended (we recommend a limit of no more than fifteen minutes), the students should share their feelings about the teacher, and tell the teacher what strengths worked best. The teacher can share his/her feelings of frustration and inadequacy. If the class had a note taker, he should provide feedback at this time. This brainstorming session can lead to new ideas for finding strength and gaining control for the teacher.

7. Teachers can repeat their lessons at a later time to see if they have found and internalized new strength as a result of the discussion. We recommend that before teachers repeat their lessons, they have the opportunity to role play students.

DIRECT CONTACT

Direct contact is an approach designed to allow the out-of-control student a chance to make public his anxieties and feelings which affect classroom behavior. The teacher may use this approach alone, but for the best result, we strongly urge the use of an outside colleague, preferably someone who is not a regular part of the school. The outside agent should be knowledgeable about education and have some background in working with difficult children, perhaps a school psychologist, guidance counselor, or professor of education at a local college. The agent's role is to elicit feelings from the difficult students.

DIRECT CONTACT PROCEDURE

1. The agent is introduced to the class as a helper for the teacher. His/her role is described as a giver of information for the teacher to help him/her improve teaching by collecting feedback.

2. The agent asks each student to finish the following sentence as honestly as possible, anonymously, by stating the strongest, most important feelings.

   Miss/Mrs./Mr. (teacher's name) _____ makes me feel _____ when he/she _____ because _____

3. After the students finish the sentences, the agent collects them and leaves class for the day. Later, the teacher may or may not read all of the statements. The purpose of this activity is not to provide direct feedback, although feedback can certainly be of interest to the teacher. We suggest that the teacher decide whether or not he/she wants this feedback at this time.

4. On the following day, the agent returns to the class and gives each student one of the sentences. No student has the sentence he/she wrote unless it occurs accidentally. Papers should be divided randomly among the students, but it is important that the one or two out-of-control students are given sentences that reflect as closely as possible their potential negative feelings. In other words, if a student demonstrates hostility, that student should be given the most hostile sentence other than the one he wrote. Because the sentences were anonymous, the agent should carefully note the one or two sentences by the out-of-control student as they are collected. This tactic may seem underhanded in some ways. If you are uncomfortable with this aspect of this technique, it may prove unsuitable for your use. Remember we said that each of these methods is extreme and is to be used with extreme problems only.

5. With the classroom teacher present, the agent then asks some student to read his/her sentence and asks for a show of hands from any student who has experienced feelings similar to those expressed in the sentence being read. After two or three students have read their sentences, the out-of-control student has his/her turn.

6. After the student has read the sentence, the agent asks the student if he/she has ever felt that way. The agent may have to push to ensure that the student acknowledges his feelings while making sure that the student is not pushed into confessing something that would generate much discomfort.

7. After the student has agreed or not agreed that he has felt the same way, the teacher is asked to respond by sharing how he/she feels about what the student has said. A discussion can then occur, facilitated by the agent, dealing with the feelings of the teacher and student.

The direct contact approach has had beneficial effects with students who have hidden feelings which are affecting his/her relations with the teacher. It is not that useful with students who make their feelings known. The following episode occurred with a teacher who used this approach.

Gladys Hughes taught a tenth grade English class which had one very bothersome student. After consulting a colleague who was familiar with the direct contact technique, it was decided to try an experiment. Permission was granted by the principal prior to any action. The agent followed the format described above and noticed that one student wrote, "Mrs. Hughes makes me feel horny when she writes on the blackboard because she wiggles her ass." It was not the out-of-control student who wrote it. On the next day, he randomly gave sentences to the other students, but gave that sentence to the biggest troublemaker in the class.

After the out-of-control student read that sentence, he was asked if he ever felt horny when Mrs. Hughes wrote on the blackboard. After denying this twice, he finally admitted that Mrs. Hughes made him horny some of the time. Mrs. Hughes commented that she was flattered but she was in no way willing to have anything other than a teacher-student relationship. The student, although somewhat embarrassed expressing his feelings in front of the whole class, still expressed deep-seated feelings which were blocking his ability to maintain control and he did find some safety in the fact that he did not write the sentence himself. It was reassuring to him to know that his feelings were shared by at least one other student. After this episode, he caused no more than the usual problems of any tenth grader.

SELF-CONTAINED ALTERNATIVES

Many students with serious authority or peer problems do not fully benefit from instruction in regular education programs. As a result, many alternative methods, approaches, and programs have been geared toward helping these students realize more of their needs, while protecting others from the potential deleterious effects of their behavior. The following are some suggested programs and methods that can be effective in working with disruptive youth.

Timeout Area. The timeout area is usually an in-classroom option that temporarily removes a student from the mainstream, yet keeps him in the classroom. The area for timeout may include a desk and a chair in a pleasant, not too stimulating atmosphere. It should *not* be either a punitive or rewarding setting, but rather a pleasant place with some, but not too many, stimulating activities. An enclosed area that is apart from other classroom activities is suggested. Materials may include books, paper, pencils, and some art supplies. The teacher may send students for timeout for violation of the social contract or they may go voluntarily when they feel that they need to temporarily "get away" from the mainstream. With younger students, a maximum of five to ten minutes is recommended at any one time.

Out of Classroom Emotional Support. Some youngsters can greatly benefit from having an adult friend in school. Although the teacher can be perceived as a helpful friend, the teacher's professional role makes him/her responsible to many students, and often the student who needs friends the most is the most difficult to like.

The Primary Mental Health Project is a program geared primarily for children in the kindergarten to third grade who are having mild to moderate school adjustment difficulties.[5] Children are worked with either individually or in small groups with a project aide who is a paraprofessional person with an interest and sensitivity to the needs of children. Children are removed from their classrooms for approximately one hour per week, and the aide works with the child toward reaching the goals that are established at a meeting, usually involving the teacher, school mental health team, aide, and (when desirable), other school personnel. Parents must give their permission in order for the child to receive this service. The aide receives weekly supervision by the mental health team (school psychologist and social worker). The program is *preventive* in that early screening and identification of youngsters with signs of school or personal maladjustment leads to a program of intervention which decreases the probability of these youngsters developing more serious difficulties later on. Conferences and home contacts to assess the child's progress toward the goal(s) are held periodically.

The emphasis on early identification and the use of paraprofessionals in the role of friend or helper make the project a cost-effective way

[5] Cowen, Emory et al. *New Ways in School Mental Health* (New York: Human Science Press, 1975).

of providing needed resources to youngsters with problems and their families. In addition, the program provides support for the classroom teacher who wants help in dealing with difficult children.

Role Model.   The concept of Primary Project can be extended to include the use of older students as aides. There are a number of high school and college students who can identify with the problems that younger antiauthority children may be having. Such students can be assigned to periodically meet with younger children to talk to them, play games or take a walk with them. These friends can also be brought into class for tutoring with the out-of-control students, while the teacher is working with the rest of the class. This option allows the teacher to fulfill his/her primary responsibility while providing special attention to the problem student.

Just as some reformed drug addicts or alcoholics help those who are currently struggling with such problems, so may the reformed anti-authority student be able to provide some support, insight, and help to his younger colleague.

In-school Detention.   Some schools have adopted the practice of using in-school detention as an alternative to suspension, particularly for adolescent students. Most detention rooms are perceived as boring by the students and indeed they are. They are often stark, bleak looking bare rooms that offer little stimulation and do little to offer any comfort or incentive to the student. It seems that the goal of most is to bore the student into submitting to a return to the regular classroom. They are often staffed by teachers who would rather be elsewhere or hall aides who generally have little training in offering educational alternatives. If the goal is simply the removal of the student from the regular class, then in-school detention does serve this purpose. It is possible, however, to make in-school detention a positive experience that may serve to whet the learning appetite of the student.

Particularly with the anti-authority adolescent, a casual, relaxed atmosphere can be an asset. Rearranging the room to include comfortable furniture, old couches, stuffed pillows, magazines, newspapers, posters, and other materials can make the room a place where learning may be encouraged. The student should be assigned work from his subject teacher and receive help from the person(s) staffing the room, if needed. There should be no more than eight to ten students per adult, and, if possible, at least one adult should be a teacher, counselor, or administrator who has generally had success with troubled students.

Some might agree that such a pleasant arrangement is actually rewarding to students who misbehave and will strengthen their misbehavior so that they can return frequently to the special "room." While this may be true, the more powerful message is that school can be a pleasant, rewarding place to be, and an anti-authority student who wants to be in school is a lot easier to deal with than one who simply doesn't want to be there at all costs. And learning may occur.

Rules and Consequences.   The antiauthority student has repeatedly demonstrated a disregard for the classroom or school social contract. With this student, we advise that you keep rules to a minimum, and that the consequences be enforceable. Rules should be limited to antisocial actions such as physical violence, weapons, extortion, and threats.

In some instances, physical restraint may be necessary to prevent the out-of-control student from hurting himself or others. Avoid physical restraint if possible, but use it if necessary. It can reassure other students because it tells them that school staff can be depended upon to handle a student's destructive impulses and behaviors.

Staffing.   In-school alternative programs, either full-time or part-time programs such as the "detention room," should be staffed by carefully selected faculty who are reasonably relaxed when responding to the needs of the anti-authority student. Staff should have a strong background in counseling skills and in crisis intervention, as well as outside interests that they bring with them to the classroom.

Special Class or School.   Some students will need a fully self-contained classroom unit in which to function. Residential schools sometimes offer a comprehensive treatment program for emotionally disturbed youth. Many schools have classes which are housed in the regular school building to serve the needs of the emotionally disturbed. The decision to place a youngster in a special class or school is a very difficult one and should include all (including the parent) who are involved in the youngster's life. We believe that the prevention, action, and resolution dimensions are equally applicable to anti-authority youth in specialized settings and can be adapted to deal with the unique needs of such students. For example, as indicated earlier, rather than having rules focusing on homework, such classes may choose to place limits on only dangerous and potentially violent actions. At this level, it is even more necessary to involve the student in making decisions regarding group living, because there are fewer students and relationships can thereby intensify much more rapidly.

Since a significant amount of data is often necessary to justify a special class or school placement, the regular class teacher's record keeping in the prevention and action dimensions can show specific rules which were violated by a given student over a period of time. If you had written resolution dimension contracts that were frequently violated, these can also be used to support a special class placement.

Our feeling is that all students should remain as close to the mainstream of school life as possible, and for some, the special class or school is as close as they can come to the mainstream while ensuring the safety of themselves and others.

Special Problems

There are many different kinds of youngsters who are out-of-control and must still remain in the school setting. We wish to comment briefly on two special cases, those involved with alcohol and drugs, and those who are prone to dangerous physical violence especially with weapons.

THE DRUG AND ALCOHOL USER

There is little a school can do about most drug problems. Teachers are very reluctant to get involved with students who use drugs (and alcohol), and there are shifting attitudes at a national level about drug use. The problem in schools is that most school personnel do not want students arrested or to have police records, while at the same time they do not want to condone drug use in school. We find that this dilemma is extremely touchy for most schools, especially those with a high incidence of drug use and alcohol. It is impossible for teachers to teach and to behave rationally with students who come to class stoned on drugs or alcohol. Even more pressure is put on those teachers who see older students influencing younger ones to become involved with drugs. We suggest the following approach as one potential method of dealing with this difficult problem.

Separate the crimes of distributing and selling drugs from the crime of using drugs. Many states have already done this with new marijuana laws. Pushing, influencing, or contributing to younger children's drug and alcohol use should be considered a legal problem and reported to the police. This procedure should be announced to the entire school community and enforced without exception. The problem of catching these violators is the job of the police in conjunction with school personnel. In-service training should be provided to help teachers recognize when the problem occurs and to deal with their ambivalent feelings about reporting it to the authorities.

Drug and alcohol use should be dealt with differently. We suggest that a resolution dimension contract be established around the use of drugs in the class or school. As much as teachers want to influence drug and alcohol use after school, this is usually beyond their ability. Included in the consequence section of the resolution dimension contract should be parent notification. If the student stops drug use in school and the contract works, we feel that enough has been accomplished. To involve the parent may create distrust and ultimately alienate the student so that the contract will fail. If the contract is not followed, parents should be brought in to help. We believe that at no time during this process should the police be informed. If the student becomes involved with drug distribution within the school boundaries, the police should be notified and this procedure should be made clear in the contract. Finally, any violence, theft, or other crime that is associated with drug use should be forbidden and result in police notification. Notice the following contract:

Required of student:

1. No drug use will occur in class.
2. Any drug use in class will be reported home and a parent conference will result. The contract will then become void and a new contract will be developed with parental involvement.
3. Any distribution of drugs will result in notification to the principal's office and with his recommendation, notification of the police.
4. Any criminal actions such as stealing or violence will be dealt with the same way as drug distribution.
5. The teacher and/or school nurse has the right to examine the student's eyes and speech and if drug use is suspected, a conference will occur either on the spot or after school to discuss what will happen next.

Required of teacher:

1. There will be no notification of the police if drugs are used and no other part of the contract is violated.
2. The teacher will not contact the parents as long as no drug use occurs in class.
3. The teacher does not have the right to inspect the private belongings of the student.
4. If drug use is suspected, but there is no proof, the teacher must meet with the student before parents can be notified.

Signed: _____ (teacher) _____ (student)

We strongly recommend that these contracts be signed and copied, one for the teacher and one for the student. While this procedure can be seen as either too lenient by some teachers or too harsh by others, its main purpose is to stop drug use in the classroom with a minimum of threat while making it clear that drug use is serious and violations will result in strong action.

We do not believe that this approach will stop drug use in the school. Drug use is symptomatic of a larger social problem, and our society has not yet found ways to successfully deal with the larger drug and alcohol use problem. Our hope is that teachers can limit the use of drugs and find a comfortable alternative to either ignoring the problem or reporting to the authorities. Because of the legal implications of this approach, we strongly believe that the school as a whole accept it with administrative support.

THE VIOLENT STUDENT

Many schools have reported an increase in school violence, with attacks upon teachers and other students. Weapons have increased in schools, creating real fear on the part of teachers and students alike. The most common solution to this problem is the use of police on school grounds. While police are needed in many schools, their presence creates an atmosphere of a police state and serves to create new tensions as it reduces some, but not all, of the old ones.

In the same way that all out-of-control students are difficult, violent students create problems beyond the scope of any disciplinary approach which currently exists. We believe that violence cannot be tolerated if the school is to function.

The fear created by violent students both in the teacher and in other students can destroy most of the potential good of the school. We can offer no magical solution, nor even offer a solution we like. But we feel that chronic violent students have no place in the school. Unfortunately, there is no place for these students. Reform schools, jails, and the "street" are not acceptable alternatives. Ideally, there should be places where these students can go to receive help so that they can either return or stay a part of the school mainstream. While some places exist which offer help rather than punishment, they are hard to find. Once found it is even harder to get students enrolled because of the long waiting lists. Our first alternative is to try psychological or sociological support within the school environment. If that fails, students should be placed in alternative environments which stress rehabilitation rather than punishment. If these two alternatives fail, then the rights of the school people, including staff, faculty, and other students are paramount. Legal steps should be taken so that the violent student does not destroy the fabric of the school.

We favor the use of school suspension in dealing with the student who chronically resorts to violent behavior. The school may provide the youngster with home tutoring until such time as the student has developed a plan that he believes will make his violent behavior unnecessary. If the plan is acceptable to school authorities, then a parent-student-school conference is needed to discuss how the plan may be implemented. Everything that is mutually agreed to should be written down and signed by each party. The plan should then be monitored either daily or at most weekly to assess its effect.

We recognize the great difficulty in working with out-of-control students. Whether or not these students are involved in drug use, violence, or day to day destructive behavior, they make teaching and learning impossible. We are the first to acknowledge that every problem does not have a solution, and many of the out-of-control students cannot be dealt with reasonably without the creation of new programs and without the aid of many new resources both in terms of people and money. Yet, we are hopeful that these suggestions will help with some of these students and at least help remove the guilt and anxiety that you may have when you are confronted with one of these students in your classroom.

13

SCHOOL-WIDE DISCIPLINE

School-wide discipline problems differ from classroom problems in many ways. One major difference is that in the classroom there is usually one teacher and twenty to thirty students. (In nontraditional classrooms there may be two or three teachers and teacher aides.) By contrast, there may be a range of from 20 to 200 teachers and several thousand students who must interact within the boundaries of the total school. Further, in the class the students see one authority figure with a given set of expectations and behaviors. In the school there are teachers, principals, vice-principals, guidance counselors, school nurses, librarians, secretaries, custodians, and older students. All have some degree of authority, all have either explicit or, more likely, implicit rules to follow, and all have different and sometimes unknown methods of enforcement.

With the increase in sheer numbers of people involved, there are other problems related to school-wide discipline. In most schools that have serious school-wide discipline problems, the definitions of misbehavior vary greatly among the teachers and between the administrators and teachers. In one school we visited, for example, we asked the staff how many students (what percentage) were chronic discipline problems. We defined chronic to mean "broke the rules at least three times a week." The staff of thirty-five teachers answered as follows:

- 1–10% of the students are chronic rule breakers—6 teachers
- 11–25% of the students are chronic rule breakers—8 teachers
- 26–40% of the students are chronic rule breakers—12 teachers
- 41–100% of the students are chronic rule breakers—9 teachers

In another school, we asked teachers to estimate the number of school-wide rule violations which occur daily. The range estimated was from one to over fifty daily rule violations.

Another problem is that school-wide rules are often unclear to both students and faculty alike. Many schools have written handbooks with all the rules and regulations, and these handbooks are available to every teacher and student in the school. Yet, in many of the schools we have worked in, it was difficult and often not possible for the teachers to recall what was written in the handbook. Moreover, many teachers felt there were other rules, usually implicit, which operate in place of the publicly stated ones.

Perhaps the greatest problem in dealing with discipline on a school-wide basis is that given the large number of professionals and students, all with potentially differing perceptions, teachers may differ from their colleagues in their willingness to accept responsibility for maintaining order outside their own classrooms. Some teachers refuse to accept any responsibility while others make school discipline their personal vendetta, seeking the rule violators like bounty hunters in the Old West.

SCHOOL RULES CONTINUUM

Try this experiment. Place yourself on the following continuum as described by the descriptions below.

| Smokescreen Sam | Outdoors Ollie | Camel's Carl |

1. Sam goes hunting to suspend any student who gives a hint of smoking.

2. Ollie avoids the boys' room at all costs. He goes outside rather than pass by it.
3. Carl buys cigarettes and smokes them with the "guys."

FOLLOW-UP QUESTIONS

1. Why are you where you are? What fears do you have?
2. If you had no fears, where would you be?
3. Write a brief paragraph describing your place and why you are there.

_____

_____

_____

_____

Now, try to see how many of your colleagues place themselves in the same place as you. Conduct an informal survey of the teachers in your department and school and see where they place themselves.

The differences in willingness to accept responsibility cause some of the following situations to occur:

1. Some teachers enforce all the rules, others do not.
2. When violators are caught they are punished rather than taught what correct behavior is.
3. Punishments are administered inconsistently.
4. Students are shuffled to the principal's office when they break rules and are accorded no follow-up attention.
5. Some teachers openly denounce school rules as too strict, too lenient, inadequate, and stupid.
6. Some teachers never go near places where students congregate, such as student rest rooms, for fear of finding rule violations. These teachers would rather the bounty hunters take over.
7. Faculties tend to feel uncomfortable about their views of discipline and polarize into cliques based on these views.

Given the fact that the school is filled with teachers with different perceptions about the nature and scope of school-wide discipline problems and given that there is a wide discrepency between teachers' willingness to accept responsibility for the school, what can be done to improve school-wide discipline problems?

Step One: Support from the Principal

In order for policy changes to be effective in a school, the support of the principal is essential. Since the principal is often asked to intervene with students who misbehave, any attempts to institute school-wide discipline procedures must have his/her cooperation and backing. One important finding in a recent report by the National Institute of Education, titled "Violent Schools; Safe Schools," was that a single person—the principal—can turn a violent school into a safe school. The study indicated that the principal's involvement with the students, an adhered to school policy of strict and fair discipline, the principal's ability to stir school spirit, and parental and community involvement were major factors in turning violent schools into safe schools.

While there are many variables that must be considered, one that is essential is the attitude of the principal. While administrative styles range from the principal who needs to be involved in all decision making to the one who has a laissez-faire "do your own thing" attitude, the fact is that despite style, support is necessary. Ideally, this support is in the form of an active principal who encourages input from faculty and is willing to make his/her own views known without coercing others to agree. Involvement with students, and a spirit of compromise and negotiation with those who disagree with his/her own views, are additional support factors that are needed from the principal.

Step Two: Sharing Perceptions

The next important step is for the school personnel, including teachers, administrators, secretaries, custodians, and especially students, to reach a common understanding of the nature and scope of school-wide discipline problems. This means an increased awareness by everyone involved in the school of what is really happening (that which is testable and measurable) and what is perceived to be happening (what each and every school person thinks is happening).

At first glance, it may appear that only the facts are relevant and that it is not necessary to examine perceptions. However, we have found that people act on how they perceive their environment regardless of information which may or may not support those perceptions. When different ways to measure the types and amounts of behavior problems and the many different educational philosophies are considered, the perceptions of the school personnel are critically important.

This step involves a sharing of perceptions to find common ground between two critical variables. The first is how people see the school as it is, and the second is how people want the school to be. In working with various faculties we have found it helpful to use faculty meetings, questionnaires, small group discussions, and other forums to begin the process. We have found it a difficult and arduous process to help a faculty begin to see that others have different equally valid points of view regarding school-wide discipline.

Given the emotionally laden topic under discussion, it is not at all uncommon for disagreements, resentments, blame, and frustration to occur. This is a necessary, albeit unpleasant, part of the process, but one that can clear the way toward group problem solving. A thorough sharing of different views is necessary prior to a search for solutions.

Some staff might have considerable reluctance to share their views, particularly those who silently disagree with what they imagine to be the prevailing opinion of those in authority positions. Should this be a factor, then we would suggest the use of a technique that encourages the sharing of perceptions and feelings, while protecting the anonymity of staff. The group facilitator may direct each staff member to write down on a slip of paper "one obstacle that you believe gets in the way of solving school-wide problems. Please be specific." The facilitator then collects and reads each written statement and then opens things up for discussion. At times, the obstacles can lead to the expression of feelings and discussions that may move the focus away from the immediate task. This is okay, for it allows the issues of greatest prominence to emerge, to be shared and hopefully to be resolved.

We are reminded of a large inner-city junior high school that invited us to help them set up an effective program of school-wide discipline. After a few hours, we realized that there were issues among the staff that needed attention prior to any school-wide plan. There was a great deal of anger and frustration in many teachers, very poor teacher to teacher communication, and a new energetic principal who had not yet gained respect and trust from her staff. Our two-day focus moved from the initial intent of setting up a school-wide social contract to helping staff personnel make meaningful contact with each other. To have manipulated them into accepting a school-wide plan would have been similar to expecting an infant to walk before he has crawled. Unlike the classroom where the teacher's philosophy is rarely challenged, school-wide discipline is a no man's land.

Step Three: Attending to the Problem

The next step is deciding on which problem(s) will be attended to. These may include cafeteria misbehavior, hall or corridor problems, bathroom vandalizing, student smoking in restricted places or others that are problematic to a given school. We suggest the use of the brainstorming technique at this point, in which staff members are encouraged to list all school-wide problems that come to mind. This list is written down on a sheet of newsprint or on a blackboard so that everyone can see. If the school staff is quite large (over twenty-five), then having small groups do the brainstorming may ensure that all staff members have a chance to voice their own opinions.

After the list(s) have been compiled, a thorough discussion of each item is needed to ensure that all staff is clear on how the problem is defined.

Step Four: Reaching Agreement

Agreement is reached in the same way as described in our discussion of social contracts in Chapter 9. Remember, at this point, the staff's task is to reach agreement on *what* specific school-wide problem is to be addressed. In most schools, there are usually two or three major problems and a host of minor ones that are identified. We strongly suggest that no more than one or two problems be tackled at first, and that the staff reach either unanimous consensus or consensus on which one or two to deal with. We advocate gradual school-wide changes that minimize the potential of the creation of the chaos and frustration of many changes occurring too abruptly.

Step Five: How Will the Problem be Solved?

Problems may be solved in many different ways. A range of possible alternatives is as follows:

1. The principal is responsible for finding solutions.
2. A committee is formed to examine the problem and make recommendations for change, which are then reviewed and discussed by the total staff.
3. A committee is formed and is given the authority either by the principal or total faculty to solve the problem, with an understanding

that their findings and recommendations will be adopted by everybody.
4. All staff who are interested in problem solving are involved in meetings.
5. The total school staff is expected to participate in developing a school-wide plan.
6. Interested faculty, community, and student representatives are selected to tackle the problem.

We prefer the second, third, and sixth alternatives, although in some situations, one of the other described methods may have appeal. If the third alternative is selected, then it is important to ensure that the committee's formation include staff members with a range of philosophies that are representative of the total school staff. This criterion can be discussed with the total staff, and then volunteers may be solicited. If a good mix of staff does not occur, then another problem-solving method is preferable.

Step Six: Developing a School-wide Program

The final step is to formulate a workable plan that clearly spells out the problem, and the rules and consequences that are developed to resolve the problem. The following program was developed with the use of three-dimensional principles.

A MODEL PROGRAM FOR SCHOOL-WIDE DISCIPLINE

The three-dimensional approach grew out of our work with schools and teachers who wanted help in dealing with discipline. One school in particular was helpful in formulating our ideas on the three-dimensional approach. In the account that follows we describe the process and end result of our working with a school for over one year to help resolve school-wide problems. For the sake of this book, we have renamed the school, Valley View School, and while the name is fictitious, the events are real. Valley View School is an inner-city elementary school with grades four through six.

The biggest and most noticeable feature of Valley View school is children. Their presence is everywhere. During the school day there is no place in the school without them. They move about, clearly demonstrating their belief that Valley View school is theirs. After school, the childrens' presence is immediately felt, even when there are no children present. The school atmosphere is warm, supportive, creative, and energetic. Yet, discipline problems were a real part of the school, and we were asked to help the school devise and implement a program that would resolve these problems without destroying the openness of the school.

Our first step was to talk with a representative group of teachers who met regularly as the Instructional Council. This group reflected the various subject areas and age groups of the school. They identifed an inconsistency throughout the school between the philosophy of the principal and the teachers and the actual methods used by administration and teachers. The more we talked the more the gap seemed to widen. Further, we heard teachers say that openness is fine, but there was a significant population of students who abused the system and rendered it dysfunctional.

We needed to know at this point whether or not this inconsistency was a major incompatibility of ideas and/or behaviors, or rather a communication dysfunction. After careful data collection, we discovered that although there was a wide range of philosophical interpretations, teachers shared a similar view of the basic goals of the school. Further, the problems as perceived by the staff were remarkably similar. But the staff never had open discussions about the goals and purpose of their school. Thus differences were imagined. And these differences were intensified by individual teaching styles and the need for communication.

Once the staff was confronted with the data we collected, things began to happen. First there was a need for greater communication among themselves and with the administration. In fact they were willing to work during the summer without pay to establish a viable communication program. Second, they were able to identify specific problems in the school that were sore spots for them. By dealing directly with these problems they could relate better with everyone. They could allow their differences to co-exist and their similarities to provide a unity and consistency that was previously lacking.

We decided to deal with the immediate problems first. In a total staff meeting we brainstormed all the school problems that the teachers could not solve individually. These were the overall problems that the openness of the school created. Once the list was completed, we began to perceive ironic circumstances. The students' freedom of movement throughout the school, the same factor that gave the school its vitality and student centeredness, was a breeding ground for a wide variety of problems. It seemed that unrestricted movement of students allowed, and in some instances encouraged, students to aimlessly float, to make disturbances that interfered with ongoing classes, and to cause other related problems. Each teacher handled the disturbances differently; some ignored them, others were strict, some referred violators to the principal, others punished students themselves. This inconsistency was the largest contributor to the teachers' differences in their perceptions of the school's goals. When asked, the teachers felt that between ten and forty percent of the students were chronic problems.

At this point a combination of insights were synergistically created that enabled the staff to understand the nature of the problem in a new way. One by one the following points were noted leading up to the identification of a most creative problem-solving alternative.

1. The school needed a consistent policy accepted by all teachers and the principal.
2. The policy needed to be flexible to allow various alternatives for different situations.
3. The majority of students should not be restricted because of a large minority.
4. The minority of students who created problems should not be ignored because of the needs of the majority.
5. Students should be encouraged to assume responsibility, and any policy should be based upon improvement, not punishment.
6. The problems of Valley View were mostly related to traffic and movement outside the classroom. Discipline and instruction within the classroom posed no significant problem.

Finally, an idea was conceived, modeling a real life system with which all students were familiar, and one that met all the preconditions just listed. The plan shows how the three-dimensional approach can be used and adapted to a school-wide situation. The staff developed a list of rules that encouraged free movement, but did not allow fighting, loud noises, or aimless wandering. Each student received a list of the rules and discussed them during class time. A test would be administered to any student who wanted it, and the students who passed were issued "movement permits." This step is the same as the testing step in the prevention dimension. These permits signified permission to have freedom of movement throughout the school. If a student was caught breaking a rule, he/she would have an infraction recorded on his permit. Three infractions would revoke the permit until the offender met for three group meetings with other offenders, two teachers, and the school psychologist. The purpose of the meetings was to help the offenders learn how to cope with responsibilities, not to punish them. As long as a student had no permit, he had to travel with a partner, or "chauffeur" who did have a permit (this included bathroom privileges). After a two-month trial period, each student who had either less than three infractions or had attended three sessions was issued a permanent laminated license, complete with his/her picture. Three offenses against this license would result in loss of the license and would require attendance in three group sessions. Fighting was one rule violation that resulted in immediate loss of license. (This was also the only rule that was extended to include classroom behavior.)

This system has worked well, and the reasons for its success are applicable to Valley View or any school for that matter.

1. The teachers accepted the system, because it grew out of their needs and from their own efforts.
2. The principal genuinely supported the system.
3. Because all teachers accepted them and followed the rules, they created a consistent atmosphere for the students who always knew what was expected of them.
4. No one teacher was responsible for loss of the student's privilege. It took three infractions to cause a loss of license.
5. The system was built upon the need to give students responsibility. Those students who could take responsibility were given it. Those that could not, received help, not punishment.
6. The students understood the system, because of the familiarity of the drivers license analogy, and accepted it.
7. The effects of misbehaving were immediate. The infraction was immediately listed on the permit.

There were additional management problems that the teachers faced when the system first began. The younger students lost many permits, over and over again, most likely because they had difficulty understanding the system. There was a great increase in paperwork for all the teachers. Some students found loopholes and were able to beat the system (by accidentally losing a permit that recorded an infraction). But the staff handled these problems in stride and found ways to solve them.

The permit/license concept enhanced the enthusiasm of the entire school and the community at large because everyone could relate to the concept. More important, however, was the interaction between teachers and principal. First the staff began to talk about their goals, beliefs, and philosophies in a positive and supportive atmosphere, which enabled them to focus on a cooperative school environment rather than thirty isolated minicosms. Secondly, they were able to discern the difference between a goal and the methods used to reach that goal. This was a most critical step in the development of solutions. In addition, they saw the need to help students learn to be responsible by giving them more responsibility. Those that needed help could now receive it, without resorting to a restrictive and closed school environment. Finally, they participated in the development of an ongoing communication system among themselves and with the principal.

What we can learn from the Valley View experience is that there are a number of factors that contribute to successful programs for school-wide discipline. The same basic factors which make the three-dimensional approach successful in the classroom are important for school-wide problems. It is not necessary to develop an elaborate plan such as movement licenses, although the concept can work in most schools regardless of grades or location. What is important is communication and consensus.

Communication.   It is essential that good communication exist between teachers and between teachers and administrators. We have developed a list of questions which we ask most faculties when we work in schools. These questions are asked at faculty meetings when the entire faculty and administration is present. The participants indicate their answers by a show of hands and the results are tabulated on large sheets of newsprint or on dittos and copies are sent to each participant.

QUESTIONS:

1. How many of you think serious school-wide problems requiring a dis-cipline response, exist here?
2. How many of you have serious classroom management problems?
3. How many of you know someone else who has serious classroom man-agement problems in his/her class?
4. How much teaching time do you lose due to classroom management issues?

   0–5%

   5–15%

   15–30%

   over 30%
5. How many of you must send at least one student per week to the prin-cipal or vice-principal for discipline reasons?
6. How many hope that by the end of the day(s) to have a different pro-cedure for dealing with classroom management?
7. How many hope that by the end of the day(s) to have a different pro-cedure for dealing with school-wide discipline problems?
8. How many of you think that finding a solution to classroom discipline problems is hopeless?
9. How many of you think that finding a solution to school-wide prob-lems is hopeless?

10. How many of you have tried something new in dealing with discipline in the last month?
11. How many of you think that if other teachers observed your classroom, they might learn something that would help in dealing with discipline?
12. How many of you stop yourself from expressing what you really want from students for fear of any number of things happening?

These questions begin the process of communication of thoughts and feelings regarding discipline. Before a faculty can move to Step two, it is important that open communication about discipline be started by all school personnel.

Reaching Consensus.   We have found that unanimous consensus for an entire school is close to impossible, but we feel that a consensus on most issues will enable the school to work successfully. If a consensus cannot be reached, it might be impossible for any further work to be done. This is an important ground rule, for once a staff truly sees the need for consensus, they are usually more willing to actively work toward it. Consensus must be reached on the following two points:

1. Where is the school now in terms of the most important problems in discipline?
2. Where does the school want to be if a solution is found?

To discover where the school is involves a clear statement about what the faculty can agree are the most important disruptions. These may include such things as fighting in the halls, noise during class time, littering, vandalism, theft, students in the halls with no place to be, or smoking in the lavatories. We suggest that the school only try to resolve the behaviors around which a consensus can be reached. If one or two teachers do not agree in a population of thirty or more, a majority of over ninety percent is sufficient.

Once consensus has been reached on the nature of the problems to be solved, the school must then write clear, specific rules which prohibit the negative behaviors and describe what positive behaviors are allowed. To prevent fighting a school may have the following rule: No fighting is allowed on the school grounds. Disagreements may be solved through discussion, through negotiation with a third party such as a teacher or counselor, or by cooling off for a day or two.

Each rule must have a range of alternatives. Both the formulation of rules and consequences must follow the guidelines established in the prevention dimension as discussed in Chapter 4.

If a true consensus has been reached, all of the teachers have agreed that a real problem exists which is worth stopping, and that the rule established for dealing with the problem is worth enforcing. If the consequences are clear and provide a range of alternatives designed to instruct more than punish, and if the staff agrees to administer a consequence whenever a rule is broken, there will be the necessary consistency for setting up a preventive environment.

Student Involvement

The heart of the three-dimensional approach is student involvement. We suggest that the problems identified by the staff be discussed with the students through a school-wide assembly (which can be effective even with primary grade students) or through class discussions led by each teacher in the school. The rules and consequences can be presented to the students at this time. (If there are teachers using the three-dimensional approach in their classes, the students will be familiar with the approach and easily adapt. Further, should a school adopt a version of the three-dimensional approach, it will be that much easier for teachers to use the model in their classrooms.)

The advantage of having permitted student involvement in the development of the school-wide plan is now evident. If representative students were involved in the formulation of the plan, then the chances of the majority of students seeing the school-wide plan as autocratic and authority imposed is lessened. The responsibility for the plan rests with both the students and teachers (and administrators). The shared responsibility typically results in a shared sense of commitment.

Just as the classroom social contract is on trial for a month or two, we suggest that the school-wide plan be given a similar trial period. A committee of teachers and students can be organized to monitor the effectiveness of the program, to suggest change, and to solicit feedback from all who wish to be heard.

The students can be allowed to think of rules and consequences for the faculty and each other, in the same way as they do in the classroom version. This may be done in the assembly or in classrooms either prior to or immediately after the assembly.

Once all the rules and consequences have been developed for the entire school a vote can be taken in much the same way as described for a classroom. The only difference is that consensus is often not attainable with a large group, and a 65 to 75 percent acceptance rate is usually sufficient. We also suggest the notion of flagged rules. These are rules which are to be implemented regardless of the vote because the faculty sees them as critical to the welfare of the school. Some examples of flagged rules are fighting, bringing weapons to school, and the use of drugs in school. Since flagged rules deal with illegal activities or are so important that a vote is not appropriate, students can easily understand the reasons for them. It is not a good idea to flag all of the teacher rules and none of the student rules.

After an explanation of the rules and consequences, a test for comprehension is administered. Passing the test insures the students of school privileges; for example, a movement license as in the Valley View school.

The final step is to notify parents through a mailing of the school-wide plan accompanied by an explanation describing the trial period and the problems that the plan is trying to solve. We suggest that the letter be sent from the principal and that questions and clarifications be dealt with through the office of the principal. The important factors in the school-wide approach are as follows:

1. Consensus of faculty, staff, and administration.
2. Student involvement.
3. Clear rules describing acceptable and unacceptable behavior.
4. A range of alternative consequences designed to teach, not punish.
5. Testing for comprehension and granting privileges to those who pass.
6. Monitoring the school plan during the trial period.
7. A total community spirit for problem solving.

School-wide problems can be extremely difficult to deal with and may require a great deal of energy. As we have stated earlier, discipline problems have no easy solution, and while some gimmicks effect immediate positive change, lasting effects require school-wide commitment, resources, and cooperation.

14

RESOURCE PERSONNEL

There are a variety of resource programs and personnel in schools throughout the country whose function it is to assist the teacher, parent, or child in developing to his/her full potential. Such resources include the principal, assistant principals, guidance counselors, reading and math resource teachers, speech and language therapists, teachers for the emotionally disturbed, learning disabled, and mentally retarded, school psychologists, nurse-teachers, school social workers and substitute teachers. While each resource person has certain specialties which separate him or her from others, our experience has shown that despite any formal title, each specialist will be required to intervene in situations related to discipline at one time or another. Resource personnel can use the three-dimensional approach to help a teacher, a student, or a parent with a discipline problem.

The Principal's Role

The school principal, by far, plays the most important and influential role in establishing a tone or climate in the school which will set the stage for the success or failure of the three-dimensional approach (particularly with school-wide discipline). Since the approach advocates feelings, awareness, and negotiation, the principal must honor such values to help the program succeed in each classroom. We advocate an active, involved approach by the principal for school-wide implementation.

The following activities are designed primarily for the school principal in order to help him foster successful communication of the three-dimensional approach.

MY DISCIPLINE STYLE

Complete the following sentences by checking the responses most appropriate for you:

1. When a teacher says or does something that I dislike, I usually
   a. Tell him/her.
   b. Pretend I didn't see what happened.
   c. Feel resentful but rarely say anything.
   d. Send or place a letter in the teacher's personnel folder.
   e. Negotiate a solution with the teacher.
   Give a specific example:

   _____

   _____

2. When a student says or does something that I dislike, I usually:
   a. Scold or threaten.
   b. Call the parent.
   d. Paddle the student.
   d. Pretend I didn't see or hear.
   e. Feel resentful but rarely say anything.
   f. Negotiate a solution with the student.
   Give a specific example:

   _____

   _____

3. When a discipline problem occurs outside my office, I wish that:
   a. The teacher would handle it without me.
   b. The teacher would inform me.

c. The teacher would leave me alone.

d. Other _____

Give a specific example:

_____

FOLLOW-UP

Write a paragraph indicating how your responses reflect your view of discipline. List ways that you can be more supportive of the three-dimensional approach. Share your paragraph with others. (A small group discussion is equally useful.)

WHAT ARE THE DISCIPLINE PROBLEMS AROUND HERE?

In the previous chapter on school-wide discipline, we stressed that although most people in a school have some awareness of what a discipline problem is, individual definitions and responses to problems have a wide variance in any school. As principal, your first step (particularly when you want to resolve school-wide problems) is to identify what a discipline problem is from the point of view of your staff. In addition, it can be helpful for you to know what teachers are expecting from you and when they want you to intervene.

Explain during a faculty meeting that you'd like some data from your teachers to determine what the discipline problems are in the school and in each classroom, and that you'll be sending around a brief survey for them to fill out. To minimize any fear they may have of being judged, tell them to answer the survey anonymously. Stress the importance of each teacher's response.

SAMPLE SURVEY

I'd like to know how each staff member views discipline in our school. Please fill out this survey. I am interested only in gaining a total school perspective, so you may fill out this form anonymously. Thank you for your cooperation.

1. List those discipline problems (in order of severity) that occur primarily in the classroom:

    a. _____

    b. _____

    c. _____

    d. _____

    e. _____

2. List those problems (in order of severity) that you define as school wide:

   a. _____

   b. _____

   c. _____

   d. _____

   e. _____

3. What do you see as some "in school" causes of these problems and if you could, what would you do to resolve them?

   _____

   _____

   _____

   _____

   _____

4. Do you feel that the school administration is responsive to your needs related to discipline?

   _____ yes   _____ no

   Please explain.

   _____

   _____

   _____

   _____

FOLLOW-UP

After you have received these responses, we suggest that you share them with your staff and allow some time for your reaction and that of your staff. This feedback can lead to lively discussion out of which some alternatives for change may emerge.

Intervention

The principal or assistant principal is usually the person expected to deal with students with which teachers have had little success. In many elementary schools the teachers simply send students to the office when they have had enough misbehavior. At the secondary level, students are usually referred to the principal or the assistant principal for discipline, and he/she is then expected to take some kind of action. In many instances, the administrator hears both sides of the story (from the student and teacher), but does so without both parties present. This often puts the administrator in the role of a middleman; that is, he tells the student of the teacher's complaints and the teacher of the student's complaints. As a result, the teacher perceives his/her authority as undermined, or the student sees the principal as the ally of the teacher.

We feel that the administration can avoid many problems by learning the principles outlined in the resolution dimension (positive student confrontation) and implementing them when conflict occurs between teachers and students. Through an atmosphere of openness and a willingness to negotiate, many solutions acceptable to both students and teachers can be found.

Many resource personnel can assume the role of coach in positive student confrontation. Solutions between the teacher and student that are facilitated by a resource person need monitoring to see how well they work. The negotiation process should include a monitoring procedure whereby a date is set (a few weeks later at most) for all parties to get together and assess how things are going. At that time, any changes, grievances, or modifications of the previously agreed to solution(s) can be discussed. Although your role is primarily to facilitate, you may be able to break through an impasse between the parties by offering suggestions of your own. Just as a labor mediator can at times get the grieving parties together and break a deadlock, so can the "coach" at times serve the same purpose.

We defined a discipline problem as a situation or event in which either authority or group needs are in conflict with individual needs. It is therefore incumbent upon the resource person to observe how these needs are conflicting, to provide nonjudgmental feedback to the teacher or student, and to offer suggestions as to how future conflicts may be avoided.

Classroom observation can be a powerful way of understanding the classroom dynamics that are interacting to create discipline problems. Although most resource professionals recognize the value of observation, few are taught the skills that are necessary to effectively observe. As a consequence, many resource people work with the student away from the classroom and give themselves little opportunity to deal with the classroom causes of discipline problems.

Joseph, eight years old, was referred to the school counselor by Miss Miller because he was not attending to his assigned work and instead was annoying other children. Although his behavior was not overly aggressive, he would push, shove, tickle, and touch other students when they were doing their work. This would often cause classroom disruption, as the other children would be distracted from their work, and the teacher frequently had to intervene to make Joe stop.

On several occasions, Mr. Henry, the school counselor, observed the class, and his report yielded the following information:

1. Joe was capable (intellectually) of doing most of the assigned work.
2. Joe appeared to attend well to films and to stories read aloud.
3. Joe's annoying behavior occurred mostly during independent seatwork time.
4. Joe seemed to calm down when Miss Miller touched him.
5. Joe's behavior worsened shortly after the teacher praised him.
6. Joe was sitting apart from the rest of the class (because he couldn't behave himself).

On the basis of these observations, a plan of action was formulated with Miss Miller.

Plan of Action:

1. *Goal:* To reduce the frequency of such disturbing behaviors as tickling, pushing, and shoving other children.
2. *Suggested activities to meet the goal:*
   a. Miss Miller would touch, hold, or hug Joe at times when he's doing what is required.
   b. Joe would earn one point for completing each assignment. Each point would earn him a trip to the library where he would be permitted to watch a film or listen to a story on tape.
   c. Joe would start each day seated with the group. He would be removed from the group only after three reminders from Miss Miller to stop misbehaving.
   d. Miss Miller would keep Joe in close physical proximity to her, particularly during independent seatwork time, although he could cash in his points for library trips at this time if he knew he could not use the independent time for classwork.
   e. Miss Miller would thoroughly discuss this plan with Joe prior to implementation.

DEVELOPING YOUR OBSERVATION SKILLS

Observing a classroom is tedious, difficult, and sometimes boring. No observer should observe more than twenty minutes and he/she should have clearly defined, specific things to look for.[1] The following list may be helpful in setting up a program of observation.

1. What is the student doing at the time of the observation?
2. How much attention is being given the student, and by whom?
3. Does the student initiate contact with others; if so, how?
4. Where is the student seated?
5. For what period of time is the student "on task" (doing what's expected)?
6. What happens when he/she is on task?
7. What is the task?
8. What is the teacher doing (in relation to the student)?
9. How much contact is he/she having with the observed student (note eye contact and physical proximity as well as verbal behavior)?
10. What is the quality of the contact (e.g., reprimands, punishing statements or put-downs, reminders to get back to work, praising behavior, acknowledging the student when he's behaving appropriately, and so forth)?
11. List all interactions (verbatim, if possible) that you observe between the teacher and observed child.
12. What is the nonverbal interaction like (what do you see as the unspoken messages that convey feelings)?
13. What does this child do to provoke others?
14. What do others do that provoke him/her?
15. What are the implicit and explicit rewards in the classroom?

On the basis of your observation, what suggestions or recommendations would you make?

FOLLOW-UP

When you write up your observation, it is very important that you avoid blaming or criticizing what you saw. Stick to the observable record and be as specific as possible (e.g., When Joe left his seat, Miss Miller pointed her

[1] Three excellent books which will help you improve your observation skills are: Weinberg and Boehm, *The Classroom Observer* (New York: Teachers' College Press, 1977); Curwin and Fuhrmann, *Discovering Your Teaching Self: Humanistic Approaches to Effective Teaching* (New Jersey: Prentice-Hall, 1975); and Goldhammer, *Clinical Supervision: Special Methods for the Supervision of Teachers* (New York: Holt, Rinehart and Winston, 1964).

finger at him and said, "Sit down"). You lose credibility when you say, "Joe got out of his seat and this made Miss Miller angry at which time she got up and forced him to sit down." You can see her finger, and hear her words but you cannot observe "force" or "anger." You can only assume that this is what you saw, and your assumptions must first be checked out.

The purpose of an observation is to help the teacher be aware of what the student is doing, how the teacher or other students are responding, and how these interactions may perpetuate classroom conflict. Your suggestions should be specific and should take into account the teacher's range of responses. The teacher who attributes all the responsibility of misbehavior to the student and has little awareness of how he/she contributes, needs to be worked with differently from one who readily accepts feedback and is more than willing to make changes. Your sensitivity to the needs of the teachers you work with is your best guide to specific recommendations you make.

It is important for you to share your observations with the teacher you observed as soon as possible after the class and discuss your notes. Never withhold data you collected, because if the teacher feels you are selective in your feedback, you will break down trust and be less effective.

Substitute Teachers

In Chapter 2 we asked you to choose between two situations, one with no rules and the other with complete and absolute rules. (See page 80.) Frequently a substitute's presence in the classroom is a signal for the students to work as hard as possible to create situation A (no rules) while the substitute tries to create situation B (total rules). In most classrooms the students come closer to achieving their goal than the poor substitute, who is usually content to finish the day with some degree of sanity. Those substitutes who do set up strict rules and have the ability to enforce them are often viewed by students with fear and mistrust, so that little positive learning occurs.

However, there are a great many substitutes who have the ability to come into a classroom as a stranger and in a very short time win the students' respect in positive ways. We believe that three-dimensional discipline can help substitutes do more than survive in the classroom.

WHAT THE TEACHER CAN DO TO HELP THE SUBSTITUTE

If you are using the three-dimensional approach with your class, there are a number of things you can do to help your substitutes function smoothly in your class.

1. Include in the classroom social contract at least one rule (usually an implicit rule) and set of consequences covering classroom behavior when a substitute is present. For example:

   Rule: When a substitute is present, students will follow the social contract exactly as if the regular teacher was present.
   Consequences:
   a. Loss of privileges for three consecutive days for any student who repeatedly violates the contract.
   b. All work that is not completed on the day that the substitute is present will be made up within two days.
   c. Students will write a letter of apology to the substitute and send it to him/her.

2. Leave the social contract with the substitute explaining how it works and what the substitute can do to enforce it. This is best done in writing because you may not know in advance of your absence nor have time to sit down and discuss the contract with him/her. It is also helpful to leave a copy of your social contract with your principal or assistant principal who may help the substitute use it if he or she needs help during the school day.

3. If you work with a substitute, who takes your place on a regular basis, you can invite the substitute in and spend a class period developing a special social contract with him/her which only goes into effect when you are absent. This not only gives the substitute an opportunity to add a few rules and consequences of his/her own, but gives the students an opportunity to add a rule or two for the substitute. This new social contract will not replace the original one developed by you and your class. We suggest that it be brief, containing no more than two or three rules and sets of consequences.

4. Brainstorm with your class a list of things to do when substitutes take over the class. There can be two lists, one for behaviors that will make life easier for the substitute (a modified set of rules without consequences) and the other a list of academic activities that the students would enjoy. The list can be left for the substitute who can then refer to it when necessary. Having a choice gives the substitute more flexibility to do what he/she may find enjoyable.

5. Design a "problem list" (you may use or adapt the "disruptive behavior checklist") to give to your substitutes to record all classroom student behavior which represents major problems. Minor incidents are not to be included because the substitute should be able to handle them alone. After you have used a substitute three or four times, or have had three or four substitutes, examine the list for recurring

problems and present them to your students. Develop a social contract to prevent these from occurring in the future.

WHAT A SUBSTITUTE TEACHER CAN DO WITHOUT THE TEACHER'S HELP

If you are a substitute teacher, you may take over for a teacher who has never heard of three-dimensional discipline. As you know, there is little time to get to know the students and there is not enough time to develop social contracts unless you are a long-term substitute. But there are some things you can do to prevent discipline problems from occurring and to resolve them when they do occur. You may find the following list of suggestions helpful:

1. Develop your own list of rules and consequences. Unlike a social contract, it is not a good idea to have a rule for everything. Limit your list to three or four important rules. Check with the principal or assistant principal for help in designing enforceable, realistic consequences. If you substitute for a teacher on a regular basis, work with him/her to think of rules and consequences for that class. Once you have a good list of rules and consequences, design a cardboard display to present to the students at the beginning of class.

2. Ask the students for one rule they would like you to follow, and then follow it. Consequences are important but can be left out if you are only taking over for one class period. If you know the rule is not good for you, negotiate so that their need is met and yours is too. Change the rule so that it fits for you and the students.

3. Talk to any teacher for whom you will be substituting on a regular or semiregular basis and express your need to have the teacher discuss classroom behavior for substitutes. If possible come into class one day when the teacher is present and co-teach a lesson; this will help you get to know the students and they will get to know you. If possible try to inform the teacher about social contracts and maybe the two of you can develop a social contract for use when you take over. If the teacher likes the idea and develops his/her own social contract, so much the better for you because the students will be familiar with the system and most of the major problems will be in the process of improvement.

4. When individual students continually give you a hard time, try a modified version of positive student confrontation; this can occur in front of the other students. For example, "Steve, you have been

jumping up and down for ten minutes. I want you to stop. Is there something I can do for you to make it easier for you to stop?

5. Keep a list of the major classroom problems which occur in the class. If you are working in one class over a period of time, maintain the list for three or four times. Discuss the problems with the teacher and see if together you can resolve them or prevent them from occurring. Bring the list with you the next time you take over that class and begin by stating the problems that you and the students have when you are together; then design a mini-social contract to eliminate them. State what you need and ask the students what they need to stop the behaviors. If you work in a variety of classes, see if any problems recur in all of them. Look for patterns of student behavior. If you find that many problems continually appear in a variety of classes, the problem may rest with you. See if there are any ways you contribute to the problem or set it up. You may set it up by acting defensive or overly aggressive, or by setting up consequences you can't enforce; for example, "Johnny if you speak out again, you will stay after class everyday for a week." Try to think of creative ways to prevent these problems. You may try fantasizing what it's like to be a student in the class in which you are substituting, and see if your teacher behaviors would work for you, the student.

6. Substituting is hard work. Use the activities in Chapter 7 ("Expression of Feelings") to take care of your own needs so that you have the energy and strength to act positively.

7. The use of the nonverbal techniques, particularly those described in the action and resolution dimensions (Chapters 10 and 11) can be very effective in stopping misbehavior before things get out of control.

CONCLUSION

In general, resource personnel can be very important to the successful implementation of the three-dimensional approach. Help may range from providing a teacher a safe place to scream to setting a positive tone, to providing training for an entire faculty and staff. We find that schools in which teachers and administrators support, confer, and resolve problems together are the most positive places for students, teachers, and administrators. Students model what they see and all too often, principals treat teachers as if the teachers were discipline problems. The more positive interaction students observe between teachers and administrators and between teachers and other teachers, the more likely they will demonstrate the same kind of behaviors. Widespread use of the three-dimensional approach offers consistency, respect, and cooperation between all school personnel.

15

WORKING
WITH
PARENTS

There are many parents and teachers who spend time and energy looking for the culprit responsible for the lack of effective school and classroom discipline. While they are busy blaming and judging each other, they become defensive and hostile and deny any responsibility for themselves. Some teachers claim that because of disinterested parents and lack of affection and supervision at home, students come to school without the academic and/or emotional tools to find school a successful place to be. They point to the growing numbers of parents who do not come to parent-teacher conferences, the numerous single parent homes in which the parent is too busy working to attend to child rearing, and too much free out of school time for students which may lead to trouble.

Parents are frequently complaining about the teacher's lack of interest in their child, too much freedom in the school, too many electives, parental exclusion in curriculum development, and school disciplinary procedures that are not strict enough.

It seems that during any given period of time, the pendulum of blame swings back and forth, with parents and teachers arming themselves against attack from each other. While it is unlikely that this pattern

Parents and teachers can communicate various ways of helping children overcome misbehavior.

will ever be extinguished, there are many things that can be done to improve communication and to enhance cooperative effort in the alleviation of classroom and school discipline problems.

Within the last few years, parents and teachers have in many instances worked together more closely through parent volunteer programs, the inclusion of teachers in previously all parent organizations, and the presence of parent representatives on important decision-making school committees. We applaud these efforts. As teachers and parents become more familiar with the role that each plays in a child's development, an atmosphere of empathy and understanding replaces one of hostility and antagonism. The fact is that parents and teachers are often beset by similar problems in different environments. The child who doesn't pay attention to his/her parents' directions at home will often have a similar problem following the teacher's directions. The child who is frequently fighting with his brothers and sisters at home will often be fighting with other kids in school. The student who is tardy to class is usually tardy to mowing the lawn or washing the dishes at home. The student who takes what belongs to somebody else in school will usually do the same at home. The student who has little respect for school authority generally has little respect for parental authority. The student who survives in school by demonstrating his inadequacy appears stupid and helpless at home.

Although a child's actual behavior or misbehavior may vary in different settings, the response pattern (what the child does to get what he needs) is often very similar both in school and at home.

We feel that there is a great deal of common ground upon which parents and teachers can communicate various ways of helping children who seek misbehavior as a response. There is much that the teacher can do to set a positive tone with parents, which can elicit their cooperation rather than their protective resistance.

This chapter will focus on how you, the teacher, can extend the three-dimensional approach to both include and encourage parental participation. Developing a rapport with parents before discipline problems are evident can serve to help you when their cooperation is needed.

We include the following suggestions and activities to help you gain the cooperation of parents for support of your three-dimensional program.

Open House

Shortly after school begins, many schools have an "open house" in which parents are invited to meet the teacher in what is generally a social setting. In most cases, parents are informed that the open house is *not* the time to discuss individual children and their progress, but rather to explain the curriculum and to consider general issues of concern to either the teacher or the parent. Due to the limits placed on what can or cannot be discussed, such an encounter often yields a lot of game playing with little meaningful contact actually established. We believe that this early year open house is an excellent time to discuss the three-dimensional approach and to invite parental reaction to your plan. We suggest that you discuss the prevention dimension, social contracts, how you plan to keep records in the action dimension, and individual contracts (resolution dimension).

Another format that we have found to be more useful because it generates more enthusiasm is the experiential method. The few experiential activities which follow can be done during open house or at some other time. If you cannot use open house, we suggest you find another time to meet with parents shortly after school begins.

QUESTIONNAIRE: MY CHILD'S INTERESTS

Just as we suggested that an awareness of your students is important in the prevention of discipline problems, we also feel that knowledge of your students through the eyes of their parents can be a positive factor in involving parents in the three-dimensional approach. In this regard the following questionnaire can be very helpful. It can also serve as a means of comparing how parents assess their child's interests and how your students see their own interests.

DIRECTIONS

Briefly explain three-dimensional discipline to your group of parents. Let them know that part of the program involves your (teacher's) awareness of what interests each student has and a knowledge of what interests you (the parent) think your child has. Ask them to please fill out your questionnaire and explain that it is for your use only; their responses *will not* be discussed with their child.

QUESTIONNAIRE

1. List three things that your child likes to do.

   _____
   _____
   _____

2. What three things does your child like to do best in school?

   _____
   _____
   _____

3. If your child could avoid three things in school, what would they be?

   _____
   _____
   _____

4. What are some things that I (the teacher) should know about your child that would help me to make school a happy place for him/her? Write a brief paragraph.

   _____
   _____
   _____
   _____

5. How would you rate your child's academic achievement in school thus far (including his past school history)? Circle as many as apply.

   a. Works up to potential.

   b. Tries hard but has difficulty learning.

   c. Could do better in school if he/she tried harder.

   d. Does better in school than I expect.

   e. Is above average in achievement.

f. Is average in achievement.

g. Is below average in achievement.

6. How would you rate your child's social development in school thus far?

   a. Is popular and has a lot of friends.

   b. Has a few close friends, but not many.

   c. Is easily led astray by others.

   d. Spends most of his/her time alone.

   e. Is a "social organizer" or group leader.

7. Complete the following. Please be as specific as possible.

   a. My child's feelings about school are _____

   b. What he/she needs most from a teacher is _____
      _____

   c. I'd like to see my child _____

   d. My child's reaction to criticism is _____

   e. My child's most successful or productive school year was_____
      _____

SCHOOL AND HOME DISCIPLINE: WHERE DO I STAND?

The following survey, to be administered to parents, gives you an opportunity to become aware of their thoughts, values, and feelings regarding discipline both at home and at school. One problem that has often been cited as a cause of discipline events is the lack of consistency between teacher and parents in their approaches and methods to both defining and resolving discipline problems. An understanding of what approaches, techniques, and attitudes the parents have about discipline can provide you with insights into how congruent your beliefs are with those of your students' parents. You can then use this feedback to mirror the attitudes of the community or to express how you differ with their attitudes if you choose the latter approach. It is important that you *not* judge, but simply express how you and your expectations are different. In this way, at least everybody can be clear on where each person stands.

DIRECTIONS

Introduce this activity by saying that you value knowing the thoughts, attitudes, and methods that each parent uses in disciplining, so that you can see how similar or different their views are from your own.

1. Place a check mark next to those items that you believe represent significant student or teacher misbehavior.

_____ Student comes to class late.

_____ Student talks back to the teacher because he/she feels they've been unfairly treated.

_____ Student doesn't turn in his homework assignment.

_____ Student cuts class.

_____ Student cheats on exam.

_____ Student takes the belongings of another without permission.

_____ Teacher doesn't give homework assignments.

_____ Teacher "chews out" your child in front of the class.

_____ Teacher deals with student swearing by listing every four-letter word on the blackboard and asks students to define each word.

2. For each misbehavior checked, what do you believe would be a fair consequence? (You may list more than one thing that should happen as a result of such misbehavior.)

_____

_____

_____

_____

3. What, if anything, does your child do at home that requires you to discipline (please be specific)?

_____

_____

_____

_____

4. For each misbehavior listed in Question 3, what do you do?

_____

_____

_____

_____

5. What methods or techniques work best for you in the management of your child's behavior (e.g., taking away privileges, rewarding good behavior, spanking, and so forth)?

_____

_____

_____

_____

6. Place a + next to the statements with which you agree, a − next to those with which you disagree, and a 0 next to those with which you have no opinion or can't decide.

_____ Kids have too much freedom in school.

_____ Parents are primarily responsible for misbehavior that occurs in school.

_____ The teacher is primarily responsible for misbehavior that occurs in school.

_____ Teachers or administrators should let the parent know each time their child misbehaves.

_____ The school is too strict and should allow students more freedom.

_____ The school for the most part cares very little about the needs of the individual child.

_____ Students should respect authority at *all* times.

_____ Those in authority should respect students at *all* times.

_____ Teachers should provide special activities and help for those students who misbehave.

_____ I am an advocate of "Spare the rod, spoil the child."

_____ Students who misbehave should be punished.

7. What would be acceptable to you if and when your child misbehaves?

_____ Contact me either by phone or in writing.

_____ Work it out with my child without my involvement.

_____ Use your judgment to deal with the situation.

_____ Leave the child alone.

8. What are some qualities in your child that you appreciate?
I appreciate my child _____

_____ .

9. What if any of your child's behaviors have you attempted to eliminate, but have had little if any success? or What is your child still doing that you've repeatedly tried to get him/her to stop doing?

_____

_____

_____

_____

_____

_____

10. I would be willing to discuss my responses to this questionnaire with you at some time in the future. _____ yes _____ no

FOLLOW-UP

After you've obtained the questionnaire and home and school discipline responses, you may want to invite reaction and feedback from your parents. "Would anybody like to share any thoughts or feelings on these tasks?" We hope that you give yourself (teacher) permission to share any of your thoughts or feelings with the parents that you determine to be appropriate.

SOCIAL CONTRACTS

We suggest that you take parents through a shortened version of social contract setting to familiarize them with the process. Explain to them that one of your methods toward the prevention of discipline problems is to give everybody in the class a voice in deciding the rules of the classroom and the consequences of misbehavior.

1. Divide the group into subgroups of no more than five or six parents each. Each group should contain people who either do not know each other or have very limited interaction.

2. When groups are formed, tell them that you would like them to imagine that they are students in the class (the same age as their own children). Tell them that this classroom belongs to everybody, and therefore everybody should have a say in what goes on here. The task for each group is to develop one rule that they would like to have in the classroom to govern the teacher's behavior. (Give examples as you might a group of "real" students). All group members must agree upon the content of the rule (explain limits such as it must not violate state, federal, local laws, or school rules). Allow approximately five to ten minutes.

3. When each group has developed a rule, have them think of as many consequences (positive or negative) as they can that they feel should be implemented if the rule is violated (negative consequences) or followed (positive consequence). Allow five to ten minutes.

4. Have each group record their rule and consequences on a sheet of newsprint or on the blackboard.

5. Have them repeat the same process in developing one rule for students (each other) and consequences (approximately ten to twenty minutes).

6. Add any rules and consequences to the list that you (teacher) have for your students.

7. If you are short on time, then stop and spend a few minutes explaining the remaining steps in the process (e.g., discussion of rules and consequences, including role playing, voting, testing, and the transition into the resolution dimension).

8. If you have sufficient time, then continue the process of social contract setting to completion (as detailed in Chapter 9).

DISCUSSION

The following questions might be helpful as a way of concluding the activity.

1. What do you think of social contracts?

2. Can you think of ways in which social contracts might be useful at home?

3. How do you imagine your child would react to this procedure?

4. How do you feel when you are given a chance to develop rules and consequences that affect your life versus being told by an authority what the rules and consequences are and having no say in their development?

Trying vs. Doing

One message that many of us have been taught is that as long as we try, we are to be commended. Because trying to do rather than doing is often rewarded, the familiar phrase, "I'll try," has become one of the favorite excuses and cop-outs used by some children. Those children who become adept at "trying" wind up "trying the nerves" of people around them. The statements, "I'll try not to fight with Billy again," "I'll try to remember to do my homework assignment," "I'll try not to blurt out in class," "I'll try to find time to mow the lawn on Saturday," are but a few specifics that tell the wise parent or teacher that the child has little if any intention of action. After all, how can anybody make demands from cute little Mary who does nothing but tries everything; or pudgy Sammy who tries not to eat four Devil Dogs every afternoon but eats them anyway; or poor Tommy who has been trying not to push other kids around for years but keeps pushing them?

We believe that when an adult is firm with a child and expects that child to behave appropriately, then any child who is not seriously handicapped can. The students who try rather than do, usually see themselves as inadequate and are afraid to risk failure. When we accept the "trying" excuse, we are confirming to the child that we also see him/her as inadequate. Since the child believes this about himself and receives confirmation of his/her inadequacy from the environment, there is nothing to motivate the child to exert anything more of himself.

When we speak of the difference between trying and doing, we are not referring to children who try but have difficulty in completing the task. There are many times when students may try and not do; for example, when a young child tries to tie his shoe laces and after several attempts stops without success. In this case, the child has tried in a very different way from the child who uses trying as an excuse for not doing or the child who sets his sights so low that doing is seen as impossible from the beginning. Teachers and parents should know the difference between an honest attempt and using the notion of trying as an avoidance procedure. One way to tell might be to ask the child or adolescent to show what steps were taken or in what ways did he/she try.

> *Parent:* Mary, did you clean up your room?
>
> *Mary:* I tried to find time, but I couldn't.
>
> *Parent:* What did you do to find time? (asked in a straightforward manner similar to the adult to adult communication in Transactional Analysis, see pages 92–93).
>
> *Mary:* I thought about it, but I could not do it.
>
> *Parent:* Tell me the steps you went through to help you find time. Maybe we can work together in planning so you can clean your room. Remember your job is to clean your room, not to find the time.

In the next example, you can see how accepting trying while examining the process can be helpful.

> *Teacher:* John, I asked you to clean up your work table when you finished your project.
>
> *John:* I tried, but that's the best I could do.
>
> *Teacher:* I am glad you tried. That is important, and it is also important that your table be cleaned. What ways did you try?
>
> *John:* I put away the paste, but Bill was playing with the cap and it got lost. Also, I didn't know where the crayons were supposed to go. I tried to wash the desk, but there were no clean sponges and I didn't know how to clean it.
>
> *Teacher:* I am glad you tried to do each of the things you are supposed to do during cleanup time. That makes me happy. If there are things about cleanup that you do not know how to do or if you do not know where things are supposed to be, please come and ask me. The crayons are put away in the cabinet behind my desk and in the drawer next to that cabinet are extra sponges. Please take one if you ever need one. It is your responsibility to see that other students do not play with your materials. Now, I think the next time you must clean up, you can do it. If you have any problems, feel free to talk with me.

It is important that you become aware of how you accept excuses and that you stop this practice. The same is to be said for parents. When parents and teacher believe and expect the child to behave a certain way, they can work together with the child to help performance match expectation. Since each child has had a say in determining the social contract and has demonstrated a thorough knowledge of its contents, we advise you to send home a copy and suggest that each parent discuss it with his/her child. For those students who believe themselves to be inadequate and who just "can't" follow the contract, then we believe that a parent-teacher-student conference might be helpful in showing the student how the parent and teacher can work together to make demands of the student.

We offer the following method for dealing with such a student. This method can be used by either teacher or parent.

1. *Teacher:* Mark, I expect the homework to be done on time.

   Mark: I tried, but it is just too hard.

   Teacher: I want to see how you tried. Show me what you did and where you had trouble.

   Mark: I forgot to bring my assignment to class.

   Teacher: Mark, I will accept no more excuses. When you are given a homework assignment, I expect it to be done. If you need extra help, then tell me about it, and I am sure we can work something out.

   Mark: I will try.

   Teacher: Trying is not enough. I expect homework done, not tried. Now tonight's assignment is _____. If you would like, you can take a look at the assignment before you leave school. If it looks too hard, then you let me know, and I will give you some extra help right after school.

2. *Parent:* Mark, please take out the trash (several minutes go by and the trash is still in the house).

   Parent: Mark, I want you to take out the trash.

   Mark: Okay, I will try to find time as soon as I'm done with my model airplane.

   Parent: Mark, when I want you to do something, you always seem to have an excuse. Now, I would like that trash removed.

   Mark: Later.

   Parent: We each have responsibilities in this house and yours is to remove the trash after supper.

   Mark: (no response)

   Parent: (yelling) Take that out right now or I will have your father give you a beating!

   Mark: (with resignation) All right.

This example illustrates the nagging parent. She winds up yelling at her child who has learned to be irresponsible and find excuses. Now contrast the nagging approach with the following:

3. *Parent:* Mark, from now on, I expect you to take the trash outside after supper.

   Mark: I'll try to remember.

> *Parent:* Your job is to do it, not to try to remember to do it.
>
> *Mark:* Okay. (After supper, the trash remains.)
>
> *Parent:* (walks up to Mark, takes him by the arm, leads him to the trash, and points the way outside)
>
> *Mark:* (unhappily takes out the garbage)

Even though Mark is unhappy, the nonnagging message was followed, not forgotten.

FOLLOW-UP

If you are comfortable with parents who often ask the teacher for a myriad of child-rearing advice, you may suggest and even role play this technique with them (either in a group or individually). In this way, you can jointly develop a plan of action for those students who are "tryers" both at home and at school.

Do You Know Something I Don't?

Stanley, aged 10, was having a terrific year according to his special education teacher. He had been placed in this class because of his refusal to do any work in a regular class and because he set himself up for constant scapegoating from other students; he had had no friends. In his special education class, his teacher saw him as an outstanding student who appeared happy.

The school year ended, and as Stanley was about to return to his special education program in the fall, he told his mother that he would not go back. After all, his teacher had expected him to help other students with academic problems, which he did. But, unused to his new "helper" role, Stanley put a lot of pressure on himself and was often coming home with a headache, and he would occasionally leave for school with an upset stomach. Stanley never complained to his teacher and never failed to complain to his mother. But the teacher did not know of Stanley's pressures, and his mother never informed the teacher.

Except for pre-planned parent-teacher conferences, most teachers contact the home only when a problem has occurred. By meeting with parents at times prior to the eruption of problems, you can have a better working relationship when a moment of crisis occurs. In this way, you can avoid or minimize parental defensiveness and antagonism.

Just as we emphasize *prevention* with children, we extend this concept to include the parent(s) of the child. It is likely that if Stanley's teacher knew how upset Stanley was, she would have intervened in some way to help him work through his self-imposed pressure.

We suggest that the teacher periodically reach out to parents by inquiring how they see the child's school functioning. There are many possible ways of doing this, and the one which seems the least time consuming is to address a letter to the parents inviting their feedback. Our suggested format is as follows: .

Dear Parent,

Although I work with your child/adolescent for _____ hours each day, sometimes children/adolescents have thoughts or feelings which escape my attention. I am especially interested in knowing (1) how your child/adolescent deals with his homework assignments, (2) whether or not you think he/she sees my class as a place he/she wants to be, (3) if your child/adolescent has any complaints such as frequent headaches or stomachaches which you feel are related to school, (4) and if you have any other concerns or thoughts about your child's progress in school.

Since I value the feedback that I receive from both students and parents, I would very much appreciate your sending me a short note or letter that addresses these issues or others. I can also make myself available to meet with you in person should you so desire. Thank you for your cooperation.

Sincerely,

_____

Some Parents Are Hard to Reach

The activities we have suggested in this chapter can be effective in establishing good working relationships between parents and teachers. Yet, often the parents who come to meetings and return feedback forms are more than willing to cooperate with the school. It is usually the parents who don't come and don't return feedback whose children are in most trouble at school. There are many reasons for this. Some students live in homes where parents don't get along or in homes where their parents do not have time for school. Some parents feel uncomfortable with the risk of exposing their own difficulties to school personnel. Some parents with children who have experienced failure in school feel they have failed as parents and begin to experience guilt. These parents would rather not have salt rubbed in their wound and would prefer as little contact with the school as possible. As we have said previously, many times children misbehave at home the same way they do at school. Parents of troublesome children do not want reminders of how inadequate they have been in parenting. There are many more reasons ranging from benign neglect to alcoholism to lack of awareness. Regardless of the reason the teacher is still faced with either uncooperative or possibly hostile parents.

There is little a teacher can do to make these parents come to school, to show an active interest in their children's education, or to work cooperatively with teachers. We have seen various experiments in some schools which may help. We offer these to you.

1. One school did not send home report cards. The only way for parents to receive them was to come to school personally and have a conference with the teacher. While this plan took a lot of work, it was only done early in the year. The teachers made personal contact with every parent, a working relationship was established, and parents were more willing to meet with the teachers later in the year. Not every parent cared enough to come and passed up seeing the report cards, but many of the more reluctant parents came to school for the first time in a long while.

2. Set up a preschool conference day prior to the beginning of school and provide teachers with extra pay. No student can register for school until at least one parent has had the conference. The thought of having summer vacation extended is strong motivation for many parents.

3. Call home or make a home visitation. While many teachers and educators feel this violates the teacher's limit of responsibility, it may prove very beneficial for reaching some parents. We feel that a personal call from the teacher rather than the principal has a better chance of success because the threat from authority is reduced.

These suggestions may help bring the parent in contact with the teacher. If your school has a problem with many parents who won't come, it may be helpful to have a faculty meeting devoted to thinking of other ways to initiate contact.

Once contact has been made, it is extremely important to do everything possible to ensure that the experience will be positive. The following list of guidelines are helpful for interacting with the hard to reach parent:

1. Be friendly, supportive, and listen. This is not the time to win points or be defensive. You may be right and never see the parent again.

2. Ask questions in an interesting way. Do not sound like the receptionist at the hospital, taking Blue Cross information when the patient needs immediate care. Use questions because you care and want to know as much as possible so you can be helpful.

3. While it's nice to tell parents your educational philosophy, don't do it. They are not meeting with you to discuss education, they are most interested in their children. Remember, you do not have to prove your competence and knowledge of education at this meeting.

4. Do not attack, criticize, or put down their children. If the parents feel like failures they will be hurt, angered, or made to feel guilty by hearing a list of their childrens' faults.

5. Do not discuss problem behaviors. We feel that in the first meeting with a parent, especially a hard to reach one, it is almost always inappropriate to get into the business of problem solving the child's behavior. The first contact should be confined to establishing a working relationship between parent and teacher.

6. Encourage the parent to join you in a team effort for the good of the child. Talk of cooperative efforts that might be helpful in making the school year a positive experience for the child.

7. Be prepared. Know who the children are and be familiar with their history. Show the parents that you are a professional and that you care. Parents do not like talking with someone who appears to be uninformed.

8. Don't be rushed. Even though you have twenty-seven things to do after the meeting, plan enough time so you can stay with the parent for as long as he/she wants. Never look at your watch or the clock. Give the parents the impression that their meeting with you is one of the most important parts of your job and mean it.

    This step is difficult because of the load most teachers have, and it should be reserved for only those parents who rarely come to school. Be specific and be sure to include positive behaviors that you see in the child, no matter how small. Express both your concerns as well as the strengths that you observe in the child. Parents should leave you with some encouraging news.

9. Finally, set up another appointment before they leave. Agree on a plan so that the next meeting will have specific input from both parent and teacher. For example, encourage the parents to monitor how well their children do their homework and how long it takes. Meet a week later to discuss the results and modify your homework for that child if the parents provide data that it is too hard or easy, too long or short, too boring or whatever they tell you. Show them that what they say makes a difference in the quality of education for their children.

Notice the following two exchanges between a parent and teacher:

1. *Teacher:* Hi, Mrs. Ryan. The reason for this meeting is that Patrick has been acting up in class and I want to tell you about it and have you work with him at home.

   Parent: (*surprised and defensive*) Well, what's he doing?

   Teacher: He has been hitting the girls in class and making fun of them. It's driving me crazy.

   Parent: This is the first time he's acted that way. No teacher ever told me this before.

   Teacher: Well, I don't know anything about that. Does he act badly at home? Does he listen to you when you tell him to stop? Does he have any brothers or sisters and do they act the same as him?

   Parent: (*flustered*) He has an older sister but we have very little trouble at home. (*Defensively and untruthful*). We think the problem must be in his class.

   Teacher: My philosophy is that in my class all children must behave and do as they are told. And Patrick just does not listen. I have told him many times to stop fighting and I have sent him to Mr. Aronsen's office (principal), but it doesn't help. I think that maybe a few good paddlings might straighten him out.

   Parent: (*confused*) Well, I don't want Pat spanked.

   Teacher: It's four-thirty and I have another conference in five minutes. If Patrick's behavior doesn't improve, then I'll be referring him to the psychologist so that he can be in a special education class. Feel free to call me if you'd like to speak with me again.

2. *Teacher:* Hello Mrs. Ryan. I'm glad you could come and talk with me. I know you have a busy schedule and it is not easy for you to get to school.

   Parent: Hello, has Pat done something wrong?

   Teacher: No, I wanted to meet to see if there are any questions you have about my class and to see if you had any information which might be helpful to me in making this year a good one for Pat.

   Parent: No I don't know anything to tell you and I have nothing to ask.

   Teacher: That's fine. Maybe I could ask a couple of questions to help us get started. You see, my goal this year is for each student to enjoy school and to learn as much as he can. I want Pat to have a successful year and I thought we could work together to achieve that. Does Pat talk about school with you?

   Parent: No, not really. He doesn't like school very much.

   Teacher: Can you tell me one thing he often complains of, and maybe you can remember one thing he has said that he likes about school.

   Parent: He has complained of teachers punishing him too severely at times and that he gets bored when the work is too difficult for him. He usually likes to work in the library. He talks a lot about going to the library and reading books on cars.

Teacher: Does he say what kinds of punishments are too severe for him?

Parent: No, not really. I don't really have much more to say and I need to get back home to make supper.

Teacher: Fine, I am willing to speak with you as long as you want, but I understand the pressure of making supper. I make supper for my family when I get home after work and it gets busy sometimes. Before you go, I want to ask you to help me to improve things for Pat. Can you write down the things he says he likes about my class and the things he doesn't like about it. Don't write a lot, just a few words for each like and dislike. We can meet later and I will try to use that information to improve school for Pat.

Parent: Well, I don't have a lot of time, but I guess I can do it.

Teacher: I am glad, maybe together we can provide Pat with more positive experiences than I could by myself. I want to set up a time right now for us to meet to discuss your list. How about next week at this same time?

While the teacher in the first example was stricter than the teacher in the second, the real difference was in their communication style. The first teacher tried to make points, place the blame at home, and end the meeting in control of both Pat and his mother. In the second example, the teacher established contact and was facilitative without pushing too far. Pat, his mother, and the teacher won in this exchange. It is extremely difficult to get hard to reach parents in the school to meet with teachers. Once they are there, the interactions must be positive and supportive so the parents will return and see school as a place where they have a voice and their children's needs can be met.

16

CONCLUSION

Many teachers who are struggling with discipline want immediate relief. A recent study indicated that stress related to classroom management is the most influential factor in failure among novice teachers.[1] Little research is needed for experienced teachers who are *subject* to the stressful effects of dealing with discipline daily.

After concluding a workshop in three-dimensional discipline, a teacher asked us, "What if I do everything exactly as you taught me; I become aware of myself and my students, I express my feelings, I learn all there is to know about alternative theories of discipline, I establish social contracts, I keep records, I implement the best alternative consequences, I develop individual contracts with those students who need them, I work closely with parents and other school personnel, and I still have discipline problems? What do I do then?" Our answer was that discipline is not a disease, and the three-dimensional model is not a cure. Preventing and resolving discipline problems is a continuous process which has no final solution. To eradicate discipline problems would mean the elimination of individual differences among people. We see this as neither desirable nor possible.

---

[1] Jack O. Vittetoe, "Why First Year Teachers Fail," *Phi Delta Kappan*, January 1977, p. 429.

Throughout this book we have resisted the temptation to explain why students misbehave. We have not listed reasons for every disruptive classroom event. Rather we have focused on action—what can be done to improve discipline utilizing cognitive, psychomotor, and emotional energy. We believe that you, the teacher, are the best judge of how to adapt the numerous principles and activities to your unique teaching style.

Teachers who have used our approach report positive and beneficial effects for themselves and their students. A sense of commitment and personal energy that comes from self-awareness and ownership of values, behaviors, and feelings are responsible for these positive results. We used feedback from teachers who were generous enough to share their thoughts and feelings about our approach. We now hope that you will apply your own creativity to developing a three-dimensional approach to your school or classroom which will generate excitement and enthusiasm for you in your teaching. We would greatly appreciate your thoughts and feelings and invite you to communicate your feedback to us.

For information concerning three-dimensional discipline workshops write: For You Associates, P.O. Box 9931, Rochester, New York, 14623.

BIBLIOGRAPHY

Abidin, Richard. *Parenting Skills: Trainer's Manual.* New York: Human Science Press, 1976.

Alschuler, Alfred; Tabor, Diane, and McIntyre, James. *Teaching Achievement Motivation.* Middletown, Conn.: Education Ventures, Inc., 1971.

Ballard, Jim. *Circlebook.* Amherst, Mass.: Mandala, 1975.

Bandura, Albert and Walters, R. H. *Social Learning and Personality Development.* New York: Holt, Rinehart and Winston, 1963.

Becker, Wesley C. *Parents are Teachers.* Champaign, Ill.: Research Press, 1971.

Berne, Eric. *Games People Play.* New York: Grove Press, 1964.

Bessell, Harold. *Methods in Human Development.* San Diego: Human Development Training Institute, 1970.

Borton, Terry. *Read, Touch and Teach.* New York: McGraw-Hill, 1970.

Brutten, Milton; Richardson, Sylvia O., and Mangel, Charles. *Something's Wrong with My Child.* New York: Harcourt Brace Jovanovich, Inc., 1973.

Canfield, Jack and Wells, John. *100 Ways to Enhance Self-Concept in the Classroom.* Englewood Cliffs, N.J.: Prentice-Hall, 1976.

Carrington, Patricia. *Freedom in Meditation.* Garden City, N.Y.: Anchor Books, 1978.

Cowen, Emory L. et al. *New Ways in School Mental Health.* New York: Human Science Press, 1975.

Curwin, Richard L. and Curwin, Geri. *Developing Individual Values in the Classroom.* Palo Alto, Calif.: Learning Handbooks, 1974.

Curwin, Richard L. and Fuhrmann, Barbara. *Discovering Your Teaching Self: Humanistic Approaches to Effective Teaching.* Englewood Cliffs, N.J.: Prentice-Hall, 1975.

Curwin, Richard L. and Fuhrmann, Barbara. "Mirror, Mirror on the Wall-Developing Teacher Congruency." *The Humanist Educator.* Sept. 1978, Vol. 17, No. 1.

Curwin, Richard L. and Mendler, Allen. "Three-Dimensional Discipline: A New Approach to an Old Problem." *American Middle School Education.* Univ. of Georgia, Athens, Ga., 1979, Vol. 1., No. 4.

Dodson, Fitzhugh. *How to Discipline With Love.* New York: Rawson Associates, 1977.

Dodson, Fitzhugh. *How to Parent.* New York: New American Library, 1971.

Dollar, Barry. *Humanizing Classroom Discipline: A Behavioral Approach.* New York: Harper & Row, 1972.

Dreikurs, Rudolf. *Children: The Challenge.* New York: Hawthorn Books, Inc., 1964.

Ernst, Ken. *Games Students Play.* Millbrae, Calif.: Celestial Arts, 1972.

Fantini, Mario and Weinstein, Gerald. *Making Urban Schools Work.* New York: Holt, Rinehart & Winston, 1968.

Frankl, Viktor E. *Man's Search for Meaning: An Introduction to Logotherapy.* New York: Pocket Books, 1963.

Galbraith, Ronald E. and Jones, Thomas M. *Moral Reasoning: A Teaching Handbook for Adapting Kohlberg to the Classroom.* Minneapolis, Minn.: Greenhaven Press Inc., 1976.

Ginott, Haim. *Teacher and Child.* New York: Macmillan, 1972.

Glasser, William. *The Identity Society.* New York: Harper & Row, 1972
———. *Reality Therapy.* New York: Harper & Row, 1965.
———. *Schools Without Failure.* New York: Harper & Row, 1969.

Gordon, Thomas. *Teacher Effectiveness Training.* New York: Peter H. Wyden, 1974.

Harris, Thomas. *I'm OK—You're OK.* New York: Harper & Row, 1967.

Hart, Harold H., ed. *Summerhill: For & Against.* New York: Hart, 1970.

Hendricks, Gay and Roberts, Thomas B. *The Second Centering Book.* Englewood Cliffs, N.J.: Prentice-Hall, 1977.

Holmes, Monica; Holmes, Douglas, and Field, Judith. *The Therapeutic Classroom.* New York: Jason Aronson, 1974.

Locke, John. *Some Thoughts Concerning Education.* London: Cambridge, University Press, 1934.

Marquis, John N.; Morgan, Wesley G., and Piaget, Gerald W. *A Guidebook for Systematic Desensitization.* Palo Alto, Calif.: Veteran's Workshop, 1971.

Maslow, Abraham. *Motivation and Personality.* 2nd ed. New York: Harper & Row, 1970.

Maslow, Abraham. *Toward a Psychology of Being.* 2nd ed. New York: Van Nostrand Reinhold, 1968.

Neill, A. S. *Summerhill: A Radical Approach to Child Rearing.* New York: Hart, 1960.

Pearson, Craig, ed. *Resolving Classroom Conflict.* Palo Alto, Calif.: Learning Handbooks, 1974.

Postman, Neil and Weingartner, Charles. *Teaching as a Subversive Activity.* New York: Dell, 1969.

Poteet, James. *Behavior Modification: A Pracitcal Guide for Teachers.* Minneapolis, Minn.: Burgess, 1973.

Raths, Louis, et al. *Values and Teaching.* Columbus, Ohio. Merrill, 1966.

Rogers, Carl. *Freedom to Learn.* Columbus, Ohio: Merrill, 1969.

Schein, Edgar. *Process Consultation: Its Role in Organizational Development.* Reading, Mass.: Addison-Wesley, 1969.

Schrag, Peter and Divory, Diane. *The Myth of the Hyperactive Child.* New York: Pantheon Books, 1975.

Silberman, Charles E. *Crisis in the Classroom.* New York: Random House, 1970.

Simon, Sidney B.; Howe, Leland W., and Kirschenbaum, Howard. *Values Clarification.* New York: Hart. 1972.

Sloane, Howard N. *Classroom Management: Remediation and Prevention.* New York: John Wiley and Sons, Inc., 1976.

Snygg, D., and Combs, A. W. *Individual Behavior.* New York: Harper, 1949.

Stellern, John; Vasa, Stanley F., and Little, Jack. *Introduction to Diagnostic-Prescriptive Teaching and Programming.* Glen Ridge, N.J.: Exceptional Press, 1976.

Stevens, John O. *Awareness: Exploring, Experimenting, Experiencing.* New York: Bantam Books, 1973.

Thorndike, E. L.: *The Elements of Psychology.* New York: Seiler, 1905.

Tyrell, Ronald; Johns, Frank, and McCarthy, Frederick. *Growing Pains in the Classroom: A Guide for Teachers of Adolescents.* Reston, Va.: Reston, 1977.

Weinstein, Gerald and Fantini, Mario. *Toward Humanistic Education: A Curriculum of Affect.* New York: Praeger, 1970.

Weinstein, Gerald; Hardin, Joy, and Weinstein, Matt. *Education of the Self.* Amherst, Mass.: Mandala, 1976.

Wolpe, Joseph, and Lazarus, A. *Behavior Therapy Techniques.* Oxford: Pergamon Press, 1966.

INDEX